Complete
Pasta Cookbook

Complete
Pasta Cookbook

Bridget Jones

angus

A QUANTUM BOOK

Published by Angus Books Ltd
Swift Distribution
Units 1 – 6 Kingsnorth Industrial Estate
Hoo, Nr. Rochester
Kent ME3 9ND

This edition printed 2007

Copyright ©MCMXCIV
Quintet Publishing Limited

ISBN 978-1-84573-301-8

QUMPBI-N

This book is produced by
Quantum Publishing
6 Blundell Street
London N7 9BH

Printed in Singapore by
Star Standard Industries Pte Ltd

The material in this book has appeared in previous publications.

CONTENTS

INTRODUCTION
An Historic Food 6
The Origins of Pasta - Some Ancient Stories of
Art and Travel 6
A Different Place, A Different Form 7
Ideal for Today's Busy Cook 8

THE WORLD OF PASTA 9
Using the Pasta Glossaries 9
Selecting the Right Pasta for the Meal 9

GLOSSARY OF ITALIAN PASTAS 10

SPECIALIST PASTAS 14

FLAVOURED PASTAS 16

SWEET PASTAS 18

ORIENTAL PASTAS 19

EXAMPLES OF PASTAS FROM
OTHER COUNTRIES 22

PASTA ON THE PLATE 24

PASTA IN THE DIET - Putting it into Perspective 25

SERVING STYLES 28

PASTA KNOW-HOW
Making Pasta at Home 30
Cooking Pasta 34
Storing and Freezing Pasta 37

THE RECIPES 38

THE DOUGHS 40

ESSENTIAL SAUCES AND
CONTEMPORARY DRESSINGS 50

SUPERLATIVE SOUPS 76

HOTPOTS AND STEWS 94

MAIN COURSE SAUCES 106

STUFFED AND FILLED PASTA 148

BAKED PASTA DISHES 178

ORIENTAL SPECIALITIES 194

PASTA SALADS 212

INDEX 221

Introduction – An Historic Food

(49)-2018-Macaroni drying in the dirty streets of Naples, Italy.
Copyright Underwood & Underwood.

Pasta – the practical food for today's busy cook – has a long tradition, set in the history of many nations and steeped in the controversy of international culinary claims. Pasta goes so far back in the history of food that it is talked of as one of the first palatable forms of using grain and ways of preserving the milled grain. It is undoubtedly the continued popularity of pasta that has brought about discussion of its origins.

The Italians have to be thanked for making pasta the 'varied and multinational product it has become, but whether or not it is fair to say that they invented pasta dough is unclear. From research into writings on the topic, it seems that pasta is a food that has evolved in different corners of the world in parallel, rather than stemming from one particular source.

The Origins of Pasta – Some Ancient Stories of Art and Travel

One popular theory is that the explorer Marco Polo discovered pasta on his travels to China during the 13th century and took the idea home to Venice. The Chinese were making noodles long before Marco Polo visited their country, but there is also evidence that the Italians were producing an equivalent food. References to pasta-making equipment date back before Marco Polo's travels, and there were recipes for vermicelli and filled pasta in a 13th-century publication that also preceded his return from the Orient. The Etruscan art of early Italian civilization includes

cooking equipment that could well have been used for making pasta. It is suggested that the first Italian experiments may have been along the lines of a Greek dough.

Apart from these two popularly discussed sources of pasta, Indians and Arabs were also making pasta by (if not before) the 13th century, so either could well have introduced the idea to Europe. The names sev or seviyan, for Indian vermicelli, have evolved from sevika, an early name for pasta, meaning thread. Other names for the first pastas indicated that it was long and thread-like, and spaghetti is derived from spago, meaning string. Later, macaroni was to become the generic term for pasta. By the 18th century, the same term was used for young men who travelled to Italy with the fashionable intention of improving their cultural outlook, but who, instead, indulged in the pleasures of consuming pasta – dandy macaronis indeed.

A Different Place, A Different Form

It is interesting to look at the shapes and types of pasta and similar doughs that have developed in Europe. The Italian-like filled pasta of Poland, for example, was brought to the country as a result of a marriage with

Above: Commercial pasta production, Italian style.

Ideal for Today's Busy Cook

One of the first forms of convenience food, pasta still provides an excellent variety of culinary opportunities: there are instant forms, ready meals, quick-cook mixtures and fresh doughs. Thankfully, there are good-quality dried pastas (which have to be boiled for the traditional 10–20 minutes) and these still predominate. With specialist Italian, Oriental and Indian shops in most large towns and cities, the supermarket supply of familiar pasta shapes and noodles can be readily supplemented by the more unusual forms. High-quality fresh pasta is now mass-produced and widely marketed, and inexpensive hand-turned pasta machines are sold in most good cookshops, so it is not difficult to make a batch of noodles at home.

The exciting aspect of pasta is that it can provide whatever you need, be it a really tasty, satisfying supper, a romantic dinner for two or a stunning dinner party dish. It is all things to all people, from inexpensive novelty shapes for the under-fives to a gourmet topic of conversation for devotees of unusual ingredients.

The Italians still dominate the world in terms of the quantity of pasta that they produce – 2.203 million tons in 1991, with a capacity for an even higher figure of 2.7 million tons. Italian pasta finds its way all over the world, but it is still as popular as ever at home, with an average annual consumption of 25 kg (55 lb) per person in Italy – that is over 450 g (1 lb) pasta per person, per week. The rest of us have a way to go before we catch up. Switzerland is leading, at the 9.1 kg (20 lb) per person mark, the USA clocks in at round 8 kg (17½ lb), and Greece manages 7.7 kg (17 lb). The Canadians may be hot on the trail at 6.3 kg (14 lb), but the United Kingdom has still got some way to go, with an average consumption of just 2.3 kg (5 lb) per head.

Enough facts and figures, controversy and history, though, and on to the real business of pasta: buying, cooking and eating it. The ever-increasing choice makes pasta cookery a real pleasure, and I hope you will enjoy exploring the diverse world of pasta.

Italian royalty, and then there are the robust noodles of Germany. Potato, cheese and flour are all used as bases for pasta doughs that range from dumpling-like gnocchi to curly spätzle and noodles similar to tagliatelle.

Oriental forms of pasta are distinctly different to these, having a lighter texture. As well as doughs based on wheat flour, rice flour and flour made from inung beans are used to make rice sticks or clear, cellophane noodles. Oriental methods used to shape pasta also differ from those of other countries, with noodles being formed by a technique of twirling and stretching the dough. Swinging the dough round rather like a short skipping rope extends it rapidly and makes exciting entertainment for a hungry audience in restaurants. As the dough flies, it thins and it is folded and swung time and time again to create the long, slim noodles that everyone eagerly awaits.

THE WORLD OF PASTA

This section provides an overview of the different groups of pasta that are available world-wide but, first, a few useful notes.

Using the Pasta Glossaries

Italy is by far the most prolific producer, so it makes sense to begin by listing and illustrating the many shapes and styles of pasta *alla Italiana*. You will also find information on oriental pasta and the better-known types from other countries. In addition, there is a section on flavoured pastas with tasting notes.

There are also tips on an equally important group of specialist items; wholemeal, gluten-free, egg-free and even low-protein pasta, or alternative grain pastas.

Selecting the Right Pasta for the Meal

Suggestions for which pasta to serve with a particular sauce are included throughout the recipes. There are some traditional partnerships, with the long thin pastas being served with thin sauces, whilst the chunky pastas and those in shapes to catch juices would be offered with meatier or more substantial mixtures, but there are some unusual combinations to try, too.

I also make comments occasionally about the appearance or the substance of the pasta. This is as they may vary when cooked. You may have come across advice on selecting pasta that suggests that the bright yellow-coloured products are superior to the paler more opaque types. If you extend your view of pasta beyond the narrow confines of the one or two most commonly found Italian sauces by shopping, tasting and testing, you will find that this is nonsense. There are many traditional, rather murky looking pale pastas that are more starchy – dare I say it, stodgy – when cooked, but they are ideal for rich, meaty sauces and not at all inferior to the clearer, more yellow shapes. As a general rule, the only pastas I sometimes felt could be called inferior were some of the really speedy quick-cook types that resembled traditional Italian pasta in

GLOSSARY OF ITALIAN PASTA

AGNELLOTTI, AGNOLLOTTI OR AGNOLOTTI (1)
Cushions of stuffed pasta, round or semi-circular, attributed to Piedmont region.

AGNOLINI (Not shown)
Small ravioli.

AMORI/AMORINI (2a & b)
Knots. They do not resemble knots, but are hollow spirals that may be ridged.

ANELLINI (Not shown) Tiny rings, for use in soups.

BAVETTE (Not shown) Oval spaghetti.

BIGNI (Not shown)
Local name for spaghetti.

BIGOLI (Not shown)
A type of spaghetti.

BUCATINI (3) Thick, hollow spaghetti.

CAMPANELLE (4)
Bells. Small cones of pasta with frilly edges. Good for trapping sauce.

CANDELE (5)
Meaning candles, the pasta shapes are, in fact, pipes, about 1-1.5 cm (½-¾ in) in diameter.

CANNELLE (Not shown)
Meaning pipes, and including cannellini, cannolicchi, cannelloni and canneroni.

CANNELLONI (Not shown)
Popular pipe shapes, used for stuffing, coating with sauce and baking.

CANNERONI (8)
Larger than canneroncini, these are short pasta tubes.

CANNERONCINI (7)
Short lengths about 1 cm (½ in) of narrow pipes.

CAPELLINI (8)
Thin hairs. Very fine spaghetti.

CAPELLINI SPEZZIATI (9)
Short, broken lengths of capellini.

CAPPELLETTI (10)
Little hats. Small circles of pasta indented in the centre or with a pinched pleat, which forms their hat shape.

CASARECCIA (11)
Slightly twisted lengths of "S"-shaped pasta.

CASONSEI (Not shown)
Stuffed rings of pasta from Bergamo.

CICATELLI DI SAN SEVERO (12)
One of a range of handmade pasta from the Puglia region. These opaque, white, curled shaves of pasta are made from wheat flour and water but no egg. They swell significantly on cooking and are recommended for serving with long-cooked meat sauces. They remind me (slightly) of the spätzle that I made.

CONCHIGLIE (13 & 15) Shells. They come in many sizes, from conchigliette, for soup, to large conchiglioni, for stuffing.

CONCHIGLIE RIGATE (14)
Large shells with a ridged texture. Ideal for boiling, draining, stuffing and baking or grilling with a gratiné topping.

CORALLINI (16)
Tiny soup pasta that look like little slices of hollow spaghetti.

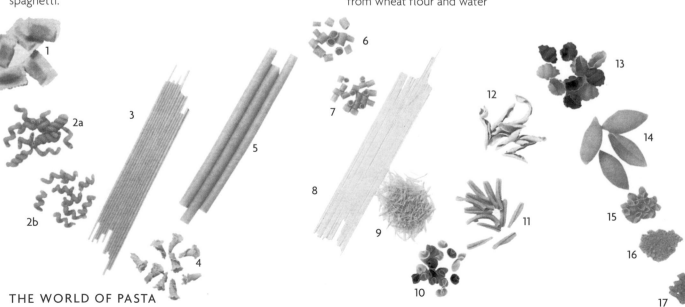

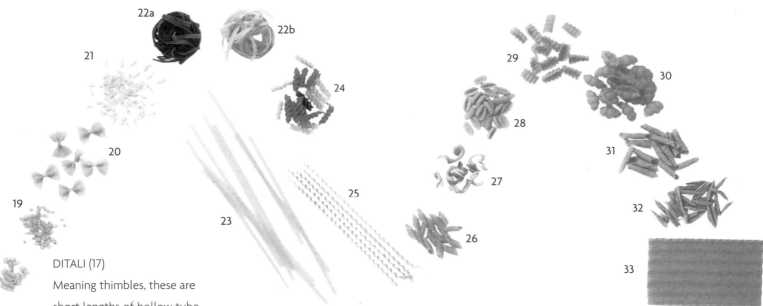

DITALI (17)
Meaning thimbles, these are short lengths of hollow tube, slightly smaller than the end of your little finger. Good for salads and for a chunkier pasta in soup.

DITALINI (19)
Smaller than ditali both in length and diameter, with proportionally thicker pasta.

FARFALLE (20)
Butterflies. The term "bows" is also sometimes used for the same pasta shape. Made from thin, flat pasta, these shapes tend to cook quickly for their size. Good for adding to hotpots or layered (moist) dishes in which the pasta is cooked from raw.

FARFALLINI (21)
Wonderful, tiny farfalle, for soups or when small shapes are required. Very decorative.

FETTUCCINE (22a & b)
Flat noodles. This is the alternative Roman name for tagliatelle. Readily available fresh.

FISIETTI (18)
Little whistles. Thin macaroni.

FRESINE (23)
Straight noodles, slightly narrower than tagliatelle and in similar lengths to short spaghetti.

FUSILLI (24)
Spirals, which may be long or short depending on the region of origin. Apparently, they were originally made by wrapping spaghetti round knitting needles, which gives some indication of the size and thickness of the pasta.

FUSILLIER COL BUCO (25)
Long, slim spirals (about the same length as short spaghetti).

GENOVESINI (26)
Presumably attributed in origin to Genoa, these are short, diagonally cut lengths of fairly thick tube pasta. Rather like short, plump penne.

GLI STROZZAPRETI (27)
The basic shape as casareccia, but the cut lengths are curled round into "C" or "S" shapes.

GNOCCHETTI SARDI (28)
Small versions of gnocchi, they are ridged, opaque and pale in colour. Good with meaty sauces.

GNOCCHETTO (29)
More yellow in colour than gnocchetti, ridged and semi-tubular in shape. Look more like an average pasta shape than the more gnocchi-like types of dried pasta.

GNOCCHI (30)
Little dumplings. The dried pastas are shaped to resemble gnocchi which are marked with a fork. There are many types of fresh gnocchi (see pages 42-45).

GOMITI (Not shown)
Hollow corners of pasta, like elbows, lumache (small) or pipe.

GRAMIGNA (Not shown)
Couch grass. Pasta shaped like grass.

I GARGANELLI ROMAGNOLI (31) Squares of pasta rolled diagonally to make slim rolls with pointed ends.

IS MALLOREDDUS LUNGHI (32) Like small, pale (creamy white), distinctively ridged gnocchetti but tightly curled.

LASAGNE (Not shown)
Wide strips or squares of pasta. Available fresh or dried.

LASAGNETTE (33)
Small lasagne. The same as malfade, this is a type of wide ribbon noodle with frilly edges.

LE EMILIANE (Not shown)
A name for nests of pappardelle.

LINGUINE (Not shown)
Little tongues. Narrow noodles or flat spaghetti, readily available fresh.

LUNETTE (Not shown)
A term used on some brands of semi-circular stuffed pasta.

LUMACHE (34a & b)
Snails. Available in different sizes, the large ones are ideal for stuffing. I also found this name attributed to ridged shell shapes – presumably snail shells!

LUMANCHINE (35)
Small snail shapes as above, but not as distinctive in shape. For salads, stuffing vegetables (peppers) or when a reasonably chunky soup is required.

MACARONI OR MACCHERONI (36)
Hollow tubes of pasta, larger than spaghetti. Originally sold in long lengths, wrapped in blue paper packets and still available as such from better delicatessen sources. Quick-cook, short-cut macaroni and elbow macaroni (another term for elbows or slightly longer right angles) are the most popular and readily available types.

MACCHERONCINI (Not shown)
Very small macaroni.

MACCHERONI RIGATI (Not shown)
Ribbed macaroni.

MAFALDE (37)
Wide, flat noodles with fluted or ruffled edges.

MAFALDINE (Not shown)
Flat noodles with fluted or ruffled edges, narrower than mafalde.

MALFATTINI (Not shown)
Finely chopped.

MISTA PASTA (38)
Mixed pasta. Mixed shapes sold together.

MISTO CORTO (39)
Mis-shapen. A mixture of tubes, spaghetti and broken pieces of similar length.

NIDI (40)
Nests. Small, rounded bundles of tagliatelle or fettuccine, these unravel when cooked. Pasta nests as a base for serving a sauce are created by arranging the cooked pasta in a nest shape on the plate.

OFFELLE (Not shown)
Stuffed pasta of ravioli type from Trieste.

ORECCHIETTE (41)
Little ears. Opaque pasta, paler than usual shapes and slightly thicker than

some. With a slightly softer texture when cooked, ideal for rich sauces (vegetable ragoûts or meaty sauces). Look as though they have been formed as the result of someone pressing their thumb into a piece of pasta.

PAGLIA E FIENO (42a & b)
Straw and hay. Green and white linguine or very narrow flat noodles mixed together. Also available as pink and white, flavoured with tomato and plain.

PANSOTTI (Not shown)
Stuffed pasta of Ligurian origins, usually triangular.

PAPPARDELLE (43)
Wide, ribbon egg noodles. Traditionally an accompaniment for rich meat or game sauces, such as hare or meat sauces.

PASTA A RISO (44)
Pasta in the shape of

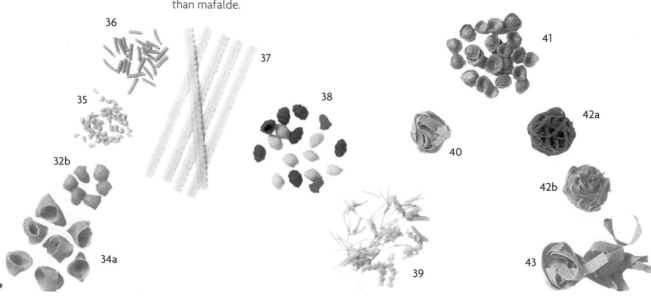

small grains of rice. This cooks quickly and may be used instead of the Greek equivalent, known as orzo or minestra.

PASTINE (Not shown)
Small pasta shapes; soup pasta.

PENNE (45)
Quills. Hollow pasta cut into short lengths, at a slant.

PENNE, MEZZANI (46)
Small penne, slimmer and slightly shorter.

PENNE, MEZZANINE (47)
Yet smaller penne, shorter and slimmer than both the above.

PERCIATELLI (Not shown)
Thick, hollow spaghetti, thicker than bucatini.

PERLINE (Not shown)
Little pearls. Small soup pasta.

QUADRETTI (Not shown)
Small squares of pasta for soup.

RADIATOR! (48)
Radiators. Deeply ridged, pale pasta like old-fashioned radiators.

RAVIOLI (Not shown)
Small, stuffed pasta shapes. May be square or round, depending on their region of origin.

RIGATONI (49)
Ridged tubes, like large ridged macaroni. Good with meat sauces and for baked dishes.

RUOTI (50)
Wheels. Cartwheel shapes.

SEDANI (Not shown)
Ridged, curved tubes of macaroni type, resembling celery sticks.

SPAGELLINI (51)
Short, thin pieces of spaghetti.

SPAGHETTI (52)
Long, slim, solid pasta. The majority is now shorter than it used to be, but it is still available in long, blue packets.

SPIGANARDA (53)
Similar to pasta a riso, but consists of longer grains.

STELLINE (54)
Tiny stars. Soup pasta.

TAGLIATELLE (55)
Familiar ribbon noodles. See also Fettuccine.

TORCHIETTI (56)
Small torches. Slightly swirled lengths of ridged pasta.

TORTELLINI (57a & b)
Stuffed pasta, formed from squares or circles, filled and folded in half, then pinched together into rings.

TORTIGLIONI (58)
Ridged tubes, like rigatoni, but curved, with the ridges forming a slight spiral on the pasta.

TRENETTE (Not shown)
Finer than linguine or similar to flattened spaghetti.

TUBETTI (59)
Small tubes. Small, short lengths of hollow pasta.

VERMICELLI (Not shown)
Thin worms. The Neapolitan term for spaghetti, which is slightly thicker than the familiar form. However, on an international basis, this is the term ascribed to fine spaghetti.

ZITI (60)
Spinsters or batchelors. Thick macaroni.

ZITONI (61) Thicker than ziti.

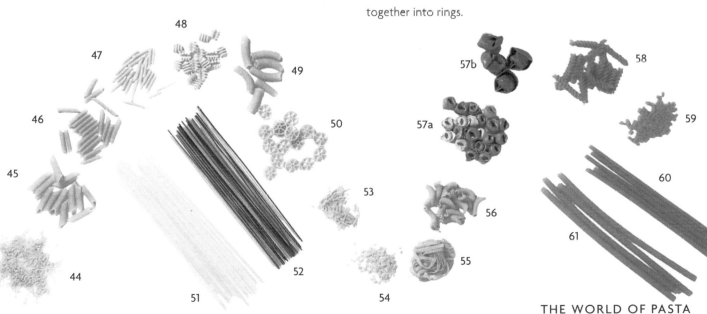

SPECIALIST PASTAS

The familiar wheat flour pastas are also available in organic forms and as wholewheat types from larger supermarkets as well as delicatessens and healthfood shops. However, those who may suffer from an allergic reaction to the protein content of wheat and some other grains will be pleased to know that there is a good choice of wheat-free pasta products. They also provide an exciting range of ingredients for any interested cook. The following is a sample of the range located, but there are many small shops offering a variety of different products, so see what you can find.

Glossary of Speciality Pasta

RICE PASTA (1)

There is a variety of rice pastas, including VEGETABLE RICE PASTA, RICE (1b), RICE, TOMATO AND BASIL PASTA (1a), and garlic and parsley rice pasta. They are gluten-free and made without eggs and are available in a number of shapes, refined and stoneground.

The flavour of rice comes through clearly (especially in plain rice pasta) and this makes a pleasant change. Good with thin sauces as the texture is rather stodgy compared to traditional pasta. Take care with the cooking process as undercooking gives the pasta an unpleasant grainy "bite" whilst overcooking makes it soft. Use the largest available saucepan for cooking.

LOW-PROTEIN PASTA (2)

Made from blended vegetable starches, including potato and maize. Unusual in appearance for its white colour and a real surprise in terms of texture and flavour. The texture was firm with a good bite (this was a product that suffered very slightly if the timing was not exact, either under or over, when cooking). Apart from its usefulness for those on a special diet, it is an interesting ingredient that looks and tastes good. The lack of salt is noticeable, but this is not a problem if the pasta is tossed with butter or seasoned olive oil before serving.

COOKING NOTE

I found that some of the cooking times suggested by manufacturers of specialist pastas were quite inaccurate. In particular, some of the very short cooking times were too short and the pasta was just not cooked. When using a new product, it is worth checking the pasta at different stages during boiling. Also, you will need a large saucepan for some specialist pastas as they make the water starchy.

BARLEY PASTA (3)

A stoneground product produced from barley, it is wheat-free and without eggs. Check the details on the packets as differences may occur between brands. This has a nutty flavour and a slightly soft texture, with the wholemeal adding interest to the texture. Take care not to overcook this pasta.

SPELT PASTA (4)

Spelt is a registered trade name for this American pasta. Organic and wholegrain, and made from a wheat-related grain. It is not necessarily suitable for those following a gluten-free diet, but more information is available from the Coeliac support groups.

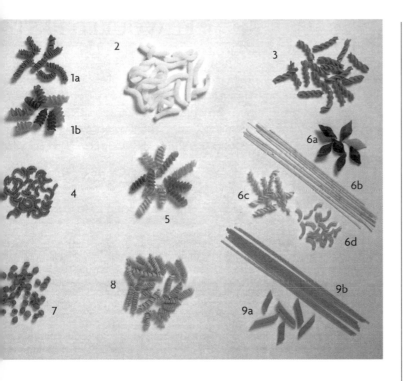

CORN PASTA (6c & d)

Pure corn pasta, made only from maize without any added starch and binders, is gluten-free and made without eggs. Available in a variety of flavours, including:

CORN AND PARSLEY (6b)

Corn, chilli and tomato, and corn and spinach. Shells, spaghetti, twists and rigatoni.

I was delighted with the results from the various corn pastas I tried. The texture was good in all cases and it compared very well with Italian wheat pasta. Also, the flavour was delicate and pleasing and would go well with any pasta sauce. The types I tried were not temperamental in the cooking, so a couple of minutes too little or long did not spoil them.

WHOLEWHEAT PASTA (7)

There is a wide variety of wholewheat pasta products available, from supermarkets as well as specialist shops.

RICE AND MILLET PASTA (8)

Stoneground, wholegrain pasta that is wheat-and gluten-free. It is also made without eggs.

KAMUT PASTA (9a & b)

Kamut is a registered trade name for a range of Italian pasta products. Marketed as wholegrain and organic, the information on the packet provides promotional information on the ingredients without giving details of exactly what goes into the pasta product, other than a reference to *Triticum polonicum* after the trade name. *Triticum* is the Latin name for a wild species of grain from which wheat developed (the Latin name of durum wheat is *Triticum durum* for this reason). It should not be eaten by those following a gluten-free diet.

When cooked, the pasta I tried became quite pale. It was firm and *al dente* in texture. Anyone used to eating a high-fibre wholemeal wheat pasta would probably find the texture too smooth, light, soft or plain, and it cannot be compared directly with wholemeal pastas in terms of texture. I found it to be similar to white bread with fibre added.

The Spelt Elbows I tried had a smoothness to their texture that is not usually associated with wholemeal pasta. Lovers of Italian pasta would find the texture and flavour disappointing, and anyone used to wholemeal products may find it lacking in bite.

ORGANIC PASTA (5)

Prepared using organic ingredients, a wide choice of refined and wholewheat pastas, as well as products prepared from other grains are available.

CORN AND VEGETABLE PASTA (6a)

Colourful pasta shapes made from polenta with spinach, beetroot, tomato, celery and onion. Attractive and gluten-free, without eggs either.

Lighter than stoneground and wholemeal types, these are a good choice for serving when catering for "traditionalists" and those who may be avoiding gluten or eggs. The pasta I cooked was good, with excellent texture and a tasty flavour that was not too strong, but justified the pasta being labelled as "vegetable".

Spinach varieties are always a good test of the quality of a pasta, and I could taste the spinach in these, as well as the onion and other vegetables of the other varieties.

FLAVOURED PASTAS

There is a wide choice of flavoured pasta products and the quality is equally varied, but then this is true of all food products. The information that follows applies to the dried pastas that I tried. Some of the flavoured fresh pastas, particularly the less expensive brands, can be rather coarse and raw in taste. By way of contrast, some of the best fresh pastas really are a treat.

Glossary of Flavoured Pasta

PORCINI PASTA (1)

Delicious pasta flavoured with dried ceps or porcini. A distinctly flavoured pasta that will stand alone if dressed with a little butter, oil, cream or other very simple sauce. Clever mushroom shapes enhanced the image. Would be terrific in a hearty mushroom soup (it was a shame to drain away their cooking water) or in hotpots and moist stews. The expensive Italian brand I tried really was worth it.

CORN AND SPINACH PASTA (2)

See Speciality Pastas. The combination of corn and spinach were good in flavour and colour. Good spinach colour.

BLACK SQUID (3a & b)

Cuttlefish or squid ink is used to enrich rather than strongly flavour the pasta. Although squid ink pastas do not have a "fishy" flavour, they are tinged with seafood and I would not serve them with a poultry sauce or meat. Best for seafood or vegetable-based sauces.

ASPARAGUS (4)

At first taste, a bit "grassy", but better when tossed with melted butter. Serve with a light, creamy or milk sauce.

SMOKED SALMON (5)

The pasta smelled strongly of smoked salmon, but the flavour had diminished markedly after boiling. For the price, I recommend buying plain pasta and spending the price difference on fresh smoked salmon to toss into it.

CORN, TOMATO AND CHILLI (6)

See Corn pasta in the Glossary of Speciality Pastas. Quite distinctly tasted of chilli, but the tomato does not come through. Good in flavour and texture.

CHAMPIGNON (7)

From a French range, the "pâtes aux oeufs frais aromatisées" that I tried were flavoured with dried trompettes de mort mushrooms. A good flavour, milder than porcini pasta. Serve plain with butter, oil or cream and cheese. Toss with sautéed mushrooms to accentuate the flavour or, toss with butter and serve as a base for creamy chicken mixtures or milk-based seafood sauces. Take care not to drown the delicate mushroom pasta.

BASIL (8)

Quality is important when buying herb-flavoured pasta. I tried a French-made brand of tagliatelle that had a good, mild basil flavour. Good tossed with oil or butter as a base for a topping or simply with cheese.

SPINACH (9)

Qualities vary widely, but expensive types are worth the extra for a good spinach flavour.

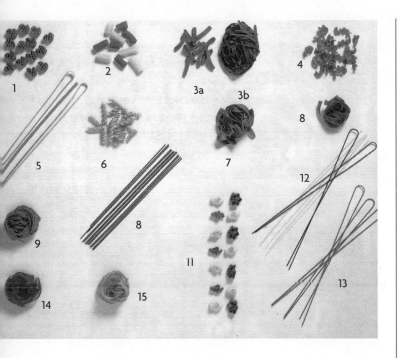

The garlic tends to overpower the tomato, so the latter contributes colour rather than flavour.

FASTA PASTA

There is a wide range of quick-cook pasta, instant noodles and sauced pasta. Here are just a few of them.

BOIL-IN-THE-BAG PASTA: Perforated boiling bags containing slim pasta spirals (or other shapes) that cook in about 7–8 minutes. Easy to drain, but the texture is not as good as "proper" pasta.

INSTANT CHINESE NOODLES: These are soaked in freshly boiled water instead of having to be boiled. They are great; a real boon for supper in-a-hurry dishes.

INSTANT OR VERY SPEEDY PASTAS: These are usually in cake form, like Chinese dried noodles, and vary considerably in quality and flavour. In general, I find that the more they offer in the way of flavouring, the less like real food they tend to be.

QUICK-COOK PASTAS: Spaghetti in a major Italian range cooks in 3 minutes to give excellent results, but some larger shapes tend to have a slightly slimy texture. Quick-cook macaronis vary: some are ready in 3 minutes, others in 7 minutes. I found the latter to be excellent.

SAUCED DRIED PASTA: There is an ever-increasing and changing range of dehydrated sauce and pasta mixes, rather like flavoured rice mixes. Frankly, with fresh pasta so readily available, I would opt for a bowl of pasta topped with a little oil or butter and some grated cheese.

GARLIC AND CHILLI (10)

The Italian brand I tried was good (spaghetti), with a pronounced pep coming from the chilli.

CHIANTI SPECIALITY (11)

Novelty pasta in the shapes of red grapes (beetroot), white grapes (plain) and leaves (spinach). This was very good, and the spinach flavour was the best of all the spinach pastas that I tried specifically for this chapter. Looks terrific!

BLACK AND WHITE SPAGHETTI (12)

Flavoured with black squid ink and plain. A good combination that makes an elegant base for seafood. A smart option for appearance rather than flavour.

BLACK OLIVE SPAGHETTI (13)

This is good! A light flavour of black olives that is just sufficient to assert itself. Ideal for tossing with olive oil and garlic and topping with pecorino. Would be lost with a strong (meat-type) sauce, milk or cream. Diced fresh tomatoes or sun-dried tomatoes would go well, especially with fresh basil or parsley.

TOMATO (14)

As for spinach, the quality varies significantly and some pink pasta tastes rather bland.

SWEET PASTAS

I have not explored sweet pasta here beyond including some examples of filled pastas with sweet fillings as there were so many savoury recipes I wanted to include, but there are traditional sweet pasta dishes and many modern ways in which Italian-style pasta is used in sweet recipes.

Glossary of Sweet Pasta

Above: Plum and blackberry compote.

FRUIT COMPOTES FOR PASTA
Stewed fruits may be served with noodles and plain pasta. Cherries, plums, apricots and other full-flavoured fruits should be used. There are Eastern European and Italian dishes of this type.

FRUIT-FILLED PASTAS
Pasta shapes filled with whole cherries, plums, apricots or other fruit, boiled and served with butter, sugar and soured cream are popular in many Eastern European cuisines.

LOKSHEN PUDDING
A Jewish pudding of noodles (tagliatelle or ribbon noodles) in which boiled noodles are baked with eggs, dried fruit, cinnamon and sugar.

MACARONI MILK PUDDING
A British pudding. Macaroni is baked in milk and sugar until the milk has been absorbed and the pasta is tender and creamy. Vanilla, lemon rind or a cinnamon stick may be added.

MOHN NUDELN
Austrian dessert of noodles tossed with butter, sugar and poppy seeds.

SUESSEN NUDELAUF
An Austrian dessert of noodles layered with apples or plums and sugar, then baked. Fried breadcrumbs form a crisp topping and soured cream is served with the pudding.

POLISH POPPY SEED PUDDING
A traditional Christmas Eve pudding. The cooked ribbon noodles are tossed with butter, sugar and poppy seeds. Noodles with poppy seeds is also a popular combination for sweet puddings in other Eastern European countries.

SEVYIAN
An Indian milk pudding with vermicelli (vermicelli being known as sev, or sevyian). The vermicelli is broken into small pieces and simmered in milk. Green cardamoms, raisins or sultanas, pistachio nuts and almonds are added. Rose water is used and cloves may be added. The sweet mixture is cooked until the milk has been absorbed and the pasta is thick and creamy delicious warm or cold.

SWEET-FLAVOURED PASTAS
A popular American concept, pasta may be flavoured with chocolate, fruit or other foods and served with sweet sauces or with butter and sugar or cream.

ORIENTAL PASTAS

Chinese egg noodles are readily available from most supermarkets and many wholefood or healthfood shops sell a variety of oriental pasta, notably Japanese noodles. Specialist Chinese or oriental supermarkets are the places to find a large range of different rice sticks as well as fresh egg noodles and won ton wrappers.

Above: Japanese rice sticks.

The following is a guide to some of the main types. Inconsistencies in terms of translations and local names, as well as the general similarity between some types of noodles in Chinese, Thai, Malaysian and Singaporean cooking, make this a difficult subject on which to offer a definitive list, but the following glossary provides a good starting-point for discovering the delights of oriental pasta. If you make a new discovery, study the packet as there are often diagrams showing how to cook the pasta. Also, I find that the shopkeepers are always keen to help by explaining how they cook the product. The fun part of shopping this way and pleading ignorance is that most of the other customers in smaller stores readily join in to contribute ideas and anecdotes about their cooking.

A note about cooking times: most packets give instructions and they should be followed as the products vary enormously. I have given some indication of the times I have used or come across, and they may be of help in the absence of other guidance. As a general rule, though, the finer and less dense the noodles, the shorter the cooking time (with the exception of egg noodles). Generally, the Japanese method of cooking noodles is to soak or boil them, then to rinse them in cold water before using. Personally, unless I am serving the noodles cold, I find that they do not have to be rinsed if they are used immediately. If there is any delay after cooking though, rinse in cold water to arrest the cooking process.

GLOSSARY OF ORIENTAL PASTA

SAIFUN NOODLES (1)
Japanese dried, very fine, opaque white noodles, made from sweet potato starch and potato starch. An alternative to shirataki, these can be served in dishes such as sukiyaki or they can be served cold. They are cooked for 3–4 minutes in boiling water or soaked in hot water for 2–3 minutes before adding to a hotpot.

MUNG BEAN THREAD OR TRANSPARENT NOODLES (2)
Clear, shiny noodles. The Chinese type are usually made from rung bean flour. Various other cellophane noodles, particularly Japanese varieties are made with buckwheat flour, yam flour and wheat starch.

CHOW MEIN NOODLES (3)
Cakes of dried, yellow noddles, made from wheat flour, possibly with egg (check ingredients listed on packet) or with colouring; see Egg noodles.

SANUKI SOMEN (4)
Soumen, or somen, noodles. Dried, white and made from wheat starch, these are round and fine, as for marufuji somen and somen. They should be cooked in boiling water for 4–5 minutes, or until tender.

NAENG MYUN (5a & b)
Fine, vermicelli-like, Japanese noodles for adding to pang myun soup. Made from wheat flour, buckwheat flour and sweet potato starch. The noodles themselves are fine, round and shiny and light brown.

DRIED WHEAT FLOUR NOODLES (6)
Long, white, narrow noodles.

SHIRATAKI (7)
Japanese white noodles prepared from a plant known as the devil's tongue plant, a root vegetable similar to yam. The root is used to make a flour that is formed into a cake or loaf known as konnyaku. The same dried flour is used to make the noodles. Sold tinned or in sausage-shaped plastic tubes, the noodles are kept in water. They are ready cooked for adding to dishes, such as sukiyaki.

SOBA (8)
Japanese pasta, made from buckwheat flour, with or without wheat flour, possibly with yam flour added. There are many types, some containing a larger proportion of buckwheat flour than others.

NAI YAU MEIN (9)
Chinese dried, flat, narrow white noodles with milk powder added.

EGG NOODLES
(10a, b, c, d & e)
The most popular type of oriental noodles, used in Chinese, Japanese,

SINGAPOREAN (Hokkien); Malaysian (Mee); and Thai (Ba Mee) cooking. Available fresh and dried, they may be thin or fine, thread noodles or medium. There are also slightly thicker fresh noodles (comparable to linguine of Italian origin). In general, the noodles seem to vary slightly in thickness. They are packed in cakes or bundles and cook quickly. Some dried types are simply soaked in boiling water for about 15 minutes, whilst others may be boiled for just 2–3 minutes.

FRESH EGG NOODLES
(Not shown)
Larger Chinese supermarkets sell two or three types, of different widths. They may be rounded or thin and slightly flattened, slightly thicker than spaghetti or wider and more like narrow Italian noodles. The noodles are folded in small bundles, dusted with cornflour. They keep well in the fridge for about a week or they freeze well and may be cooked from frozen. They cook quickly (in 2–3 minutes) when added to boiling water.

TOMOSHIRAGA SOMEN (11).
Dried, white somen noodles.

RICE STICKS AND RICE VERMICELLI (12a, b, c, d & e)
Noodles made from rice flour, available in a variety of widths from fine vermicelli (yinsi rice vermicelli) to wide ribbon noodles. Sometimes sold cut flat, but more often formed into large or small bundles, rather like skeins of wool. Also known as Singaporean or Malaysian BEE HOON or MEE HOON or Thai SEN MEE, or Indian SEV.

BEE HOON OR MEE HOON
Singaporean and Malaysian names for Chinese rice vermicelli, see Rice sticks.

SEN MEE (Not shown)
Thai term for rice vermicelli. Thin and semi-transparent.

SEV (Not shown)
Indian rice vermicelli.

HO FUN, HOR FUN, KUA TEAW OR KWAY TEOW (13)
Chinese noodles made from wheat flour and cornflour or rice flour. White and quite wide, they are similar to short tagliatelle or ribbon noodles.

UDON (14)
Japanese white noodles, thicker than somen.
Also available in form of wholewheat udon (dried) in healthfood shops. Fresh noodles are most common in Japanese supermarkets – find them in chilled vacuum packs possibly cooked ready for serving with soup.

ISHIGURO YAHAIMO SOBA (15)
A variety of Japanese dried, fine noodles made from wheat flour, buckwheat flour and yam flour.

MARUFUJI SOMEN (16)
Fine, round, white Japanese noodles made from wheat flour. *See* Sanuki Somen.

OTHER ORIENTAL PASTAS NOT ILLUSTRATED

ARROWROOT VERMICELLI
Fine white noodles made from arrowroot.

LAKSA NOODLES
Fresh rice noodles, these are white and slightly thicker than spaghetti (Malaysian/ Singaporean).

HARUSAME
Japanese bean starch noodles.

HIYAMUGI
Japanese, medium-thick white noodles that are usually served cold in the dish of the same name. They are cooked for about 7–8 minutes until softened.

RAMEN NOODLES
Fine, white Japanese wheat noodles, served in a soup.

SEN LEK
Thai rice flour noodles, slightly thicker than sen mee.

SEN YAI
Thai term for white rice flour noodles that are thicker than sen mee and sen lek.

WON TONS
Fine, egg noodle-like dough, stuffed and boiled or deep fried. Won ton wrappers are small, square wrappers, sold fresh. They freeze well. Won ton wrappers may also be used for making dim sum.

WOON SEN
Thai term for fine bean thread vermicelli.

EXAMPLES OF PASTAS FROM OTHER COUNTRIES

What follows is just a sample of the pasta-type foods that are popular in countries other than Italy and the orient. In eastern and northern Europe, there are many dumplings that are similar to filled pasta and indeed, it can be difficult to decide where to draw the line between pasta and dumpling. I have not included the many German dumplings, but have restricted the examples to smaller shapes.

Glossary of Pasta from Other Countries

CSIPETKE
Tiny flour, egg and water dumplings from Hungary. The dough is rolled out to a 1 cm (½ in) thickness and cut into narrow 1 cm (½ in) wide strips. Then tiny pieces are pinched off and rolled into small balls, the size of little beans. These are boiled or cooked in a stew. Served with goulash.

FIDEOS
Spanish version of vermicelli, available in different thicknesses; used in soups and for a variation on paella.

GALUSKA
Hungarian dumplings made from a soft dough of flour, eggs and milk. The mixture is placed on a wetted board and small pieces cut into a saucepan of boiling water, a method similar to making spätzle.

KASNUDLN
Austrian filled pasta or noodles, shaped as squares, folded and stuffed with different fillings, such as meat, ham, mushrooms, cottage cheese or leftovers. Eaten as a main dish, tossed with butter and served with salad. Similar to uska or tortellini. Also made with sweet fillings, such as ground poppy seeds or dried fruit and dusted with sugar.

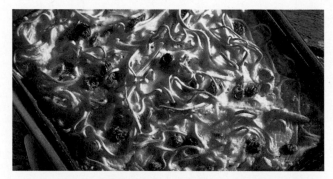

Above: Savoury noodle kugel.

Above: Lasanki with cabbage.

KNEDLE
Λ potato and flour dough is used to make these stuffed pasta-like dumplings. The stuffing may be savoury or sweet.

KNEDLIKY
Small, Austrian dumplings that may be based on a dough with bread or potatoes, these are similar to knedle, which may be compared with potato gnocchi of Italian cooking. Czechoslovakian cooking also includes its own version.

KNEIDLECH
Jewish matzo balls, made from matzo meal enriched with chicken fat and egg and rolled into tiny balls.

KOPYTKΛ
Polish equivalent of Italian potato gnocchi.

KREPLACH
Triangular, filled pasta or dumplings.

LASANKI
Polish pasta squares. An egg pasta dough, cut into tiny squares. Good with cabbage, sauerkraut, butter, garlic and onion. These are a supper dish or may be served as a side dish with stewed meats.

LENIWE PIEROGI
Lazy pierogi. A Polish quick alternative to cheese-filled pierogi (see Pierogi), a dough of potatoes, cottage cheese, bread and flour is shaped into short sausages.

LOKSHEN
Jewish name for egg noodles, the same as tagliatelle.

LOKSHYNA
Russian name for egg noodles.

MATZO MEAL NOODLES
Jewish soup noodles, made from a batter of matzo meal cooked in the form of a pancake, then cut into 5 mm (¼ in) wide strips.

NOKY
Czechoslovakian noodles, made in the same way as galuska.

ORZO
Also known as minestra, orzo is similar to pasta a riso. It is added to braised dishes and hotpots.

PELMENI
A Siberian filled pasta, made from a dough of flour and eggs and filled with ham, pork or game to make semicircular shapes. Served with butter, or lemon juice and parsley.

PIEROGI
Polish filled dumplings that are similar to ravioli. Pierogi are semicircular and may be filled with meat, cheese or other fillings, such as sauerkraut.

SCHLICK KRAPFEN
Austrian filled pasta similar to ravioli, served in soup or with butter and cheese.

SPÄTZLE
German noodles, made from a thick batter of potatoes, flour, eggs and water. The batter is cut into short strips and these are slid off a board into boiling water. Alternatively, the batter may be piped into the water and short lengths cut off. Good with meaty stews. The spätzle may be flavoured with herbs or other seasonings, and vegetables may be used in the batter. I have also seen reference to stiffer spätzle from a dough, but the batter is the original and lighter form (see pages 46-47). Sold fresh and chilled in vacuum packs in some delicatessens.

TARHONYA
Hungarian noodle dough that is dried and coarsely grated into pellets. Said to be one of the oldest of noodle doughs and an early way of preserving food, the noodles take the name of barley noodles for their grain-like shape. The nomadic Magyar tribes originally made the dough, and tarhonya is still popular today. The pellets can be cooked by simmering and then frying (they can simply be cooked until the liquid has evaporated, with butter added to start the frying process) or they can be boiled and drained as for ordinary pasta. Served with goulash.

TRAHANA
Grated noodle dough, as for tarhonya.

USZKA
Polish dumplings filled with dried mushroom stuffing (see page 173). Similar to tiny tortellini.

VARENYKY, OR VARIENIKI
Russian filled dumplings, semicircular in shape and filled with sauerkraut or cheese. Similar to ravioli in texture. May be filled with sweet cheese mixture and served with fruit or filled with fruit. There are several variations on these, both savoury and sweet. Lithuanian varenyky are filled with meat, and old recipes call for large amounts of kidney fat or suet.

ZACIERKI

PASTA ON THE PLATE

What sort of image does pasta have in your household and when does pasta immediately spring to mind as the ideal ingredient for a meal?

The popular image of pasta is Italian, quick, easy, nutritious, slimming and ... creative.

Let us pause to take a longer look at some of these ideas. Does our experience of cooking and eating pasta reinforce or dispel these popular ideas?

I think pasta is a terrific, versatile ingredient; better still, it can be delicious and different to eat in very many ways. I hope that the following pages expand your repertoire.

The important factor to remember about pasta is that it is not eaten on its own. Therefore, its true food value in the diet is subject to the accompaniments offered with it or the dishes for which it is an aside. This is very important.

If you have a serious interest in the food value of pasta, then you will appreciate that this varies according to the product. Apart from the completely separate types of pasta – Chinese, Japanese, Italian – there are regional specialities, foreign interpretations, fast foods and many brands.

The information manufacturers put on their packaging is erratic in the detail it provides, and it is not possible to provide accurate information to cover all pasta. However, it is helpful to offer general guidance.

Above: Linguini with green peppers and pesto.

PASTA IN THE DIET – Putting it into Perspective

First, I ought to stress that the word "diet" is used here in the nutritional sense, that is, to refer to all food that is eaten, regardless of any specific characteristics relating to individuals and specific types of diet. I do not use it to indicate a "reduced-calorie" or "calorie-controlled" diet. Also, this information is based on Italian-type pasta rather than oriental pasta, such as rice sticks or won ton dough.

A Well Balanced Diet

Advertisements bombard the public with information about "healthy" foods, but, in fact, there is no such thing as an unhealthy food. Butter, cream and other high-fat products are all relevant in a balanced diet as long as they are eaten as a *small* proportion of a varied total food intake. On an everyday basis, we should all consume significantly more starch and fresh fruit and vegetables than protein and fat; and we should consume regular and frequent supplies of dietary fibre or non-starch polysaccharides. Variety is probably the most useful key to a well-balanced diet.

Pasta: A Useful Food for Sensible Eating

Pasta is a useful food to include in a well-balanced diet. In itself, it does not have a high fat content, it provides starch for energy and it may include a small, but useful, source of protein. Egg pasta can make a valuable contribution of protein to a vegetarian diet where many different sources make up the total intake, unlike a diet based on fish, poultry or meat where concentrated sources of animal protein are eaten regularly.

As pasta is often eaten with substantial salads, it can be a useful food for promoting healthy eating.

There are many excellent sauces and accompaniments that substantiate the image of pasta as a well-balanced, healthy food. However, there is also a distinct tendency to smother pasta with olive oil, butter, cream and cheese, so it is up to us whether we eat it in a healthy or less healthy way.

Pasta for Energy: A Carbohydrate Food

Primarily, pasta is a carbohydrate food, usually based on wheat. Its main contribution to diet is starch. Depending on the type, as we have seen, the pasta may also make a contribution of protein (not that protein is a nutrient lacking in the Western diet). It also provides some minerals and contributes a small amount of certain vitamins.

To put this into context, pasta is similar to potatoes or rice in its role in our diet. Starches should be the main source of energy in the diet (as opposed to sugars and fats). The body breaks down food to obtain energy. Simple sugars are most easily broken down and starch, which does not have a high fibre content, is digested more quickly than foods that contain a significant amount of fibre.

All Important Fibre

Fibre is essential in the diet. White pasta is *not* a valuable source of fibre, but wholemeal pasta does provide a useful supply of dietary fibre, or non-starch polysaccharides as the experts would like it termed.

Above: Tagliatelle with grated carrot and spring onion.

Pasta and Fat: Comparisons with Alternatives

Pasta is often promoted as a low-fat food. It does have a low fat content in itself and, when olive oil is used in its manufacture, the greater percentage of the fat it does have may be monounsaturated. Potatoes, rice, couscous and wheat are also low-fat foods, and they may contain less fat than pasta.

For example, 100 g (4 oz) raw macaroni contains about 1.8 g fat; a similar weight of raw potato contains 0.2 g fat. As 100 g (14 oz) raw potato is hardly a representative portion and 100 g (4 oz) macaroni is a generous portion, a better comparison is between 100 g (4 oz) raw macaroni with 1.8 g fat and 350 g (12 oz) raw potato with 0.7 g fat: the macaroni has more than double the quantity of fat in the potato.

This comparison can be made between egg noodles and various other types of pasta with similar indications. It is also interesting to compare pasta with rice. Rice has a higher fat content than potatoes, but it is lower than pasta.

I am adopting a pedantic approach and splitting hairs simply to put pasta into context, but pasta, potatoes and rice are all carbohydrate-rich foods which have a low fat content. The actual fat content of pasta depends on the ingredients used to make it it is a product, not produce.

Pasta and Calorie Controlled Diets

Pasta is a useful food to eat when following a reduced-calorie or calorie-controlled diet as it provides reasonable bulk for its calorie content. The same is true of any food that has a high starch and low fat content, such as potatoes and rice.

One of the difficulties of promoting pasta as useful in low-calorie diets and when slimming is in distinguishing the low-calorie dishes with pasta from the others, which are calorific. For example, a hearty bowl of boiled pasta with steamed courgettes, tossed with fresh basil and topped with 2 tbsp of grated Parmesan cheese, plenty of black pepper and 1 tbsp of fromage frais is every slimmer's dream meal. However, the simpler alternative of pasta tossed with olive oil and garlic and served with a bowl of Parmesan or pecorino to taste will provide a far higher calorie intake, quite out of the realms of the target for a low-calorie meal. So, it is all down to what you serve it with

TEN CALORIE-COUNTED TOPPINGS

The calorie counts for the following are a guide for the ingredients given, excluding the pasta. Each idea provides a single serving.

Thinly slice 100 g (4 oz) young courgettes. Steam them over boiling water for 5 minutes, cook them in the microwave for about 1 minute or blanch them in boiling water for 1 minute. Toss with pasta, 1 finely chopped spring onion, a few grated basil leaves and plenty of freshly ground black pepper. Add 2 tbsp grated Parmesan cheese. *Kilocalories* 66

Grate 100 g (4 oz) carrot and mix with 2 tbsp orange juice. Add 1 chopped spring onion and toss this with the pasta Serve with 25 g (1 oz) grated mild Cheddar cheese. *Kilocalories* 151

Hard-boil and roughly chop 1 egg. Press 50 g (2 oz) cottage cheese through a sieve and toss with the pasta. Add the egg, 3 tbsp snipped chives and 3 tbsp chopped fresh parsley. Season with a little grated nutmeg and freshly ground black pepper. *Kilocalories* 137

Melt 15 g (½ oz) butter in a saucepan and lightly scramble 1 egg until beginning to set. Toss with the pasta. Serve topped with 100 g (4 oz) cooked fresh spinach. Sprinkle with freshly ground black pepper. *Kilocalories* 218

Peel, de-seed and roughly chop 100 g (4 oz) tomatoes. Hard-boil and roughly chop 1 egg. Toss the egg and tomatoes with the pasta and season with freshly ground black pepper. *Kilocalories* 105

Dice 75 g (3 oz) cooked chicken breast (without skin) and mix with 2 tbsp fromage frais. Add freshly ground black pepper and 2 tbsp snipped chives. Toss with the hot pasta. *Kilocalories* 140

Flake 50 g (2 oz) tinned tuna in brine (drained) and toss with the pasta. Add a little grated lemon rind, 2 tbsp chopped fresh parsley and a squeeze of lemon juice. Serve on a generous green salad. *Kilocalories* 50

Mix 3 tbsp dry white wine, 100 g (4 oz) sliced leek, 1 sliced celery stick, 1 diced carrot and 100 g (4 oz) grated green cabbage in a saucepan. Cover and cook, shaking the saucepan often, for 15 minutes. Add 100 g (4 oz) tomatoes, peeled and chopped, plenty of salt and pepper and cook, covered, for a further 15 minutes. Toss with the pasta and serve with 1 tbsp grated Parmesan cheese. *Kilocalories* 139

Chop 1 garlic clove and mix with 1 tsp chopped fresh oregano and 25 g (1 oz) chopped walnuts. Sieve 50 g (2 oz) cottage cheese. Toss the garlic, oregano, walnuts and cottage cheese with the hot pasta. *Kilocalories* 231

Dice 50 g (2 oz) lean cooked ham. Thinly slice 100 g (4 oz) courgettes and toss with 1 tsp olive oil in a small saucepan. Cover and sweat the vegetables for 5 minutes. Toss the courgettes and gammon with the pasta. *Kilocalories* 200

LIGHT PASTA AND LOW CALORIE COUNTS: SOME SERVING IDEAS

Here are a few suggestions for serving up calorie-controlled dishes that taste as good as they look.

- First, check the calorie content of the brand of pasta you are cooking.

- Always weigh the amount of pasta you are cooking per portion (check the packet or table for details of this) so you can serve an amount for which the above calculation is easy.

SERVING STYLES

On the whole, pasta has a rather everyday image – the ideal food for family suppers, a safe option for picky children, a quick meal for busy working people and a good ingredient when the cupboard is empty, but there is some cheese in the fridge. It may also be both modern and fashionable, but it is often overlooked as a main ingredient for dinner parties, a sophisticated lunch or a celebration family meal.

Pasta Effects: Simple ways with Versatile Products

The recipes in the chapters that follow highlight a variety of ways in which pasta can be used apart from the familiar boiling or baking, then serving. The following examples may inspire you to experiment with some of your favourite dishes.

Colourful Presentations

This must be the most obvious example of how to make plain pasta look more interesting. Instead of serving pasta of just one colour, combine two or more different colours. Also, rather than mix the different pastas when cooking, so that they are simply tossed together when served, cook them separately and arrange them in a serving dish.

For results that make a real impact at a sophisticated meal, avoid the usual red, green and white novelty shapes. The longer pastas coloured with squid ink, tomato, tumeric, saffron, herbs and so on are ideal choices for such occasions. Fresh pastas are perfect for cooking separately as they cook quickly, so you can even use the same saucepan as long as you have a boiling kettle at the ready to avoid a cold start each time. Try the following ideas.

- Arrange different colours of pasta in lines on a large rectangular or oval dish. This works particularly well for tagliatelle, malfadine, spaghetti and other long shapes.
- Spoon short shapes into wedges of different colours in a round dish or alternate two colours. Arrange sprigs of fresh herbs or spoon a sauce in the middle.
- Arrange concentric rings of spaghetti of different colours on a large platter.
- Layer pasta of different colours in a deep, straight-sided glass serving bowl or soufflé dish.
- Use two or more colours of lasagne when layering baked dishes.
- Use two colours of pasta when making ravioli, tortellini and other filled shapes. Place the filling on one colour, then lay a sheet of a second colour on top.

A Different Approach to Shape

Why is lasagne always rectangular or square? Whether you make your own pasta or not, there is no reason always to make rectangular or square layered pasta bakes. As it is often difficult to find a suitable rectangular dish for many bakes anyway, simply adopt a different approach and cut the pasta to fit dishes you have.

- If you make your own pasta, then roll it out into a circle and cut it to fit the chosen dish before boiling it. You may have to trim the pasta after cooking, at least for a neat top layer.

- If you buy lasagne, simply lay the pasta in a round dish as you would in a square or rectangular one. For a neat top layer, arrange strips of lasagne from the middle outwards, leaving a circle with a diameter of about 5 cm (2 in) uncovered in the middle. Overlap the strips all round the remainder of the dish and trim their edges, then cut out a circle of pasta to neaten the middle.

- Make single portions of baked pasta by layering pasta in ramekin dishes, single casseroles or soufflé dishes. Large squares of fresh lasagne are ideal for trimming to fit small dishes.

- Instead of serving a thick sauce or vegetables on a bed of cooked pasta, when the sauce is cooked, cook squares of fresh lasagne in boiling water and layer them in the middle of single plates with the sauce. Add a gratin topping and grill to brown. This is also an excellent way of making an attractive presentation of sautéed vegetables and pasta as a side dish for grilled fish, poultry or meat. For successful results, do not spoon too much sauce or too many ingredients between the pieces of pasta, otherwise they will run out from between the layers and look unattractive.

- Home-made stuffed pastas do not have to conform to the traditions of round or square shapes for ravioli or neatly twisted tortellini. For special occasions allow your imagination a little freedom and use pastry cutters to make differently shaped stuffed pasta.

- For Valentine's Day ravioli, encase scallops or oysters between two layers of heart-shaped pasta. Serve on a White Wine Sauce (see page 56), tinted pink with a little tomato purée, and garnish with fronds of fresh dill. Make just two or three for a first course if you do not want to spend too long shaping them. Shapes that look a little wrinkled when cooked can be beautified by topping with a little grated Parmesan and grilling for a few seconds – this hides the creases that would otherwise spoil the heart shape.

Rings, Swirls, Moulds and Loaves

Once it has been boiled and drained, pasta can be used in the same way as pastry for some dishes or it can be baked into a shape. Here are a few pointers.

- Layer circles of pasta in ramekins or small soufflé dishes with mixtures that set when baked, then un-mould them when cooked.

- Line a ring mould with cooked lasagne, alternating colours for best effect, then fill with a mixture which sets when baked. Fold over the ends of the pasta to neaten the shape and unmould when cooked.

- Layer cooked lasagne with meatloaf mixture in a loaf tin, lining the bottom with non-stick baking parchment first. Start with a layer of lasagne, cut to fit the base of the tin, then build up with layers of meat and end with a layer of lasagne. Cover with foil and bake as usual. Use lasagne verde for good effect and serve on a plate flooded with tomato sauce.

- Swiss-roll style swirls of pasta are attractive. For simple impact, cook strips of lasagne until tender, then spread with a finely minced, well-seasoned mixture of fish, poultry or meat. Roll up and place in a baking dish, then add stock, wine or a sauce, cover and braise until cooked through.

A Topping Sauce

- Instead of smothering stuffed pasta shapes with a sauce, ladle the sauce on to the plate, then arrange the pasta on top. This is ideal for strong-coloured sauces, such as tomato. Add a herb garnish to the pasta, which can look a little anaemic otherwise.

- An alternative method of serving pasta and sauces is to put half the pasta in a warmed dish, top with the sauce then add the remaining pasta. Add a garnish of herbs or other suitable ingredients (tomato slices, avocado slices, pepper slices and so on, say), then take the dish to the table. This works well with attractive pasta shapes, such as porcini-flavoured pasta or the attractive grape shapes mentioned on page 16.

PASTA KNOW-HOW

Unlike delicate pastries, pasta dough withstands the touch of an inexperienced handler, so do not shy away from tempting Italian-style stuffed pastas or home-made lasagne because you have never made any before. Once you are familiar with the dough, you will probably feel inclined to experiment with flavours - and this is when it really does become worth-while because the better quality bought pasta of this type is expensive. Apart from Italian egg pasta, you will find gnocchi and oriental-style pasta in this chapter. Remember that they all freeze well, so you can have a mammoth cooking session and store enough for several meals. Have fun experimenting and, in the process, developing your pasta repertoire.

Making Pasta at Home

Freshly made Italian pasta dough, quickly boiled and tossed with lots of melted butter or warmed olive oil, pepper, a little garlic and, perhaps, some chopped parsley or grated basil, is delicious and simple to make. However, even though it is possible to make delicate Chinese-style won ton dough, the technique for making long oriental egg noodles is not one that is practical for the home cook to learn. The information that follows on mixing, kneading and boiling, therefore, applies to the Italian-style doughs, and specific notes and information are included with the various other basic pasta recipes.

Pasta is not difficult to make, but it does take a bit of kneading. Unlike delicate pastry, the dough is firm and glutinous, so some muscle power is required rather than the delicate touch practised by pastrycooks. Strong flour is used for its gluten content, giving the dough its characteristic strength and texture, and allowing it to be rolled quite thinly with smooth results.

Equipment

If you already have a reasonably well-equipped kitchen, then you will not have to buy anything special for making pasta. However, if you have never tried making pasta before you may find the following points helpful.

A Large Work Surface

This is something you do need for rolling out pasta dough. Make sure it is thoroughly clean and dry before you start. Unlike pastry making, you do want the pasta to "adhere" to the surface slightly as you roll it, so it will pick up any grime!

Rolling Pin

A rolling pin without knobs on the end is essential, otherwise you will end up with infuriating grooves running down the length of the pasta once you have rolled it out beyond a certain size.

Above: Useful equipments: Slotted spoon; pasta boiler; pasta machine and metal rolling pin.

Look out for rolling pins that have a central section that rotates on thin handles. As well as wooden ones, marble and stainless steel pins are good as they are easier to clean and they do not stick quite as easily.

Specialist kitchen shops sell extra-long pasta rolling pins but an average-length simpler implement is fine.

Pastry Wheel or Large Knife

A pastry wheel is useful for cutting between filled and covered ravioli and it will give the pasta shapes an attractive fluted edge. However, a long-bladed cook's knife will do the job efficiently.

Ravioli Tray or Tin

This is a small tray with indentations rather like a shallow roll or muffin tin and a raised, serrated cutting edge between the indentations. The rolled-out pasta dough is laid over the tin and lightly pressed into the indentations, then the filling is added to these and the pasta is brushed with beaten egg between the dots of filling. A second sheet of pasta is applied on top and rolled with a rolling pin to separate the single ravioli.

Pasta Machines

The most common and useful one for the average house hold is a hand-turned rolling machine. Small but heavy, the machine clamps to a work surface. The rollers may be set apart at different widths so that the dough can be rolled and folded several times instead of being kneaded by hand.

Cutting rollers can be fitted for making tagliatelle or linguine. A ravioli filler can also be attached. With this, folded sheets of pasta and the filling are fed in through a hopper, then the rollers do the job of filling and separating the single pasta shapes. This is useful if you want to make very small pasta shapes, which are fiddly to manufacture by hand.

Large Saucepan or Pasta Boiler

It is worth investing in a very large saucepan that will have dozens of culinary uses apart from cooking pasta. Look out for a deep saucepan, complete with an integral strainer that fits snuggly inside the saucepan to make maximum use of its capacity. Then, when the pasta is cooked, you simply lift out the perforated lining. This also prevents pasta sticking to the bottom of the saucepan.

Large Colander

A deep colander is essential for draining pasta well. A stainless steel colander can be placed back on top of the saucepan, which is extremely useful when you are juggling a colander of pasta and trying to add the finishing touches to a sauce.

Mixing Pasta Dough

Place the flour and salt in a bowl and make a well in the middle, then add the liquid ingredients to the well. Gradually stir the flour into the eggs until the mixture clumps together – a fairly flat, sturdy plastic or wooden

Above: Kneading the pasta dough by hand.

Above: Kneading the pasta dough by machine.

mixing spoon is best for this. Then, abandon the mixing spoon and use your hands to bring the dough together, scraping the dough from the spoon and the sides of the bowl with a flexible spatula. Press the dough together into a ball, rolling it round the bowl. Depending on the recipe, the dough may seem either slightly too dry for comfortable kneading or slightly too sticky at this stage, but the kneading process is important for achieving the right texture, ready for rolling out the dough.

Kneading Pasta Dough By Hand

Turn the dough out on to a lightly floured work surface and knead it well until it is smooth. Sprinkle a little flour over the work surface during this time if necessary, but try to avoid adding too much flour as this will make the dough too dry.

The secret is to keep the dough moving all the time as you knead it firmly by grasping the front of the dough with your fingers, folding it back and pressing it down with the heel of your hand. This creates a sort of "rocking" movement.

Turn the dough round and over occasionally, keeping it moving, so that it is evenly kneaded. Pasta dough is quite tough and, if it is not moved, then it is easy to end up kneading it from one side only.

When the dough is smooth and warm, place it in a polythene bag and leave to stand for 15–30 minutes. Do not chill the dough at this stage.

Kneading Pasta Dough By Machine

If you have an electric pasta-maker, then follow the manufacturer's instructions. The most popular type of pasta machine is the compact, hand-turned rolling machine that comes with different rollers and attachments for cutting noodles and filling ravioli as well as rolling pasta dough.

First, knead the dough by hand until it comes together in a fairly smooth ball. Then put this through the rollers, set to the widest setting. Fold the dough, press it together and roll it on the widest setting again. Repeat this process several times until the dough is smooth. This, clearly, is less tiring than kneading by hand and gives good results.

Once the dough is smooth, fold it and press it together into a neat lump, then place in a polythene bag and leave to stand for 15-30 minutes.

Rolling out Pasta Dough

You can either roll the dough out by hand with a rolling pin or by machine. If you have a machine, then this stage is quick and easy. Simply pass the dough through the rollers, reducing the gap between them each time.

Work with a quantity of dough that you can handle easily. Unless you have a large kitchen table or work surface and a long pasta rolling pin, cut the complete batch of dough in half or quarters for rolling out. Keep the rest covered to prevent it drying out.

Press the dough into the shape required and lightly flour the surface before rolling it out. Try to keep the dough in the shape you want, pulling the corners out, slightly as you work to make a square or rectangular shape or turning the dough to make a round.

Lift and turn the dough occasionally to prevent it sticking and keep the surface lightly floured. Do not dredge the surface heavily with flour as this will dry the dough and make it more difficult to roll. Ideally, the dough should just cling to the surface as it is rolled. Once the dough is part-rolled and has been turned a couple of times, it becomes smooth and less likely to stick, so it is not necessary to flour the surface further. Lifting and shaking the dough slightly helps it keep its texture.

As you roll the dough – particularly if you are rolling it out with a rolling pin – look out for thick areas and concentrate on rolling them out to achieve an even result. It is easy to continue rolling in one direction so that the edges or one area of dough becomes far thinner than the middle or another area. Gently smoothing the dough with your hands occasionally helps and this is a good way of thinning any thick patches.

Pasta dough can be rolled out very thinly until you can see your hands through it, but this is not necessary. Do not leave the dough thick as it makes noodles chewy and disappointingly stodgy. You should have to work fairly hard at rolling and stretching the dough without breaking its smooth surface, otherwise the chances are that it is too thick. For noodles, the dough should be like thick brown paper or thin French crêpe after rolling.

If the time allows, leave the dough to rest for 10 minutes after rolling and before cutting. This relaxes the dough and helps to prevent it shrinking when cut, but it is not an essential process. If you do leave it to relax, make sure the surface underneath is dusted lightly with flour and cover with clingfilm.

Cutting Pasta

CUTTING NOODLES BY MACHINE
This is a simple matter of changing the rollers to cut noodles. If you have rolled the pasta by hand, then the dough must be floured before cutting.

CUTTING NOODLES BY HAND
Sieve a little flour over the dough and smooth it very lightly with the palm of your hand. Roll the dough up loosely, then cut it into strips as wide or as narrow as you want to make the noodles. Cut fine strips for linguine, 1 cm (½ in) wide strips for tagliatelle or fettuccine, and 2.5 cm (1 in) wide strips for pappardelle.

As soon as you have cut the strips, shake out the pasta dough and place it on a plate dusted with flour.

CUTTING LARGE SHAPES
Lasagne may be cut into squares measuring about 10 cm (4 in) or into rectangular shapes measuring about 15 x 10 cm (6 x 4 in). However, when you make your own pasta, you do not have to comply with the convention of always making square or rectangular lasagne.

The only point to consider when cutting large pieces of pasta is the size of the cooking container available.

CUTTING DECORATIVE SHAPES
Pastry cutters and aspic cutters are ideal for stamping out decorative shapes. Flour the cutter occasionally to prevent the pasta sticking to it.

LASANKI
Lasanki are small pasta squares of Polish origin. To make them, first cut the pasta dough into strips, then cut them across into squares – they should measure about 0.5–1 cm (¼–½ in) on each side.

HAND-MADE BOWS
Cut strips of pasta, then cut these into short lengths and pinch them together in the middle to make bows. It is worth mentioning that although they are very good when home-made, honestly, it is a time-consuming process and the pasta tastes just as good in easier-to-make squares or diamond shapes!

COOKING PASTA

There are all sorts of amusing stories associated with cooking pasta, particularly when it comes testing whether or not the pasta is cooked. It is difficult to forget the kitchen in one particular male's residence at university where there was spaghetti stuck firmly to the sloping ceiling. The spaghetti was flung at the ceiling as a test of its tenderness. I would imagine, though, that if the pasta was soft enough to stick to the ceiling, it was overcooked!

Some recommend pinching a piece of spaghetti or pasta between the fingers, but the most hygienic, and satisfactory, method is to lift a piece on a slotted spoon and taste it. When it is ready, the pasta should be tender without there being any taste of uncooked flour. You should also be able to bite the pasta: it must not be soft, but tender, the ideal being *al dente*, meaning "to the tooth", that is, still slightly firm when you bite it.

Great saucepans of Water

To be perfectly practical, you can usually get away with using a large saucepan (about 3.4 l (6 pt) capacity) for cooking 350–450 g (12–16 oz) pasta, but it does not allow enough room to boil the pasta rapidly. The other alternative is to use more than one saucepan or, with fresh pasta, to have a back-up kettle of boiling water ready and cook the pasta in two or more batches.

Salt and Oil

Add salt to the cooking water, for flavour, and a little oil. The oil helps to stop the water from frothing up and over the edge of the saucepan as it boils. I have read elsewhere that oil helps to prevent pasta sticking together, but I have never found that this problem has arisen because the only time I have had pasta stick is when I have attempted to cook it in too small a saucepan with too little water.

Dried Pasta

Pasta should be added to plenty of boiling salted water and, indeed, Italian cookbooks and packets of good-quality bought pasta quote a vast volume that is beyond the capacity of most household saucepans. It is worth investing in one very large saucepan, stockpot or a special pasta saucepan that has an integral strainer. Alternatively, a pressure cooker (without its lid and weights) is often large enough to cook pasta.

Follow the instructions on the packet as the different shapes and ingredients do result in variations in the cooking time required. When adding long pasta to a saucepan, hold the pasta and lower it into the water as it softens.

As a guide, allow 12–15 minutes cooking time for the majority of pasta. Some shapes and spaghetti take 15–20 minutes, then there are quick-cook varieties that are ready in a few minutes. However, I find the texture of some of the quick-cook Italian-style types is slimy and generally unacceptable. The majority of macaroni is now short cut and quick to cook, requiring about 7 minutes. Long macaroni, in bright blue packets, is still to be found in better delicatessens and Italian shops. It is worth getting even if you intend breaking it up into small pieces for cooking and adding to cheese sauce as the taste is so much better.

Dried Oriental Pasta

Chinese egg noodles do not need to be boiled at all. You simply cover them with boiling water and leave them to stand for about 15 minutes, then drain.

The cooking time for rice sticks varies, but it is usually about 2 minutes in boiling water. Again, it is important to read the instructions on the packets as these products can become soft and soggy quite quickly after the quoted cooking time.

Above: Fresh pasta shapes.

Fresh Pasta

Fresh pasta cooks in about 3 minutes. It also swells more than some types of dried pasta. Filled pasta shapes can take longer, depending on the filling, which may need cooking or heating through thoroughly. Read the instructions on the packet carefully when buying filled pasta shapes. The information in the chapter on Stuffed and Filled Pasta (page 150) provides further advice on cooking these shapes.

Cooking Pasta Sheets

Lasagne and large pieces of pasta really do have to be cooked in a large volume of water and with plenty of room for the water to boil rapidly. If the sheets are allowed to stay still in a small saucepan of water, they stick together and cook unevenly. If you do not have a very large saucepan, cook pasta sheets in batches.

Draining and Serving

Have a warmed serving dish ready to hold the cooked pasta. If the pasta is to be served plain, then you should have butter or warmed oil ready for dressing it. Freshly ground black pepper or grated Parmesan cheese may also be added.

Drain the pasta as soon as it is cooked as a few extra minutes can ruin its texture, particularly in the case of fresh pasta.

Pasta sheets and tubes (cannelloni) should be rinsed under cold running water immediately they are drained to prevent them cooking further. Then, they should be laid out on clean teatowels ready for use. If they are left folded in a colander, stacked or closed, they will stick together and become difficult to use.

STORING AND FREEZING PASTA

Dried Pasta

Keep dried pasta in its sealed bag or in an airtight container and use within the recommended period given on the packet. Because of its long shelf-life, the pasta will not suddenly go off or endanger health if the "use by" date on the packet has expired by a couple of weeks, but the flavour and texture will gradually deteriorate with prolonged storage past this date.

Fresh Pasta

This should be kept chilled and used within a couple of days of making. Always observe the recommended "use by" date on packs of bought fresh pasta.

Cooked Pasta

Plain cooked pasta or cooked pasta dishes keep reasonably well, depending on the other ingredients used in them. Leftover cooked pasta or pasta that is cooked ahead for salads should be covered tightly to prevent it drying out, then kept in the fridge as soon as it has cooled.

The best method of reheating plain, cooked pasta is to do this in the microwave. It heats very quickly and any significant quantity should be stirred after 2 minutes to ensure even heating. Alternatively, place the covered dish of pasta over a saucepan of boiling water.

Sauced pasta can be reheated in the microwave, over a saucepan of boiling water or in the oven. When reheating pasta dishes in the oven, take care not to overcook them or to dry out the surface before the pasta is thoroughly reheated. As with any other food, when reheating pasta dishes, make sure the whole batch of food is heated throughout to its original cooking temperature before serving. Never reheat food more than once.

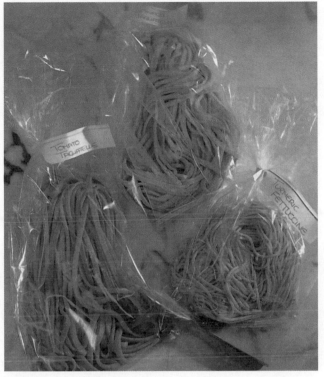

Above: Storing fresh pasta.

Freezing Pasta

Uncooked fresh pasta freezes extremely well, and it can be cooked straight from frozen, allowing a nominal extra amount of time for tagliatelle and shapes and slightly longer than this for filled pasta.

Ordinary cooked pasta does not freeze well. Although it is acceptable as a short-term measure for leftovers, which can be turned into a useful supper dish another time, it is not to be recommended as a method of cooking ahead for dinner parties and so on. This is also true of soups, hotpots or other very moist dishes (unthickened, stock-based sauces) that contain separate pieces of pasta. On thawing, the pasta is too soft and it breaks up easily.

Macaroni cheese and similar pasta dishes in which the pasta is protected by a fairly thick sauce have slightly better freezing qualities, however. Also, baked dishes containing sheets or similar large areas of pasta, such as lasagne or cannelloni, freeze very well.

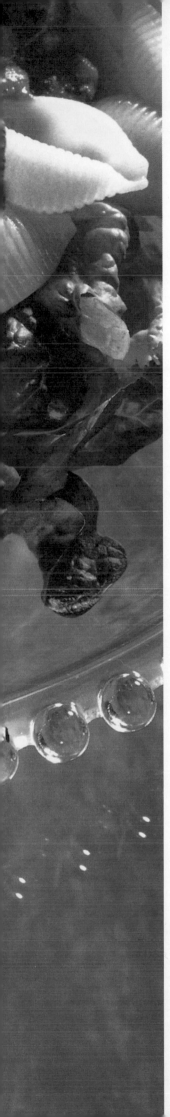

THE RECIPES

THE DOUGHS   40

ESSENTIAL SAUCES
AND CONTEMPORARY DRESSINGS   50

SUPERLATIVE SOUPS   76

HOTPOTS AND STEWS   94

MAIN COURSE SAUCES   106
Fish and Seafood Sauces   108
Poultry, Meat and Game Sauces   115
Dairy sauces   134
Vegetable sauces   138

STUFFED AND FILLED PASTA   148

BAKED PASTA DISHES   178

ORIENTAL SPECIALITIES   194

PASTA SALADS   212

THE DOUGHS

Eggless Pasta Dough

Use virgin olive oil for a pronounced flavour or a lighter oil if you prefer. Walnut oil may be used instead of olive oil to give the dough a distinct, delicious, walnut flavour. Melted butter may be substituted for some of the oil, if liked. Measure the melted butter by the tbsp so as not to disrupt the proportions and use up to 4 tbsp of butter with 2 tbsp olive oil.

MAKES ABOUT 575 G (1¼ lb) PASTA

350 g (12 oz) strong white flour

1 tsp salt

6 tbsp olive oil

scant 150 ml (¼ pt) water

Mix the flour and salt together in a bowl, making a well in the middle. Add the oil and two-thirds of the water, then mix well with a spoon until the flour clumps together.

Use your hand to continue mixing, and add a little more of the water, if necessary, to bind the ingredients into a dough. This pasta dough is slightly softer than the dough made with eggs. Knead the pasta until it is smooth and allow it to rest until required (page 32).

Pasta Dough

MAKES ABOUT 575 G (1¼ lb) PASTA

350 g (12 oz) strong white flour

1 tsp salt

3 eggs

4 tsp olive oil

1 tsp water

Mix the flour and salt together in a bowl, making a well in the middle. Beat the eggs with the olive oil and water, then pour the mixture into the well in the flour. Gradually stir the flour into the eggs, first using a spoon, then your hands, following the advice for mixing pasta on page 32. Knead the pasta until it is smooth, then leave it to rest until required (also see page 32).

Rich Egg Pasta Dough

MAKES ABOUT 725 G (1½ lb) PASTA

450 g (1 lb) strong white flour

1 tsp salt

4–5 large eggs

Mix the flour and salt in a bowl, making a well in the middle. Beat the eggs, then pour two-thirds into the well in the flour.

Gradually mix in the flour, adding more egg until the mixture clumps together (I actually used 4½ large eggs to get the right consistency for a firm, manageable dough, but the dough may need all 5 eggs depending on slight variations in the absorbency of the flour and the size of the eggs).

Mix and knead the dough following the instructions on page 32 and leave to stand before using.

Rich egg pastg dough

Spinach

Beetroot

Tumeric

FLAVOURED PASTA DOUGH

BEETROOT

Use the Pasta Dough recipe on page 40. Purée 50 g (2 oz) peeled, cooked beetroot with 2 of the eggs, then press the purée through a fine sieve (if the mixture is not sieved, the pasta will be slightly speckled). Add the beetroot purée with the remaining eggs, then omit the olive oil.

CARDAMOM-SPICED

Split 10 green cardamom pods and scrape the tiny black seeds from the pods into a mortar. Grind the seeds to a powder with a pestle, then add the powder to the flour when making either the Pasta Dough or the Rich Egg Pasta Dough on page 40.

CARROT

Use the Pasta Dough recipe on page 40. Peel and boil 100 g (4 oz) carrot until tender. Drain, mash and sieve the carrot, then leave to cool until it is warm. Add the purée to the eggs and omit the oil and water from the dough.

CUMIN-SPICED

Add 1 tsp white cumin seeds to the flour.

This may be combined with the cardamom-spiced (above) or Turmeric (below) flavoured pastas, or both.

CURRY-SPICED

Split 4 cardamom pods, scrape the tiny black seeds from inside into a mortar and grind them to a powder with a pestle. Heat 25 g (1 oz) ghee or butter in a small saucepan. Add 1 finely chopped garlic clove, 1 tbsp finely chopped onion, 1 tbsp ground cumin, 1 tbsp ground coriander, 1 tsp turmeric and the ground cardamom seeds. Cook, stirring, for 2–3 minutes, then set aside to cool. Beat the spice paste with the eggs for either of the Pasta Dough or Rich Pasta Dough recipes on page 40.

HERB

Add 4 tbsp chopped mixed fresh herbs to the Pasta Dough (see page 40) or 5 tbsp if making the Rich Egg Pasta Dough (also see page 40).

Parsley, chervil, thyme, sage, marjoram, oregano, savoury, tarragon, chives and fennel are all suitable.

Balance the mixture by using more of the mild herbs, like parsley, chives and chervil with strong flavours, such as oregano, thyme and rosemary.

Tarragon, parsley and chives are a good combination. Use 1 tbsp of tarragon to 2 of each of the others if you want a mild tarragon flavour.

For oregano with parsley and sage, use 2 tbsp parsley and 1 tbsp of each of the others.

LEMON

Add the grated rind of 2 lemons to the eggs of either of the pasta dough recipes (see page 40) and chopped parsley or snipped chives if liked.

OLIVE, OLIVE AND GARLIC, OR OLIVE, OREGANO & GARLIC

Finely chop 100 g (4 oz) stoned black olives and add to the flour of either of the pasta dough recipes (see page 40). Finely chop 2 garlic cloves and add them to the eggs if liked. Mix 2 tbsp chopped fresh oregano with the flour.

SPINACH

Wash and trim 225 g (8 oz) fresh spinach and place the wet leaves in a saucepan. Cover tightly and cook over a high heat, shaking the saucepan often, for 5 minutes, or until the leaves have wilted and are tender. Spoon the leaves into a sieve placed over a basin. Use the back of a mixing spoon to press the liquid from the spinach. Then squeeze the leaves with your hand until they are as dry as possible. Stir the liquid drained from the spinach. Add 6 tbsp of the spinach liquid to the Pasta Dough (see page 40) in place of the olive oil and water. If making the Rich Egg Pasta Dough (also see page 40) add the same quantity of spinach liquid and use just 4 eggs.

TOMATO

Beat 1 tablespoon concentrated tomato purée into the eggs for either of the pasta dough recipes (see page 40). Chopped herbs, such as oregano or parsley, may be added, too, if liked.

TURMERIC

Add 1 tsp ground turmeric to the flour for either of the pasta dough recipes (see page 44).

Turmeric pasta has a mild, slightly peppery flavour.

WALNUT

Use walnut oil instead of olive oil in the Pasta Dough recipe (see page 44).

Potato Gnocchi

Potato gnocchi may be served on their own as a light supper dish – good with a crisp side salad of mixed leaves – or they may be offered as a base for rich, meaty sauces. I have given melted butter, Parmesan and pepper as the dressing here, but lightly sautéed, chopped fresh garlic in plenty of hot olive oil is a delicious alternative.

FOR THE GNOCCHI (SERVES 4)

450 g (1 lb) potatoes

25 g / 1 (oz) butter, melted

1 tsp salt

1 egg, beaten

175 g (6 oz) strong white flour

TO SERVE

75 g (3 oz) butter, melted

freshly ground black pepper or nutmeg

freshly grated Parmesan cheese

To make the gnocchi, boil the potatoes in their skins until tender (about 20 minutes), then drain and peel them under cold running water. Mash the potatoes and press them through a fine sieve.

Beat the butter, salt and egg into the potatoes, then gradually stir in the flour. Use a spoon at first, then mix the dough together with your hand. Knead the dough lightly until smooth.

Knead a hand-sized lump of dough until smooth, then roll it into a long, thick sausage shape on a lightly floured surface and cut off 2.5 cm (1 in) lengths. Use a fork or one finger to make an indentation in each piece of gnocchi.

Place the gnocchi on a well-floured plate or tray, cover and keep cool until they are to be cooked. Bring a large saucepan of salted water to the boil. Drop in the gnocchi and bring back to the boil. Boil the gnocchi for 4–5 minutes, keeping the water just bubbling, not boiling too rapidly or the gnocchi may break up.

Drain the gnocchi as soon as they are cooked as they will become soft and watery if boiled for too long. Use a slotted spoon to remove the gnocchi from the saucepan if you have to cook them in batches.

Serve freshly cooked with hot melted butter, freshly ground black pepper or nutmeg and grated Parmesan cheese.

Spinach Gnocchi

Ricotta cheese and eggs combine with spinach and flour to make these gnocchi, which are lighter than those based on a potato dough. For sure success, it is best to chill this mixture overnight before shaping and cooking the gnocchi.

FOR THE GNOCCHI (SERVES 4)

225 g (8 oz) cooked fresh or frozen spinach,
  drained and chopped

450 g (1 lb) ricotta cheese

salt and freshly ground black pepper

25 g (1 oz) freshly grated Parmesan cheese

100 g (4 oz) plain flour

2 eggs, beaten

TO SERVE

75 g (3 oz) butter, melted

freshly grated Parmesan cheese

To make the gnocchi, first press all the liquid from the spinach. Press the ricotta through a fine sieve. Mix the ricotta, spinach, plenty of seasoning and Parmesan cheese. Stir in the flour and the eggs to make a soft dough. Chill the dough for several hours or put it in the freezer until it is firm enough to shape.

Shape small ovals of dough and place them on a floured tray or plate. Bring a large saucepan of salted water to the boil. Add the gnocchi in batches and bring the water back to the boil. The water should only just boil as if it bubbles too rapidly, the gnocchi will break up. Cook the gnocchi for 4–5 minutes, then remove them with a slotted spoon and drain well. Keep cooked gnocchi hot until all the batches are ready.

Serve hot, tossed in melted butter, with freshly ground black pepper and Parmesan cheese.

Clockwise from top: 1. Potato Gnocchi 2. Spinach Gnocchi
3. Parmesan Oregano Gnocchi 4. Kopytka 5. Baked Semolina
Gnocchi.

FLAVOURED POTATO GNOCCHI

PARMESAN AND OREGANO

Add 1 tbsp chopped fresh oregano and 25 g (1 oz) freshly grated Parmesan cheese to the potatoes. Stir in a little grated nutmeg with the flour. Serve with garlic sautéed in olive oil.

RICOTTA GNOCCHI

Omit the butter. Press 225 g (8 oz) ricotta cheese through a fine sieve and beat it into the potatoes. Add 2 tbsp finely chopped parsley and a little grated nutmeg. Serve with hot melted butter and grated basil.

Kopytka

This is the Polish equivalent of Italian potato gnocchi.

FOR THE KOPYTKA (SERVES 4)

450 g (1 lb) potatoes

100 g (4 oz) plain flour

½ tsp salt

1 egg, beaten

TO SERVE

50 g (2 oz) fresh breadcrumbs

75 g (3 oz) butter

To make the kopytka, first boil the potatoes in their skins until tender (about 20 minutes). Then, peel them under cold running water. Mash the cooked potatoes and press them through a fine sieve into a bowl. Stir in the flour and salt, then mix in the egg to make a soft dough.

Next, prepare the breadcrumbs for serving. Fry the breadcrumbs in 25g (1 oz) of the butter, stirring and turning them until they are crisp and golden. Set aside to cool.

Have a well-floured tray or plate ready and prepare a small heap of flour or have a dredger nearby to dust your hands as you work. Roll small portions of the dough into balls slightly smaller than walnuts. Make an indentation in each ball with the tip of your finger.

When all the kopytka dough has been shaped, bring a large saucepan of salted water to the boil. Cook the kopytka in batches, bringing the water back to the boil, then keeping it just bubbling, for 4–5 minutes. Do not boil the water too rapidly or the kopytka will break up, but if it does not boil, they will simply sink and become soggy.

Drain the kopytka using a slotted spoon and place them in a warmed serving dish. Keep hot whilst the remaining kopytka are cooked. Melt the remaining butter for serving and pour it over the kopytka. Sprinkle with the fried breadcrumbs and serve at once.

KOPYTKA WITH PORK FAT

This sounds awful but tastes very good! Traditionally, pork fat is diced and gently cooked in a heavy-based saucepan until it renders its fat and the pieces become small and crisp. A little of the hot cooking water from the kopytka is spooned over the cooked dumplings, then they are dressed with hot pork fat and the crispy remains of the fat.

As it is quite difficult to find chunks of pork fat these days, instead, skin a piece of belly pork and melt the fat from the skin, then finely dice the meat and fat and render this in a heavy-based saucepan or by roasting in the oven. Only three or four tiny pieces should be scattered over each portion.

Baked Semolina Gnocchi

This is different to the other gnocchi recipes as it is cooked to a thick porridge in the saucepan before being chilled, cut up and baked. The shaped pieces freeze well. Rich Tomato Sauce or Light Tomato Sauce (see pages 54 and 55) may be served with these or the Parmesan Cheese Gnocchi variation. Pesto (see page 67) is also good with these lighter Baked Semolina Gnocchi.

SERVES 4
900 ml (1½ pt) milk

1 bay leaf

1 blade of mace

1 onion, thickly sliced

3 cloves

225 g (8 oz) semolina

100 g (4 oz) butter

225 g (8 oz) ricotta cheese

freshly grated nutmeg

salt and freshly ground black pepper

2 eggs, beaten

olive oil, for greasing

3 tbsp freshly grated Parmesan cheese

Heat the milk, bay leaf, mace, onion and cloves together, slowly, until just coming to the boil. Then, remove the saucepan from the heat, cover and leave the milk until cold. Heat the milk until it is about to boil again, then strain it into a large, clean, heavy-based saucepan.

Sprinkle the semolina into the milk, stirring all the time, and bring to the boil. Do not stop stirring or the semolina will cook in lumps. The mixture becomes quite stiff as it cooks and thickens, but persist in cooking it well as this is important if the gnocchi are to be of the right consistency.

Remove the saucepan from the heat and beat in half the butter. Then, sieve the ricotta cheese and mix it into the semolina with plenty of seasoning. Finally, beat in the eggs. Grease a baking tin (a roasting tin is ideal for this) with a little olive oil and spread the mixture out in it to a thickness of about 1 cm (½ in). Keep the edges neat and of an even thickness.

Leave the semolina mixture to cool, then chill it thoroughly for at least 2 hours, until it is firm enough to be cut into squares.

Pre-heat the oven to 200°C/400°F/Gas Mark 6. Melt the remaining butter and use a little to grease a shallow, ovenproof dish. Use a sharp, wetted kitchen knife to cut the semolina mixture into small squares. Arrange the gnocchi, overlapping, in the dish, preferably in a single layer, then trickle the melted butter over them and sprinkle with the Parmesan. Bake for about 20 minutes, or until crisp and golden on top. Serve at once.

PARMESAN CHEESE GNOCCHI
Prepare and cook the semolina as above, but omit the ricotta and do not stir in the butter. Instead, beat 100 g (4 oz) freshly grated Parmesan cheese into the hot semolina with the seasoning, nutmeg and eggs. Continue as above, coating the gnocchi with butter before baking.

Spätzle

This is an example of a pasta-dumpling cross from Eastern European culinary traditions. I took a deep breath before I attempted to make this thick mixture as I remember previous efforts involving much sloppy batter, great cauldrons of boiling water, wet chopping boards, a sticky cooker and general disaster, but, with careful attention to the batter, just the right number of eggs and enough flour, these worked a treat! I was so delighted with the results that I went on to cook several batches with various flavourings, the best of which I have included here. Spätzle may be treated as gnocchi and served with butter or olive oil or other simple dressings, such as soured cream and chives or dill. However, they are also the ideal accompaniment for rich meat or game sauces and good in substantial meat and vegetable hotpots or soups.

FOR THE SPÄTZLE (SERVES 4)
225 g (8 oz) plain flour
½ tsp salt
4 eggs, beaten
about 3 tbsp water

TO SERVE
50 g (2 oz) butter, melted
To make the spätzle, first, mix the flour and salt in a bowl, making a well in the middle. Add the eggs, then gradually work in the flour and beat hard until the batter is very thick and smooth. Add the water gradually so that you can beat the batter without difficulty. However, the mixture should be thick, elastic and quite "stringy" in texture, not freely pouring.

Prepare a large saucepan of boiling salted water and have a slotted spoon ready. Pour the melted butter for serving into a warmed dish and keep this hot ready to receive the cooked spätzle. Rinse a small chopping board under cold running water and wet a large, flat-bladed kitchen knife in the same way. Drop a large pat of the batter on the board. Regulate the heat under the saucepan of water so that the water is just boiling.

Use a cutting and sliding action to scrape thin, short lengths of the batter sideways into the saucepan of boiling water. Rinse the knife under running cold water every three or four cuts to prevent the batter sticking to it. The water must be boiling otherwise the spätzle will stick to the bottom of the pan. Cook the batter in batches. Once the spätzle have been in the saucepan for about 30 seconds, gently stir them off the bottom with the slotted spoon.

Boil the spätzle for 2–3 minutes, until they are swollen and firm. Drain them well and place them in the hot butter, toss them in it and keep hot until all the batter has been cooked. Serve piping hot.

COOK'S TIPS

- Beating the batter to achieve a smooth, elastic texture is important.

- If the batter feels slightly too runny, set it aside to stand for 30 minutes before adding more flour as this will encourage the starch grains to swell and the batter to become slightly less runny. Adding too much extra flour may give a stodgy result.

- I used a small, laminated board with a smooth surface for holding the batter. I suspect some of the problems I had before when trying to shape spätzle were partly due to the fact that I was using a wooden board to which the batter tended to cling.

- If you do not have a small board, the spätzle may be shaped by squeezing the batter out of a polythene bag and snipping it into short lengths. To do this, put some batter in a polythene bag (one that does not have a gusset) and rinse the blades of kitchen scissors under cold water. When the water is boiling, snip a small point off one corner of the bag and support it whilst allowing the batter to flow out slowly. Snip off short lengths of batter. This is a speedy method of shaping spätzle, but they tend to be lumps rather than the finer, long, thin shapes achieved when using a board. Take care not to cut a chunk off the end of the bag when snipping the batter!

Above: Using a ploythene bag to cut and shape the spätzle dough.

Below: Dropping the spätzle batter into boiling water.

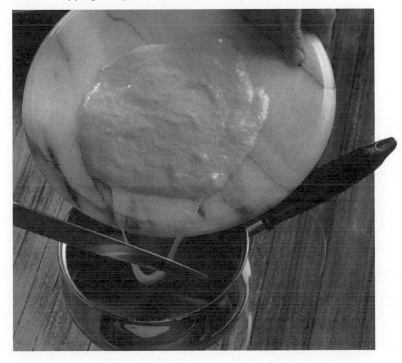

FLAVOURED SPÄTZLE

GARLIC AND OREGANO

Add 1 tbsp chopped fresh oregano or 2 tsp dried oregano and 2 finely chopped garlic cloves to the eggs.

HERB SPÄTZLE

Add 2 tbsp each of chopped parsley and chives, and 1 tbsp chopped fresh thyme or 1 tsp dried thyme to the flour.

CELERY LEAF SPÄTZLE

Finely chop the leafy tops of a head of celery and add to the eggs. Cook 2 tbsp celery seeds in the butter for serving for a few minutes, then, toss the cooked spätzle with this.

Won Ton Dough

Above: Homemade Won Ton dough.

Above: Commercially made Won Ton dough.

This is not the easiest of doughs to roll, but I find these basic quantities work reasonably well, making a mixture that can be rolled out sufficiently thinly to make light boiled or puffy, crisp fried won tons. If you happen to visit an oriental supermarket, look out for ready-made won ton wrappers, cut in small squares and dusted with cornflour. They are usually sold with the other chilled foods, such as fresh egg noodles, and often come in sizeable packs, but these may be split and frozen quite successfully.

MAKES 18 WON TONS

50 g (2 oz) cornflour

50 g (2 oz) plain flour

¼ tsp salt

1 egg, beaten

2 tbsp water

Mix the cornflour, plain flour and salt in a bowl, making a well in the middle. Add the egg and water to the well, then gradually work in the flour with a mixing spoon to make a dry dough. Scrape all the cornflour from round the bowl and knead the dough by hand until it is smooth and soft.

Dust the work surface with a little cornflour. Keep the surface lightly dusted with cornflour, but it is more important to keep the dough moving to prevent it sticking. If you dredge the cornflour too thickly, the dough will become dry on the surface and it will break easily.

Cut the dough in half for rolling out and keep the portion that is not being worked covered with cling film to prevent it drying out.

Dust the surface and rolling pin with cornflour and roll the dough out thinly, until it is about 25 cm (10 in) square. Take care not to rip the dough as it tends to stretch apart and will not rejoin easily. Trim the edges of the dough and cut it into three strips, then across into three squares. Roll out each of the squares again until quite thin and about 10 cm (4 in) on each side before filling.

The squares should be filled as soon as they have been rolled, then they should be placed on a tray dredged with cornflour to prevent them sticking.

PUFFY DEEP-FRIED WON TONS

Add 2 tsp baking powder to the flour for a dough that puffs up when deep-fried. Use it, for example, for making deep-fried Sweet-and-sour Won Tons (see page 200)

Dim Sum Dough

MAKES ABOUT 24 DIM SUM

100 g (4 oz) strong plain flour

pinch of salt

3 tbsp boiling water

25 g (1 oz) lard

cornflour, for dusting

This is a basic dough that may be used to make a variety of steamed, filled dim sum.

Mix the flour and salt in a bowl. Pour the boiling water over the lard in a heatproof jug and stir until the fat melts. Then stir the hot liquid into the flour to make a smooth, fairly soft dough. Knead the dough until smooth on a surface lightly dusted with cornflour. Use the dough as soon as it is made, keeping the portion not being worked covered in cling film to prevent it drying out.

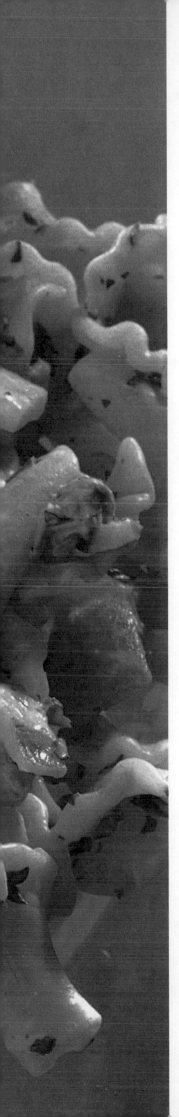

ESSENTIAL SAUCES AND CONTEMPORARY DRESSINGS

Here, you will find a classic collection of recipes alongside those that depart from tradition.

Whether you bother to make your own stock or not is entirely up to you.

There are high-quality chilled stocks available, which really are good, or some stock cubes that are not overseasoned or artificial in flavour, but avoid the strong-flavoured cubes that are very highly seasoned and bring an artificial taste to otherwise good ingredients.

You may want to make your own stock for some special dishes, or when you have a leftover carcass or the bones from a piece of meat. For many stews, poultry or meat mixture, I often rely on the flavour of the ingredients and use water with careful seasoning. One point to remember is that you do have to make the Chinese stock to get the right flavour when it is suggested in a dish.

I hope you find these recipes both useful and inspiring for quick meals as well as those occasions that demand hours of preparation in the kitchen.

Many of these sauces form a useful base for fish, poultry, meat or vegetable toppings; others are essential "ingredients" in baked pasta dishes. The chapter also includes simple dressings which can be tossed with freshly cooked pasta for a tasty lunch or supper.

Fish Stock

If you have fish trimmings, such as skin and bones, then use them to make fish stock or ask the fishmonger, who will usually be able to provide suitable stock trimmings. Do not add gills as they make the stock bitter. However, with the ready availability of excellent-quality frozen fish, there are often times when trimmings are not available, so this recipe uses a small amount of fish fillet instead.

MAKES ABOUT 1.2 l (2 pt)

225 g (8 oz) white fish fillet, such as coley, huss or haddock

1 onion, thinly sliced

1 large carrot, thinly sliced

2 celery sticks, thinly sliced

1 bay leaf

4 sprigs of parsley or the stalks from a handful of parsley

1 small sprig of thyme

1 tsp black peppercorns

1.2 l (2 pt) water

Place the fish in a saucepan. Add the onion, carrot, celery, bay leaf, parsley, thyme and peppercorns. Pour in the water and bring to the boil very slowly. Reduce the heat so that the water simmers gently. Cover the saucepan and simmer for 1 hour. Leave to cool, then strain the stock. The stock is not salted so that salt may be added to the recipe in which it is used.

Beef Stock

If you buy from an independent butcher, then you will be able to get some beef bones cut into practical sizes for putting into a large saucepan. You will also need some meat to make a decent stock. This recipe is based on shin of beef. If you can get any bones, roast them at 180°C/350°F/Gas Mark 4 for 1 hour before boiling and boil some water in the roasting tin to get all the flavour from the cooking juices.

MAKES ABOUT 1.2 l (2 pt)

450 g (1 lb) shin of beef, cubed

1 large onion, thinly sliced

2 carrots, sliced

2 celery sticks, sliced

1 bay leaf

1 blade of mace

1 sprig of thyme

6 sprigs of parsley or a handful of parsley stalks

1 tsp coriander seeds

1 tsp black peppercorns

1.75 l (3 pt) water

Place the beef, onion, carrots, celery, bay leaf, mace, thyme, parsley, coriander seeds and peppercorns in a large saucepan. Pour in the water and bring slowly to the boil. Skim off any scum that rises to the surface of the water, then reduce the heat and cover the pan. Simmer the stock gently for 3 hours. Strain the stock and use as required. Salt is not added to the stock so it can be added to the recipe in which the stock is used.

Vegetable Stock

You can vary this according to whatever is available and the strength of flavour required.

MAKES ABOUT 1.2 l (2 pt)

2 large onions, thinly sliced

2 large carrots, thinly sliced

4 celery sticks, thinly sliced

1 small turnip, diced

100 g (4 oz) closed cap mushrooms, sliced

1 bay leaf

4 sprigs of parsley or a handful of parsley stalks

1 sprig of thyme

1 garlic clove, peeled

1.25 l (2¼ pt) water

Place the onions, carrots, celery, turnip, mushroom bay leaf, parsley, thyme and garlic in a saucepan. Pour in the water and bring to the boil. Reduce the heat, cover the saucepan and simmer gently for 1¼ hours. Strain the stock through a fine sieve. Salt is not added to the stock so it can be added to the recipe in which the stock is used.

Chicken Stock

Chicken stock can be made from a meaty roast chicken carcase, from the uncooked carcase left after boning a bird, from a joint or by boiling a whole bird. Boiling a whole chicken gives by far the best stock and the uncooked bones often give a good flavour, especially when the wing ends, giblets and any other off cuts are included. The quality of stock resulting from a cooked carcase depends on how meaty it is. Using a chicken quarter is the practical choice if you want a well-flavoured stock but do not want to "waste" a whole bird. Also the meat may be diced and added to a sauce to serve with pasta.

MAKES ABOUT 1.2 l (2 pt)

1 chicken quarter
1 onion, sliced
1 large carrot, sliced
2 celery sticks, sliced
1 bay leaf
1 sprig of sage
4 sprigs of parsley or the stalks from a handful of parsley
1 sprig of thyme
1 tsp black peppercorns
1.25 l (2½ pt) water

Place the chicken quarter in a saucepan. Add the onion, carrot, celery, bay leaf, parsley, sage, thyme and peppercorns. Pour in the water and bring to the boil. Reduce the heat and cover the pan, then simmer for 1 hour.

Leave the stock to cool before straining it. Salt is not added to the stock so it can be added to the recipe in which the stock is used.

Chinese-style Stock

A combination of pork and chicken makes a flavoursome stock.

MAKES ABOUT 1.2 l (2 pt)

450 g (1 lb) meaty pork spareribs, chopped into short lengths
2 chicken drumsticks
1 onion, thinly sliced
1 carrot, thinly sliced
1 celery stick, thinly sliced
1.25 l (2½ pt) water

Place the pork spareribs, chicken drumsticks, onion, carrot and celery in a saucepan. Pour in the water and bring slowly to the boil. Skim off any scum that rises to the surface of the water, then cover the saucepan and reduce the heat. Simmer the stock for 2 hours. Strain the stock and use as required. Salt is not added to the stock as it can be added to the recipe in which the stock is used. Alternatively, soy sauce may be used as the seasoning in oriental dishes.

Japanese Stock

You will find packets of dried bonito fish and the dried konbu or kelp (seaweed) in oriental supermarkets and specialist stores. Dried bonito is sold in small sachets (or packets containing several sachets) each about 15 g (¼ oz). I find that healthfood shops also stock the dried seaweed.

MAKES ABOUT 1.2 l (2 pt)

1 piece of wakame or konbu (dried seaweed)
15 g (¼ oz) sachet dried bonito fish
1.2 l (2 pt) water

Place the dried wakame or konbu in a saucepan. Add the bonito fish and pour in the water. Heat gently until boiling. Cover the pan, remove it from the heat and leave to stand for 30 minutes. Strain the stock through a fine sieve.

Rich Tomato Sauce

This is made with bought passata and enriched with extra tomato purée as well as red wine.

MAKES ABOUT 900 ml (2 pt)

3 tbsp olive oil

2 garlic cloves, crushed

1 onion, chopped

1 small carrot, diced

1 celery stick, diced

1 bouquet garni

3 tbsp tomato purée

600 ml (1 pt) passata

300 ml (⅔ pt) robust red wine

salt and freshly ground black pepper

2 tsp sugar

Heat the oil in a large saucepan. Add the garlic, onion, carrot, celery and bouquet garni. Stir well, then cover the saucepan and cook for 15 minutes.

Stir in the tomato purée, passata and wine. Add seasoning to taste and bring to the boil. Reduce the heat, cover the saucepan and simmer gently for 1 hour.

Remove the bouquet garni, then liquidize the sauce until it is smooth. Stir in the sugar, reheat and taste for seasoning before serving.

White Sauce

MAKES ABOUT 750 ml (1½ pt)

40 g (1½ oz) butter

40 g (1½ oz) plain flour

600 ml (1 pt) milk

salt and freshly ground white or black pepper

Melt the butter in a saucepan. Stir in the flour, then reduce the heat a little and slowly pour in the milk, stirring all the time. Continue stirring until the sauce boils. Reduce the heat and simmer the sauce for 3 minutes, stirring occasionally. Add salt and pepper to taste and use as required.

COOK'S TIP

Flour, used to thicken a sauce, has to be cooked beyond simply reaching boiling point otherwise it will taste raw in the finished sauce. The flour may be cooked for 2 minutes once it has been stirred into the butter and before the milk is added. Alternatively, the sauce may be simmered for 2–3 minutes, or longer, after it has boiled.

FLAVOURINGS FOR WHITE SAUCE

BUTTER SAUCE

Whisk in 75 g (3 oz) butter, after the sauce has simmered then add seasoning to taste.

PARSLEY SAUCE

Stir in 6 tbsp chopped fresh parsley at the end of the cooking time.

TARRAGON SAUCE

Stir in 2–3 tbsp chopped fresh tarragon at the end of the cooking time.

CHEESE SAUCE

Stir in 100 g (4 oz) grated mature cheese at the end of the cooking time. Stir over a low heat until the cheese has melted.

EGG SAUCE

Stir in 4 finely chopped hard-boiled eggs at the end of the cooking time. Add 2–3 tbsp chopped fresh parsley or tarragon, or snipped chives, if liked.

MUSHROOM SAUCE

Cook 175 g (6 oz) thickly sliced button mushrooms in the butter before adding the flour. As the mushrooms begin to cook, they yield a lot of liquid, continue cooking until this has evaporated before stirring in the flour and finishing the sauce.

Light, Fresh Tomato Sauce

Above: Rich tomato sauce, and in the smallest bowl, Light fresh tomato sauce.

MAKES ABOUT 900 ml (1½ pt)

2 tbsp olive oil

2 garlic cloves, crushed

1 onion, chopped

2 small carrots, chopped

50 g (2 oz) lean rindless bacon, diced
  (optional)

1 kg (2¼ lb) tomatoes, quartered

300 ml (½ pt) young or light red wine

1 bay leaf

salt and freshly ground black pepper

2–3 tsp sugar

This sauce has a light tomato flavour and pale red colour. It is the ideal accompaniment or coating for those times when you do not want to mask delicate foods with a strong tomato flavour or when you simply want a lighter background flavour of tomato.

Heat the olive oil in a large saucepan. Add the garlic, onion and carrots. Cook, stirring occasionally, for 5 minutes. Add the bacon and stir, then cook for a further 5 minutes.

Stir in the tomatoes, wine, bay leaf and some seasoning. Bring to the boil, reduce the heat and cover the pan. Leave the sauce to bubble gently – somewhere between boiling and simmering – for 30 minutes.

Remove the bay leaf, then liquidize the sauce. Press it through a fine sieve. Reheat it and add sugar to taste with salt and pepper as required before use.

Béchamel Sauce

All the flavouring options given for the White Sauce recipe on page 54 may be applied to a béchamel sauce. The difference between béchamel and white sauces is that the additional flavourings of bay, mace and onion are infused with the milk before the sauce is made.

MAKES ABOUT 750 ml (1¼ pt)

1 small onion, halved

1 blade of mace

1 bay leaf

600 ml (1 pt) milk

40 g (1½ oz) butter

40 g (1½ oz) plain flour

salt and freshly ground white or black pepper

Place the onion, mace and bay leaf in a saucepan. Add the milk and heat slowly until it is just reaching boiling point. Remove the saucepan from the heat before it boils, cover and stand the milk aside until it is cold. Then, heat the milk gently again until it is almost boiling, then remove the onion, mace and bay leaf.

Melt the butter in another saucepan over a high heat. Stir in the flour, reduce the heat a little then slowly pour in the milk, stirring all the time. Continue stirring until the sauce boils. Reduce the heat and simmer the sauce for 3 minutes, stirring occasionally. Add salt and pepper to taste and use as required.

White Wine Sauce

MAKES ABOUT 750 ml (1¼ pt)

40 g (1½ oz) butter

1 onion, finely chopped

1 small carrot, finely chopped

1 celery stick, finely chopped

1 bouquet garni

1 blade of mace

50 g (2 oz) small button mushrooms, thinly sliced

40 g (1½ oz) plain flour

600 ml (1 pt) dry white wine

salt and freshly ground black pepper

2 tbsp chopped fresh parsley (optional)

Melt the butter in a saucepan. Add the onion, carrot, celery, bouquet garni, blade of mace and mushrooms. Stir well, then cover the saucepan and cook the mixture for 15 minutes.

Stir in the flour. Then stir continuously whilst pouring in the wine and bring to the boil. Reduce the heat, cover the saucepan and simmer the sauce gently for 15 minute Taste and add salt and pepper, then stir in the parsley.

RED WINE SAUCE

Follow the above recipe, but use red wine instead of the white wine. A robust wine may be used if the sauce is to be served with rich meats, game or duck and any cooking juices from these ingredients should be added to the sauce to enhance its flavour and suitability for the main ingredient. Also, add 2 tbsp mushroom ketchup and 1 tbsp tomato purée with the wine. For a lighter sauce, up to half the quantity of wine may be replaced with a suitable stock.

Bolognese Sauce

This is a favourite sauce for serving with all types of pasta, particularly spaghetti. It is also used in a variety of other dishes, including baked lasagne. The sauce freezes well for at least 3 months.

SERVES 4

2 tbsp olive oil

1 large onion, chopped

2 garlic cloves, crushed

2 celery sticks, diced

1 green pepper, de-seeded and diced

1 bay leaf

225 g (8 oz) lean minced beef

225 g (8 oz) lean minced pork

2 tbsp tomato purée

2 tbsp chopped fresh oregano or marjoram

1 large sprig of thyme

1 tbsp plain flour

salt and freshly ground black pepper

450 ml (¾ pt) robust red wine

2 x 397 g (14 oz) tins chopped tomatoes

225 g (8 oz) closed cap or chestnut mushrooms, sliced

Heat the oil in a heavy-based saucepan or flameproof casserole. Add the onion, garlic, celery, green pepper and bay leaf. Stir well, then cover and cook for 15 minutes. Stir in the minced beef and pork and cook, stirring for 5 minutes. Add the tomato purée, oregano or marjoram, thyme and flour. Stir well, then add plenty of seasoning and pour in the wine and tomatoes. Bring to the boil, stirring occasionally, then lightly mix in the mushrooms and reduce the heat so that the sauce just simmers. Cover and cook for 1 hour, or until the meat is tender. Remove the lid and simmer for a further 30 minutes, until the liquid has reduced slightly and the sauce is full-flavoured. Taste for seasoning before serving.

Hot-and-sour Sauce

This is an idea taken from hot-and-sour soup, which is the authentic Chinese dish that marries the flavours of pepper with vinegar. I enjoy the flavour of the soup and thought it would lend itself well to being used as a dressing for egg noodles or won tons.

SERVES 4–6

600 ml (1 pt) Chinese-style Stock (see page 53)

2 large, dried Chinese mushrooms

1 tbsp oil

1 tsp sesame oil

2 garlic cloves, finely chopped

25 g (1 oz) fresh root ginger, peeled and cut into fine strips

1 small carrot, cut into matchstick strips

1 red chilli, de-seeded and chopped

50 g (2 oz) tinned bamboo shoots, cut into matchstick strips

6 spring onions, grated diagonally

2 tbsp light soy sauce

1 tbsp cornflour

2 tbsp water

1 tsp tomato purée

¼ tsp ground white pepper

2 tsp white wine vinegar

Pour the stock into a small saucepan and add the mushrooms. Heat gently until boiling, then reduce the heat and simmer, uncovered, until it reduces to about 450 ml (¾ pt) and the mushrooms have softened. Cool slightly, then remove the mushrooms, squeezing the liquid from them into the pan. Strain the stock through fine muslin, if necessary, to remove any grit from the mushrooms. Thinly slice the mushrooms.

Heat the oil and sesame oil in a saucepan. Add the garlic, ginger, carrot, chilli and bamboo shoots, and stirring fry for 2–3 minutes. Then, add the spring onions and mushrooms. Stir well, pour in the stock and add the soy sauce. Bring to the boil, reduce the heat and cover the pan. Simmer the sauce for 5 minutes.

Blend the cornflour with the water, tomato purée pepper and vinegar. Stir in some of the hot sauce, then pour the mixture into the saucepan and bring to the boil, stirring all the time. Reduce the heat and simmer the sauce, uncovered, for 5 minutes, or until thickened. Taste the sauce for seasoning (more pepper may be added if the flavour is not sufficiently hot and more vinegar may be added for a very tangy sauce).

Garlic Cream

Cooked garlic and potatoes puréed together with cream and butter make a delicious dressing for plain, cooked pasta. Serve with any pasta and offer freshly grated Parmesan cheese as an accompaniment.

SERVES 4

6 garlic cloves, peeled

½ small onion, chopped

1 medium potato, peeled and diced

1 bay leaf

salt and freshly ground black pepper

50 g (2 oz) butter

300 ml (½ pt) single cream

2 tbsp finely chopped fresh parsley

Place the garlic cloves, onion, potato and bay leaf in a small saucepan. Add water to cover and a little salt. Bring to the boil, reduce the heat and cover the pan. Simmer until the potatoes are tender (about 10 minutes).

Drain the potatoes, onion and garlic in a fine sieve. Discard the bay leaf, then purée the vegetables in food processor or liquidizer, or press them through a fine sieve. Heat the butter and cream together in a saucepan until the butter has melted and the cream is hot, but do not allow the cream to boil. Slowly pour the cream into the vegetable purée and process briefly until smooth. Add salt and pepper to taste, then stir in the parsley and serve the sauce at once.

Above: Sweet-and-sour Sauce

Almond and Parsley Paste

SERVES 4

225 g (8 oz) blanched almonds

25 g (1 oz) parsley

100 g (4 oz) jarlsberg cheese

about 200 ml (7 fl oz) olive oil

3 tbsp snipped chives

salt and freshly ground black pepper

A food processor or liquidizer makes this a simple recipe, but it can be made by hand by first passing the nuts through a mouli grater, which will grind them, then pounding them to a paste with finely chopped parsley and finely grated cheese. Then the oil can be slowly pounded into the mixture. Toss this paste with pasta verde or tomato-flavoured pasta to make a delicious, light meal.

Grind the almonds and parsley together in a food processor (or as above if making by hand) until quite fine. Cut the jarlsberg cheese into chunks, add these to the nuts and process the mixture until it begins to bind a stiff paste. Add a little of the oil and process to a thick paste, then gradually trickle in the remaining oil as the machine is running.

Stir in the chives and seasoning to taste, then leave the paste to stand for at least an hour before serving.

Pesto

MAKES ABOUT 600 ml (1 pt)

100 g (4 oz) pine nuts

175 g (6 oz) Parmesan cheese

4-6 garlic cloves

50 g (2 oz) sprigs of basil (weigh the soft
stalk ends and leaves only, trimming off
any tough stalks that will not purée)

about 450 ml (¾ pt) good virgin olive oil

salt and freshly ground black pepper

COOK'S TIP

Pesto can be made quite easily in a
liquidizer. The important point to
remember is to process the mixture
in batches and combine them
all at the end. Pesto is not like a
mayonnaise — it does not combine
irreversibly in a liaison — so there is
nothing wrong making it in this way.

This is a classic accompaniment for plain, boiled pasta, and it is
deserving of its famous reputation. As quite a bit of oil is used, the
sauce will keep well in a jar in the fridge for many months. If you
definitely want to keep the sauce for a long time, sterilize small
airtight jars in which to keep it by washing them in a sterilizing solution
(available for home brewing or for cleaning babies' bottles). Once you
start using the sauce in a jar, use it up within one to two weeks as
it can easily become contaminated with micro-organisms from the
cutlery dipped into it. The point is to remember this and not to treat
pesto as you would a chutney or a true preserve.

Process the pine nuts and Parmesan cheese in a food processor until fairly
finely ground, but not binding together. Add the garlic and basil, then
process the mixture until the herb is finely chopped and the mixture
begins to clump together.

Pour in a little olive oil and process the mixture to a smooth, thick paste.
Then, continue trickling in the olive oil with the food processor running.
Add enough to make a thin paste. Stir in seasoning to taste. Store in dry,
sterilized, airtight jars in the bottom of the fridge. Stir well before use.

Garlic Butter

Crush the garlic over the butter, then chop the crushed part of the clove to ensure it mixes evenly with the butter.

SERVES 4

175 g (6 oz) butter
2 garlic cloves, crushed and chopped (see above)
freshly ground black pepper
2 tbsp finely chopped fresh parsley
freshly grated Parmesan cheese, to serve

Cream the butter with the garlic, then add pepper to taste and the parsley. Toss with hot, freshly cooked pasta and serve with freshly grated Parmesan cheese.

Spiced Anchovy Butter

This is delicious with pasta verde or tomato flavoured pasta.

SERVES 4

50 g (2 oz) tin anchovy fillets
1 garlic clove, crushed
2 tbsp ground coriander
1 tsp ground mace
175 g (6 oz) butter
squeeze of lemon juice
2 tbsp finely chopped fresh parsley
freshly ground black pepper

Drain the oil from the anchovies into a small saucepan. Add the garlic, coriander and mace and cook gently for 5 minutes, stirring all the time. Remove from the heat and leave to cool.

Meanwhile, pound the anchovies to a smooth paste, then beat them into the butter. Gradually beat in the spices, adding in all the oil from the saucepan, too, and add a squeeze of lemon juice. Mix in the parsley and pepper to taste.

Herb Butter

Parsley, dill, chives, tarragon, chervil, thyme, basil and oregano are all suitable for this flavoursome butter. Mint may also be used, fairly sparingly, and a little very finely chopped rosemary may be added.

SERVES 4

175 g (6 oz) butter
2 tbsp chopped fresh parsley
2 tbsp snipped chives
2 tbsp mixed herbs
freshly ground black pepper
a squeeze of lemon juice

Cream the butter with the herbs. Mix in pepper to taste and a little lemon juice.

Truffle Butter

Toss this with plain, cooked, fresh pasta and serve with a simple Good Green Salad.

SERVES 4–6

175 g (6 oz) butter
2 preserved black truffles (from a jar or tin)
1 tbsp finely snipped chives
1 tbsp finely chopped fresh parsley

Cream the butter until it is soft. Add the lemon juice from the jar or tin of truffles and beat it into the butter. Slice the truffles, then cut them into fine strips.

Beat the chives and parsley into the butter, then gently mix in the truffles. The butter may be frozen for up to 2 months.

Lemon Anchovy Butter

SERVES 4

50 g (2 oz) tin anchovy fillets in olive oil

1–2 garlic cloves, crushed and chopped

grated rind of 1 lemon

100 g (4 oz) unsalted or lightly
  salted butter

freshly ground black pepper

dash of Worcestershire sauce

4 tbsp chopped fresh parsley

Toss this butter with freshly cooked pasta and serve with lemon wedges so that diners can add a little juice to their pasta if liked. The butter is especially well suited to serving with black squid ink pasta, but other fresh pasta also tastes superb served this way.

Pound, mash or process the anchovies with the oil from the tin to make a smooth paste. Mix in the garlic and lemon rind. Soften the butter, then gradually beat in the anchovy mixture. Add freshly ground black pepper and Worcestershire sauce to taste. Finally, mix in the parsley.

Prawn Butter

SERVES 4

175 g (6 oz) unsalted butter

1 small onion, very finely chopped

½ tsp ground mace

225 g (8 oz) peeled, cooked prawns, finely chopped

3 tbsp chopped fresh dill

salt and freshly ground black pepper

Toss this with freshly cooked pasta to make a delicious supper dish. Spaghetti, mafaldine, tagliatelle, small to medium pasta shells or any long or small pasta shapes are good with this butter coating them.

Melt a quarter of the butter in a small saucepan. Add the onion and cook gently for about 20 minutes, or until it is well cooked and softened, but not browned. Stir in the mace and cook for 1 minute, then remove the saucepan from the heat.

Mix the cooked onion with the remaining butter. If the majority of the butter is quite soft, then allow the onion mixture to cool; if not, it will soften the bulk of the butter ready for mixing in the prawns. Beat in the prawns, then add the dill and seasoning to taste.

LITTLE PASTA COCKTAILS

Toss freshly cooked soup pasta with Prawn Butter, then serve in shell dishes on a base of finely grated lettuce and cucumber cut into matchstick strips. Garnish with whole, cooked prawns, lemon wedges (so that guests may squeeze a little juice over their cocktails if liked) and sprigs of dill.

Greek Yoghurt Topping

SERVES 4

5 cm (2 in) length of cucumber, peeled
   and finely diced

salt and freshly ground black pepper

1 red or white onion, finely chopped

4 tbsp chopped fresh parsley

2 tbsp chopped fresh tarragon or
   coriander leaves

4 firm, ripe tomatoes, peeled,
   de-seeded and diced

2 tbsp chopped capers

2 bottled or tinned mild green
   chillies, chopped

450 ml (¾ pt) Greek yoghurt

This is good with garlic-flavoured pasta or dough that is seasoned with spices. It is important to use a mild salad onion as an ordinary British onion is too overpowering for this topping.

Place the cucumber in a sieve over a basin. Sprinkle generously with salt and leave to stand for 30 minutes. Mop the cucumber thoroughly on doubled pieces of kitchen paper.

Mix the onion, parsley, tarragon or coriander, cucumber, tomatoes, capers and chillies. Then, stir in the yoghurt and taste for seasoning, adding freshly ground black peppers as required, but the cucumber should contribute sufficient salt. Serve within about 30 minutes of mixing.

Spicy Brazil and White Cheese Topping

This makes an unusual and delicious topping for pasta shapes. Try it on home-made spicy pasta or on ready-made chilli-flavoured pasta.

SERVES 4

100 g (4 oz) shelled Brazil nuts

2 tbsp finely crushed or coarsely ground coriander seeds

1 tbsp white cumin seeds

175 g (6 oz) white Cheshire cheese, grated

2 tbsp chopped fresh coriander leaves

Using a serrated knife, slice the Brazil nuts. Do not try to cut neat slices of an even thickness but, instead, allow some pieces to cut as part shavings, others as thin slices. Try to avoid having too many large chunks, though.

Place the nuts in a small, heavy-based saucepan with the coriander and cumin seeds. Dry roast the nuts and spices together over a low to medium heat, shaking the saucepan often, until the seeds give up their aroma and the nuts are beginning to brown. Do not overcook the mixture or it will taste bitter. Stand the saucepan aside and leave to cool.

Mix the Cheshire cheese with the coriander and stir in the cold nuts and seeds. Serve with hot, freshly cooked pasta.

Anchovy and Green Olive Paste

Lime and spring onion add a surprisingly refreshing flavour to this paste. The paste may be kept in a covered container in the fridge for up to a week.

MAKES ABOUT 300 ml (½ pt)

350 g (12 oz) tin stoned green olives in brine, drained

50 g (2 oz) tin anchovy fillets, drained

1 garlic clove, crushed

150 ml (¼ pt) olive oil

grated rind and juice of 1 lime

4 spring onions, very finely chopped

salt and freshly ground black pepper to taste

Place the olives, anchovies and garlic in a food processor or liquidizer. Add a little of the oil and process to a thick paste, then trickle in the remaining oil whilst the machine is running. Stir in the lime rind and juice, spring onions and salt and pepper to taste.

Mixed Olive and Pepper Topping

SERVES 4

6 tbsp olive oil

2 garlic cloves, finely chopped

1 mild red or white onion, quartered
  and thinly sliced

2 large green peppers, de-seeded
  and diced

2 large red peppers, de-seeded and diced

10 black olives, stoned and thinly sliced

10 green olives, stoned and thinly sliced

4 tbsp chopped fresh parsley

salt and freshly ground black pepper

lemon wedges, to serve

A colourful topping with a pleasing flavour to turn a simple bowl of pasta into a memorable lunch. Serve with a Good Green Salad and Lemon and Herb Rolls.

Heat the olive oil in a large frying pan. Add the garlic, onion and green and red peppers. Toss the mixture over a medium to high heat for 2 minutes. Remove the saucepan from the heat, stir in the black and green olives and parsley and add salt and pepper to taste. Toss the hot mixture, with all the oil from the pan, with freshly cooked pasta. Serve with lemon wedges for guests to squeeze over their bowls.

Herbed Cheese and Walnut Topping

This makes a satisfying, tasty supper of the simplest pasta. Try it on colourful shapes or toss it with some quick-cook macaroni. Dressing the pasta with a little butter or olive oil and finely chopped garlic first will suit garlic lovers. This recipe gives generous portions for decent bowls of pasta.

SERVES 4

225 g (8 oz) mature Cheddar cheese, coarsely grated

4 tbsp finely chopped fresh parsley

1 tbsp chopped fresh thyme

4 tbsp snipped chives

100 g (4 oz) walnuts, very finely chopped

Mix the cheese, parsley, thyme, chives and walnuts, then serve sprinkled over piping hot pasta and toss well.

Pasta with Garlic and Basil

Pasta tossed with lots of garlic and warm olive oil is a classic Italian snack in which generous quantities of oil may be used according to the liking of the individual diner. This is a comparatively modest dressing.

SERVES 4

6 tbsp good olive oil

3 garlic cloves, finely chopped

freshly ground black pepper

handful of sprigs of basil, grated

freshly grated Parmesan cheese, to serve

Heat the oil in a small saucepan. Add the garlic and cook gently for 3 minutes. Toss the oil and garlic with freshly cooked, piping hot pasta and add pepper to taste. Lightly mix in the basil and serve at once, with freshly grated Parmesan cheese.

Above: Pasta Shells with Garlic and Basil.

Pasta with Fresh Tomatoes

SERVES 4

2 tbsp olive oil

50 g (2 oz) butter

1 small onion, finely chopped

1 garlic clove, crushed

750 g (1½ lb) plum tomatoes, peeled (see
  Cook's Tip, page 72), de-seeded and cut
  into chunks

1 tsp caster sugar

salt and freshly ground black pepper

4 tbsp chopped fresh parsley

2 tsp chopped fresh tarragon or 1 tbsp
  chopped fresh thyme

3 large sprigs of basil, grated

Make this when ripe plum tomatoes are available or use full-flavoured home-grown fruit. Serve with Olive Bread.

Heat the olive oil and butter together in a saucepan. Add the onion and garlic. Cook, stirring, for 15 minutes, or until the onion has softened. Stir in the tomatoes and sugar and salt and pepper to taste. Cook, stirring, until the tomatoes are hot. Then stir in the parsley and tarragon or thyme. Toss the mixture with freshly cooked pasta, then gently toss in the basil.

Sweet Red Pepper Paste with Sun-dried Tomatoes

MAKES ABOUT 300 ml (½ pt)

8 sun-dried tomatoes

150 ml (¼ pt) red wine

150 ml (¼ pt) water

4 garlic cloves, peeled

2 bay leaves

4 red peppers

150 ml (¼ pt) olive oil

salt and freshly ground black pepper

This has a full, rich flavour.

Place the sun-dried tomatoes, wine, water, garlic and bay leaves in a small saucepan. Bring to the boil, reduce the heat and cover the pan. Simmer for 30 minutes, then leave to cool. When cold, drain the tomatoes, reserving the cooking liquid, and discard the bay leaves.

Meanwhile, skewer one of the peppers on a large metal fork and rotate it over a gas flame until the skin is charred. Then rub off the skin under cold water. Repeat with the remaining peppers. Alternatively, the peppers may be charred by placing them under a hot grill and turning until the skin has blistered on all sides.

De-seed and cut up the peppers, then place them in a food processor or liquidiser with the drained tomatoes and garlic. Boil the reserved cooking liquid rapidly until it has reduced to about 4 tbsp, then add it to the peppers and purée them. Trickle in the oil whilst the machine is running. Stir in salt and pepper to taste.

Pasta Carbonara

SERVES 4

450 g (1 lb) pasta

salt and freshly ground black pepper

350 g (12 oz) Parma ham

8 eggs

150 ml (¼ pt) single cream

50 g (2 oz) butter

3 tbsp finely chopped fresh parsley

The pasta must be freshly drained and piping hot when added to this creamy, lightly scrambled egg mixture. Ordinary cooked gammon or finely grated bacon (though it must be well cooked before the eggs are added) can be used instead of expensive Parma ham. This is a favourite sauce for long pasta, such as spaghetti or tagliatelle.

Cook the pasta in boiling salted water until just tender.

Meanwhile, trim any excess fat from the gammon and cut it into fine shreds. Beat the eggs with the cream, a little salt and plenty of pepper.

Melt the butter in a large, heavy-based frying saucepan or saucepan. Add the gammon and cook, stirring, for 3 minutes. Then pour in the egg mixture and cook over a low heat, stirring all the time, until the eggs are very lightly scrambled, but not setting into lumps.

Drain the pasta and add it to the pan, then turn it in the sauce for a few seconds. Stir in the parsley and serve at once.

Macaroni Cheese

FOR THE PASTA (SERVES 4)

350 g (12 oz) short-cut macaroni

salt and freshly ground black pepper

50 g (2 oz) butter

1 large onion, finely chopped

1 bay leaf

40 g (1½ oz) plain flour

600 ml (1 pt) milk

100 g (4 oz) mature Cheddar
  cheese, grated

FOR THE TOPPING

25 g (1 oz) mature Cheddar cheese, grated

25 g (1 oz) fresh breadcrumbs

Cook the macaroni in boiling salted water according to the instructions on the packet, then drain it well.

Meanwhile, melt the butter in a large saucepan and add the onion and bay leaf. Cover the saucepan and cook the onion gently for about 30 minutes, or until it has softened, but not browned. Stir in the flour, then reduce the heat a little and slowly add the milk, and bring to the boil, stirring all the time. Simmer the sauce gently for 2 minutes.

Stir in the cheese until it has melted completely, then add salt and pepper to taste. Stir in the macaroni and heat for 2 minutes. Pour into a flameproof dish.

Mix the topping ingredients, sprinkle over the macaroni cheese and brown under a hot grill. Serve at once.

Above: Pasta Carbonara.

Above (left to right): Walnut oil with thyme; Olive oil with
bay and garlic; Sunflower oil with chilli; Red wine vinegar with
tarragon; Cider vinegar with sage

Flavoured Oils

Oils may be flavoured with herbs or spices ready for dressing hot or cold pasta. The choice of base oil depends on your preference and how you intend to use it. I use olive oil, which I find is the ideal accompaniment for pasta, whether it is hot or cold in salads. Strong nut oils (walnut or hazelnut) may be flavoured with powerful herbs like thyme or rosemary, then diluted with melted butter (for hot pasta) or light oil (for cold pasta). The following are merely a few suggestions – use any strong herbs, in any combination, with garlic if liked. Use the oil as a base for sautéing ingredients for a sauce or simply trickle it over hot, freshly cooked pasta as a dressing, adding freshly grated Parmesan cheese and freshly ground black pepper to taste.

GARLIC OIL

Peel 3 large garlic cloves and cut them in half lengthways. Place in a screw-topped jar or bottle and pour in about 600 ml (1 pt) oil. Leave to stand for 2 weeks before use. If the oil is to be kept for a long period, then remove the garlic cloves after this time.

CHILLI OIL

Slit 1 green or red chilli, scrape out the seeds and rinse (take care not to splash any water into your eyes whilst doing this) and dry the pod. Place the chilli in a screw-topped jar or bottle. Pour in about 600 ml (1 pt) oil and leave to stand for 2 weeks before use. If the oil is to be kept for a long period, then remove the chilli. For a very hot oil, use 2 dried red chillies instead of the fresh chilli and leave them in the oil permanently.

SAGE OIL

Wash and dry a large sprig of sage. Bruise the leaves slightly by crumpling them with your fingers, then place the herb in a screw-topped jar or bottle. Pour in about 600 ml (1 pt) oil and leave for 2 weeks. Crush the leaves slightly, then strain the oil. This is particularly good as a base for sauces containing pork or chicken.

TARRAGON OR ROSEMARY OIL

These are two strong herbs so the resulting oil is quite powerful. Crush a couple of large sprigs of either herb and place them in the oil, making up as Sage Oil. These are good with lamb, chicken or pork.

BAY AND GARLIC OIL

Crush 4 bay leaves slightly, then place them in a screw-topped jar or bottle with 2 peeled and split garlic cloves. Pour in about 600 ml (1 pt) oil and leave for 2 weeks, crushing the bay leaves occasionally to encourage them to flavour the oil. Remove the bay and garlic if the oil is to be kept for longer periods.

Flavoured Vinegars

Vinegars may be flavoured using the same method that is used to flavour oils. The ideas given for oil are just a few of the many possibilities, and, following the same principle, many different flavours can be created. Unlike oils the flavouring ingredients can be left in the vinegar indefinitely, giving a more intense flavour, which is desirable as vinegar is used in smaller quantities than oil. White or red wine vinegar may be used as a base or white distilled malt vinegar, but the flavour of the latter is slightly harsh. I prefer to use cider vinegar, which has a milder flavour and is more suitable for use with pasta.

Another idea is to combine the vinegars with unflavoured oil to make a dressing for cold pasta. Alternatively, a little flavoured cider vinegar can be an excellent sharpening ingredient for rich sauces or for achieving a sweet-and-sour result.

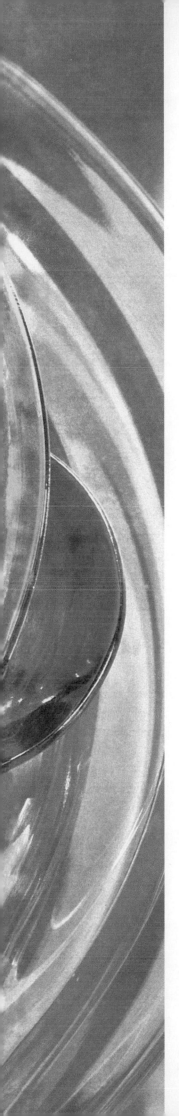

SUPERLATIVE SOUPS

This chapter aims to broaden the view that soup and pasta together spell just one thing – minestrone. All large supermarkets offer at least one or two types of soup pasta and you will find some clever miniature shapes in better Italian delicatessens. So, adding pasta to your favourite soup is a good way to make it even better.

Apart from the Italian soups, light oriental soups also use their own forms of pasta, from chunky won ton to fine vermicelli. For a dramatic dinner party starter, why not try bright bortsch served as a clear soup, complete with tiny, mushroom-filled pasta shapes.

If you make your own pasta dough, the possibilities for making clever soup garnishes are exciting. Stamp out attractive shapes to make clear soups more interesting or boil, then drain and deep-fry twists, shapes or noodles to add a crunchy contrast to hearty soups.

Crab and Sweetcorn Soup with Crunchy Pasta

SERVES 4

25 g (1 oz) butter

1 onion, chopped

1 medium potato, diced

1 bay leaf

salt and freshly ground black pepper

600 ml (1 pt) fish stock

100 g (4 oz) fresh or dried tagliatelle

298 g (10½ oz) tin cream-style corn

169 g (7 oz) tin crab meat

grated rind of 1 lemon

3 tbsp chopped fresh dill

½ tsp paprika

oil, for frying

300 ml (½ pt) single cream

This quick and easy soup looks like an oriental soup but is not based on an oriental recipe.

Melt the butter in a saucepan. Add the onion, potato, bay leaf and salt and pepper to taste. Stir well, then cover the saucepan and cook gently for 15 minutes. Pour in the stock and bring to the boil. Reduce the heat so that the soup simmers, then cover the saucepan and cook for 20 minutes.

Meanwhile, cook the tagliatelle in a large saucepan of boiling salted water, allowing 15 minutes for dried pasta or 3 minutes for fresh pasta. Drain well and set aside.

Purée the soup in a liquidizer or food processor. Stir in the cream-style corn and crab meat and heat gently to simmering point. Then, reduce the heat to the lowest setting.

Mix the lemon rind, dill and paprika. Heat the oil for deep frying to 180°C/350°F/Gas Mark 4, or until a cube of day-old bread browns in about 30 seconds. Cut up the tagliatelle slightly, then deep-fry it for a few seconds, until crisp and golden. Drain on kitchen paper and sprinkle with the dill mixture.

Stir the cream into the soup and heat gently without boiling. Taste for seasoning, then serve at once, topping portions with some crispy pasta.

Fishball Soup with Rice Vermicelli

FOR THE SOUP (SERVES 4)

1 tbsp oil

2 celery sticks, cut into fine
  matchstick strips

1 carrot, cut into fine matchstick strips

4 spring onions, grated lengthways

1 quantity Chinese-style Stock (page 53)

salt and freshly ground black pepper

100 g (4 oz) rice vermicelli

4 leaves of Chinese cabbage, grated

FOR THE FISHBALLS

450 g (1 lb) cod fillet, skinned

2 tbsp cornflour

1 spring onion, very finely chopped

grated rind of ½ a lemon

1 tbsp light soy sauce

Make the Fishballs first. Finely chop the cod or process it in a food processor, but take care not to reduce it to a soft purée. Mix the cornflour, spring onion, lemon rind and soy sauce into the fish, pounding it well until all the ingredients are thoroughly combined and the mixture binds together. Stir well, then wet your hands and shape teaspoonfuls of the mixture into small balls. Keep wetting your hands to prevent the mixture sticking.

Then, make the soup. Heat the oil in a large saucepan. Add the celery, carrot and spring onions. Cook, stirring, for 2 minutes, then add the stock and salt and pepper to taste. Bring to the boil, reduce the heat and cover the pan. Simmer for 5 minutes. Add the fishballs and simmer gently for a further 5 minutes, or until they are just cooked. Add the vermicelli and Chinese leaves, and continue to cook for 5 minutes.

Taste the soup for seasoning before ladling it into single bowls to serve.

Seafood Chowder

SERVES 4

2 tbsp oil

2 leeks, sliced

1 small onion, halved and thinly sliced

1 carrot, diced

1 celery stick, diced

1 potato, diced

600 ml (1 pt) fish stock

1 bouquet garni

450 g (1 lb) cod fillet, skinned

600 ml (1 pt) milk

8 scallops, shelled

75 g (3 oz) quick-cook macaroni

salt and freshly ground black pepper

225 g (8 oz) shelled, cooked mussels

225 g (8 oz) peeled, cooked prawns

4 tbsp chopped fresh parsley

freshly grated Parmesan cheese, to serve

Heat the oil in a large saucepan. Add the leeks, onion, carrot, celery and potato. Cook, stirring, until the leeks have reduced and the onion has softened slightly but not browned. Pour in the stock, then bring to the boil. Add the bouquet garni, reduce the heat and cover the pan. Simmer for 20 minutes.

Meanwhile, place the cod in a saucepan and add the milk. Heat gently until the milk is just about to simmer, then poach the fish for 2–3 minutes, until it is barely cooked. Remove the fish from the milk and set it aside on a plate. Poach the scallops in the milk for 2–3 minutes, until just cooked. Stand the milk aside.

Flake the cod, discarding any bones, and slice the scallops. Add the macaroni and salt and pepper to the soup, and bring back to the boil. Then, reduce the heat, cover and cook for about 7 minutes, or until the macaroni is just tender. Pour in the poaching milk and heat, stirring all the time.

Taste the soup for seasoning, then add the cooked cod, scallops, mussels and prawns. Gently stir in the parsley and heat for 2–3 minutes, or until the seafood is hot. Serve at once, with freshly grated Parmesan cheese.

Prawn and Pasta Bisque with Rouille

Uncooked prawns are sold frozen and sometimes fresh or defrosted with their heads removed. As the prawns are poached, their shells turn pink.

FOR THE BISQUE (SERVES 4)

25 g (1 oz) butter

1 onion, finely chopped

1 small carrot, diced

1 celery stick, diced

1 bay leaf

1 sprig of parsley

225 g (8 oz) peeled potato, diced

12 uncooked Mediterranean prawns, heads removed

4 tbsp brandy

300 ml (½ pt) dry white wine

600 ml (1 pt) water

salt and freshly ground black pepper

100 g (4 oz) soup pasta shells or other soup pasta

150 ml (¼ pt) single cream

FOR THE ROUILLE

2 garlic cloves, peeled

1–2 red chillies, de-seeded and chopped (see Cook's Tip, below, right)

2 egg yolks

2 tbsp fresh white breadcrumbs

2 tbsp lemon juice

200 ml (⅓ pt) olive oil

TO GARNISH

paprika

chopped fresh parsley

TO SERVE

1 short French loaf

Make the Rouille first. Purée the garlic, chillies, egg yolks, breadcrumbs and lemon juice in a food processor or liquidiser. Alternatively the ingredients may be gradually pounded to a paste in a mortar, then the yolks and lemon juice beaten in. Gradually trickle in the olive oil, with the machine running, to make a thick, fiery mayonnaise. Transfer to a serving bowl, cover and chill. Next, make the Bisque. Melt the butter in a saucepan. Add the onion, carrot, celery, bay leaf, parsley and potato. Cook, stirring, for 5 minutes. Then add the prawns. Cook, stirring gently for 5 minutes. Add the brandy and pour in the wine. Heat until simmering, then simmer gently for 5 minutes.

Remove the saucepan from the heat and use a slotted spoon to lift out the prawns. Shell the prawns and return the shells to the pan. Slice the flesh and set it aside.

Pour the water into the soup, add plenty of seasoning and bring it back to the boil. Reduce the heat, cover the saucepan and leave to simmer for 20 minutes.

Purée the soup in a liquidiser or food processor, then rub it through a fine sieve to remove any large bits of shell. Rinse out the saucepan, then pour the soup back into it and bring it to the boil. Add the pasta, reduce the heat and cover the pan. Simmer for 15 minutes, or until the pasta is cooked.

Slice the French bread fairly thinly and toast the slices until golden on both sides. Taste the soup for seasoning, then stir in the reserved prawn flesh and heat for a few seconds. Stir in the cream, heat for a few seconds without boiling, then garnish with a little sprinkling of paprika and parsley. Offer the toasted bread and Rouille with the soup.

COOK'S TIP

Chillies vary considerably in strength and personal preferences also differ widely, so adjust the number of chillies accordingly.

To prepare chillies, cut off the stalk end and scrape out the seeds (which are especially hot) and pith from inside, then rinse the shells well before slicing or chopping them.

Take care when rinsing the chillies, wash your hands thoroughly after handling them and avoid touching your eyes whilst working with them. The juices are a severe irritant to delicate skin and eyes.

Chicken Noodle Soup

SERVES 4–6

1 large, boneless chicken breast, skinned

1 tbsp oil

15 g (½ oz) fresh root ginger, peeled and
   cut into thin strips

1 carrot, cut into fine matchstick strips

50 g (2 oz) tinned bamboo shoots, cut
   into fine matchstick strips

4 spring onions, grated diagonally

1 quantity Chinese-style Stock
   (see page 53)

salt and freshly ground black pepper

about 6 fresh spinach leaves, washed and
   finely grated (optional)

100 g (4 oz) fresh wheat noodles or
   Chinese egg noodles

Cut the chicken into thin slices, then cut these into fine strips. Heat the oil in a saucepan and stirfry the chicken with the ginger until lightly browned. Add the carrot, bamboo shoots and spring onions. Stir for a few seconds before stirring in the stock.

Bring to the boil, reduce the heat and cover the pan. Simmer the soup for 30 minutes. Season, add the spinach, if using, and noodles and cook for a further 10 minutes. Taste for seasoning before serving.

Chicken and Leek Broth with Mushroom Cappelletti

This makes a hearty meal on a cold winter's day. You can substitute ready-made filled pasta for the home-made suggestion given below if you like.

SERVES 6

2 chicken quarters

1 large onion, sliced

2 large carrots, diced

1.75 l (3 pt) chicken stock

1 tbsp oil

1 garlic clove, crushed

1 bay leaf

450 g (1 lb) leeks, sliced

4 tbsp chopped fresh parsley

salt and freshly ground black pepper

1 quantity Mushroom Cappelletti

Place the chicken quarters in a saucepan with the onion and half the carrot. Pour in the stock and bring to the boil. Reduce the heat, cover the saucepan and cook for 1 hour.

Lift the chicken from the stock. Discard the skin and cut all the meat off the bones. Dice the meat.

Heat the oil in a large saucepan. Add the garlic, bay leaf and leeks. Cook, stirring, for 3 minutes, then pour in the soup and add the chicken meat. Add the parsley and a little seasoning, then bring to the boil. Reduce the heat, cover and simmer for 5 minutes.

Add the prepared Cappelletti to the soup. Bring back to the boil, then reduce the heat and simmer for about 5 minutes or until the Cappelletti are tender. Taste for seasoning before serving.

Beef and Lager Soup

SERVES 4–6

1 tbsp oil

450 g (1 lb) lean stewing beef, diced

2 large onions, thinly sliced

2 carrots, sliced

2 celery sticks, sliced

225 g (8 oz) mushrooms, sliced

1 bouquet garni

1 blade of mace

1¾ l (2 pt) water

salt and freshly ground black

300 ml (½ pt) bitter lager

1 tbsp sugar

2 tbsp tomato purée

100 g (4 oz) soup pasta

Heat the oil in a large saucepan. Add the beef and brown the pieces all over, then use a slotted spoon to remove them from the pan. Brown the onions next, cooking them over a medium heat for about 25 minutes, so that they slowly begin to brown without burning.

Stir in the carrots, celery and half the mushrooms. Return the beef to the saucepan and add the bouquet garni and mace. Pour in the water, add plenty of seasoning and the lager. Bring to the boil, then reduce the heat and cover the saucepan. Simmer the soup for 2 hours, or until the meat is very tender.

Stir in the remaining mushrooms, sugar and tomato purée, taste for seasoning, then add the pasta and simmer for 10 minutes, or until the pasta is just cooked. Serve piping hot.

Spicy Beef Soup

SERVES 4

225 g (8 oz) lean frying steak, cut into short, thin strips

pinch of five spice powder

1 red chilli, de-seeded and thinly sliced
  (see Cook's Tip, page 80)

2 tbsp oil

1 tsp sesame oil

1 small carrot, cut into fine matchstick strips

4 spring onions, grated diagonally

1 piece of lemon grass or strip of pared lemon rind

4 tbsp dry sherry

1 l (2 pt) Chinese-style Stock (see page 53) or chicken stock

salt and freshly ground black pepper

100 g (4 oz) button mushrooms, sliced

100 g (4 oz) vermicelli

Season the steak with the five spice powder and mix it with the chilli. If possible, cover and leave to marinate for several hours or overnight.

Heat the oil and sesame oil together in a saucepan. Stirfry the steak with the chilli until the meat has browned lightly. Stir in the carrot, spring onions, lemon grass or rind and cook for 1 minute. Then pour in the sherry and stock. Add seasoning to taste and bring to the boil. Reduce the heat, cover the saucepan and simmer the soup for 40 minutes.

Add the mushrooms and vermicelli, bring back to the boil, then reduce the heat and cook gently for 10 minutes. Taste for seasoning before serving.

Piquant Pork and Prawn Soup with Coconut Cream

FOR THE SOUP (SERVES 4)

100 g (4 oz) lean boneless pork, cut into very fine strips

1 tbsp oil

1 red chilli, de-seeded and finely sliced
  (see Cook's Tip, page 80)

1 garlic clove, crushed and chopped

pared rind of ½ lime, cut into fine shreds

1¼ l (2 pt) chicken stock

4 spring onions, finely chopped

5 cm (2 in) piece cucumber, thinly peeled and
  cut into thin strips

100 g (4 oz) peeled, cooked prawns, defrosted
  and drained if frozen

juice of ½ lime

salt and freshly ground black pepper

100 g (4 oz) rice vermicelli

FOR THE COCONUT CREAM

1 tbsp oil

1 tbsp finely chopped fresh root ginger

1 spring onion, finely chopped

1 tbsp smooth peanut butter

3 tbsp instant coconut milk

6 tbsp boiling water

Place the pork in a non-metallic bowl. Add the oil, chilli, garlic and lime rind. Mix well, cover and leave to marinate for 2 hours.

Turn the meat and other ingredients in the bowl into a heavy-based saucepan and stirfry in the marinade until it is cooked and has lightly browned. Stir in the stock and bring to the boil. Reduce the heat so that the soup simmers. Add the spring onions and cucumber. Cover and simmer for 15 minutes. Add the prawns and lime juice and salt and pepper to taste. Stir in the vermicelli and leave to cook very gently for 10 minutes.

Meanwhile, make the Coconut Cream. Heat the oil in a small saucepan. Add the ginger and spring onion and stirfry for 5 minutes, but do not allow the mixture to become too hot as it is likely to burn. Stir in the peanut butter, coconut milk and boiling water. Remove from the heat and transfer to a serving bowl.

Ladle the soup into serving bowls and pass the coconut cream around separately so that it may be stirred into the soup to taste just before it is eaten.

Above: Spicy beef soup.

Pistou Soup

This is the French version of minestrone, served with the paste that gives the soup its name, a close relative of pesto.

FOR THE SOUP (SERVES 6–8)

2 tbsp olive oil

2 onions, chopped

4 celery sticks, sliced

175 g (6 oz) carrots, diced

175 g (6 oz) turnips, diced

450 g (1 lb) small, new potatoes, scrubbed

450 g (1 lb) tomatoes, peeled, de-seeded and quartered

1¾ l (3 pt) vegetable stock or water

1 bouquet garni

salt and freshly ground black pepper

225 g (8 oz) shelled fresh peas

225 g (8 oz) French beans, cut into short lengths

100 g (4 oz) small courgettes, sliced

2 x 425 g (15 oz) tins flageolet beans, drained

75 g (3 oz) vermicelli

FOR THE PISTOU

handful of fresh basil

2 garlic cloves

75 g (3 oz) Gruyère cheese

25 g (1 oz) Parmesan cheese

150 ml (¼ pt) olive oil

First, make the soup. Heat the oil in a large saucepan. Add the onions, celery, carrots, turnips and new potatoes. Cook, stirring, for 10 minutes, then add the tomatoes and pour in the stock or water. Add the bouquet garni and salt and pepper to taste. Bring to the boil, then reduce the heat and cover the pan. Simmer the soup gently for 45 minutes.

Add the peas and simmer for a further 10 minutes. Then, add the French beans, courgettes, flageolets and vermicelli. Bring the soup back to the boil, partially cover the saucepan and simmer for 10 minutes.

Make the pistou whilst the soup is cooking. Place the basil, garlic, Gruyère and Parmesan in a food processor or liquidizer and process them until finely chopped. Add some of the oil, then continue processing the mixture until it forms a paste. Trickle in the remaining olive oil whilst the machine is running.

Taste the soup for seasoning. Stir in the pistou and remove the saucepan from the heat. Serve at once.

Minestrone

I love all sorts of hearty soups and this is one of my favourites. Minestrone makes a warming meal, served with plenty of fresh bread and Parmesan cheese. Try making the Olive Bread to serve as an accompaniment.

SERVES 6–8

100 g (4 oz) dried haricot beans

2 tbsp olive oil

225 g (8 oz) rindless streaky bacon, chopped

2 garlic cloves, crushed

2 onions, chopped

6 celery sticks, sliced

2 large carrots, cut in large dice

2 large potatoes, cut in chunks

1¾ l (3 pt) chicken or bacon stock

1 bouquet garni

2 x 397 g (14 oz) tins chopped tomatoes

100 g (4 oz) French beans, cut into short lengths

100 g (4 oz) courgettes, halved lengthways and sliced

225 g (8 oz) cabbage, grated

100 g (4 oz) soup pasta

salt and freshly ground black pepper

4–6 tbsp chopped fresh parsley

freshly grated Parmesan cheese, to serve

Soak the haricot beans overnight in cold water to cover.

Next day, drain the beans, place them in a saucepan and add plenty of fresh cold water to cover. Bring to the boil, boil for 10 minutes, then reduce the heat and cover the pan. Simmer the beans for 30 minutes.

Above: Minestrone soup.

Meanwhile, heat the oil in a large saucepan. Add the bacon, garlic, onions, celery and carrots. Cook, stirring all the time, for 15 minutes, or until the bacon is cooked. Then add the potatoes, stock and bouquet garni. Stir in the drained haricot beans. Bring the soup to the boil, reduce the heat and cover the pan. Simmer for 1 hour.

Stir in the tomatoes, French beans, courgettes, cabbage and pasta and bring back to the boil. Add salt and pepper to taste. Cook for a further 10 minutes, or until the vegetables are cooked and the pasta is just tender. Taste for seasoning before stirring in the parsley and serving with Parmesan cheese.

Quick Borsch with Uzska

There are many variations on this beetroot soup, but, if you want to make a soup in which to serve the tiny tortellini-type pasta, then it ought to be clear and well flavoured. This quick version bypasses the process of making and clarifying your own stock by using tinned consommé, and it works very well. If you cannot find fresh, uncooked beetroot, then use 350 g (12 oz) cooked, vacuum-packed beetroot, but do not use the type that has added acid or vinegar.

SERVES 4

25 g (1 oz) butter

1 onion, chopped

100 g (4 oz) cabbage, finely grated

1 carrot, diced

1 bay leaf

1 sprig of thyme

225 g (8 oz) fresh, uncooked beetroot, peeled and diced

2 x 275 g (10 oz) tins concentrated beef consommé

300 ml (½ pt) light red wine

300 ml (½ pt) water

salt and freshly ground black pepper

1 tbsp caster sugar

3 tbap cider vinegar

1 quantity Uszka (see page 173)

Melt the butter in a saucepan. Add the onion, cabbage, carrot, bay leaf and thyme. Cover and cook for 15 minutes.

Stir in the beetroot, consommé, wine and water. Add salt and pepper to taste and bring to the boil. Reduce the heat so that the soup just simmers, then cover the saucepan tightly and cook for 1¼ hours (do not boil rapidly).

Meanwhile, make the Uszka as given on page 173, then set them aside ready to cook at the last minute, just before serving the soup.

Strain the soup through a muslin-lined sieve. Rinse out the saucepan then return the strained soup to it. Heat the soup, then add the sugar and vinegar and stir until the sugar has dissolved. Stand the soup aside over a low heat to keep hot until the Uszka are cooked.

Cook the Uszka as given in the recipe and place some in warmed serving bowls. Taste the soup for seasoning and for the balance of sweet and sour, adjusting if necessary, then ladle it over the Uszka and offer the remaining Uszka separately. Serve at once.

Courgette Soup

SERVES 4

25 g (1 oz) butter

1 large onion, finely chopped

1 bay leaf

pared rind of 1 lemon

1 tbsp plain flour

1¼ l (2 pt) chicken stock

100 g (4 oz) pasta spirals

350 g (12 oz)   small young courgettes, thinly sliced

1 tbsp chopped fresh tarragon

salt and freshly ground black pepper

Melt the butter in a large saucepan. Add the onion, bay leaf and lemon rind. Stir well, then cover the saucepan and cook gently for 15 minutes. Stir in the flour, then pour in the stock and bring to the boil, stirring. Reduce the heat, cover the saucepan and simmer for 10 minutes.

Add the pasta to the soup and bring it back to the boil. Then, reduce the heat, partially cover the saucepan and continue to simmer for 15 minutes. Stir in the courgettes and tarragon, together with salt and pepper. Bring back to the boil, then cover and simmer for a further 5 minutes, or until the pasta and courgettes are tender. Taste for seasoning before serving.

Cabbage Soup with Spätzle

SERVES 6

25 g (1 oz) butter

1 large onion, halved and thinly sliced

2 garlic cloves, finely chopped

2 large carrots, halved and sliced

2 celery sticks, sliced

1 bay leaf

450 g (1 lb) lean bacon or gammon, for boiling in one piece

1¾ l (3 pt) water

½ quantity Spätzle (see page 46)

450 g (1 lb) cabbage, grated

salt and freshly ground black pepper

6 tbsp chopped fresh parsley

Melt the butter in a large saucepan. Add the onion, garlic, carrots, celery and bay leaf. Cook, stirring, for 5 minutes. Place the piece of bacon or gammon in the saucepan and pour in the water. Bring slowly to the boil and, as the water boils, skim off and discard any scum that rises to the surface. Reduce the heat, if necessary, to keep the water just simmering, then cover the saucepan and cook for 45 minutes.

Meanwhile, make the Spätzle batter and cook as given on page 46. Drain them and set aside.

Remove the meat from the saucepan and dice it, discarding any fat. Return the meat to the soup and add the cabbage. Taste for seasoning, stir in salt and pepper, bring back to the boil, then reduce the heat and cover the pan. Simmer for 15 minutes. Add the Spätzle and parsley and cook for a further 5 minutes, then serve piping hot.

Artichoke Soup with Walnut-dressed Pasta

SERVES 4–6

25 g (1 oz) butter

1 small onion, chopped

450 g (1 lb) Jerusalem artichokes,
    peeled and diced

1 bay leaf

600 ml (1 pt) chicken or vegetable stock

salt and freshly ground black pepper

100 g (4 oz) orecchiette

300 ml (½ pt) milk

2 tbsp walnut oil

50 g (2 oz) Gruyère cheese, finely grated

2 tbsp finely chopped walnuts

2 tbsp finely chopped fresh parsley

Melt the butter in a large saucepan. Add the onion, artichokes and bay leaf. Stir well, then cover and cook for 10 minutes. Pour in the stock and add a little salt and pepper. Bring to the boil, reduce the heat and simmer for 20 minutes.

Cook the orecchiette in a large saucepan of boiling salted water for 15 minutes, or until tender.

Meanwhile, purée the soup in a liquidiser or food processor. Rinse out the saucepan then return the soup to it and stir in the milk. Reheat the soup without boiling it, then taste for seasoning.

Drain the pasta and toss the oil, cheese, walnuts and parsley into it. Serve the soup and spoon some of the hot pasta into the bowls. Offer the remainder separately.

Thin Tomato Soup with Spinach Tortellini

SERVES 4

1 tbsp oil

25 g (1 oz) butter

1 garlic clove, crushed

1 large onion, halved and thinly sliced

2 celery sticks, diced

1 large carrot, chopped

4 tbsp tomato purée

½ tsp sugar

2 x 275 g (10 oz) tins concentrated
    beef consommé

600 ml (1 pt) water

salt and freshly ground black pepper

½ quantity tortellini with Spinach and
Ricotta Stuffing (see pages 157) or 225 g
    (8 oz) ready-made spinach tortellini

3 sprigs of basil, grated

This is an ideal recipe for ready-made tortellini or other filled pasta.

Heat the oil and butter in a saucepan. Add the garlic, onion, celery and carrot. Cook, stirring, for 5 minutes, then stir in the tomato purée and sugar. Pour in the consommé and water. Add salt and pepper to taste and bring to the boil. Reduce the heat, cover the saucepan and simmer gently for 20 minutes.

Cook the tortellini in boiling salted water, allowing about 3 minutes for home-made pasta or otherwise following the instructions on the packet for bought pasta. Drain the tortellini, then add them to the soup and taste for seasoning. Stir in the basil and serve at once.

Carrot and Parsnip Soup with Crispy Spiced Pasta

Carrots and parsnips marry well in this simple, delicious soup. If you do not want to make your own pasta for the crunchy garnish, then deep-fry ordinary cooked pasta shapes and toss them with good curry powder cooked in a little butter.

FOR THE SOUP (SERVES 4–6)

1 tbsp oil

1 large onion, chopped

450 g (1 lb) parsnips, cut into chunks

225 g (8 oz) carrots, sliced

1 medium potato, cut into chunks

900 ml (1½ pt) chicken or vegetable stock

salt and freshly ground black pepper

150 ml (¼ pt) single cream or yoghurt

TO GARNISH

about 100 g (4 oz) Curry-spiced Rich Egg Pasta Dough
  (see page 40)

oil, for frying

chopped fresh coriander leaves

First, make the soup. Heat the oil in a large saucepan. Add the onion, parsnips, carrots and potato. Stir well, then cover and cook for 10 minutes. Pour in the stock and bring to the boil. Reduce the heat, cover the saucepan and simmer for 20 minutes, or until the vegetables are tender.

Purée the soup in a food processor or liquidiser, rinse out the pan, then return the soup to it. Add salt and pepper to taste.

Now, prepare the pasta garnish. Roll out the pasta thinly and stamp out decorative shapes using aspic cutters or cut it into strips, then into small triangles. Cook the pasta in boiling salted water for 3 minutes, then drain it well.

Heat the oil for deep frying. Toss the pasta in a little flour, then fry the pieces until crisp and golden. Drain thoroughly on kitchen paper. Heat the soup, then stir in the cream or yoghurt and heat for a few seconds without boiling. Taste for seasoning and serve sprinkled with coriander and topped with the pasta.

Mushroom Soup with Watercress

SERVES 4

1 tbsp olive oil

1 onion, chopped

450 g (1 lb) closed cap mushrooms, sliced

2 tbsp plain flour

900 ml (1½ pt) chicken stock

salt and freshly ground black pepper

100 g (4 oz) ditali

300 ml (½ pt) milk stock

1 bunch watercress

Heat the oil in a saucepan. Add the onion and half the mushrooms. Cook over medium heat, stirring often, until the mushrooms are well reduced and the liquid that they yield has evaporated. Stir in the flour, then slowly pour in the stock and bring to the boil, stirring all the time. Simmer for 5 minutes. Purée the soup in a liquidizer, rinse out the saucepan, then return the soup to it and add seasoning to taste.

Bring the soup to the boil. Add the remaining mushrooms and the ditali. Reduce the heat, cover the saucepan and simmer for 15–20 minutes, or until the pasta is tender.

Stir in the milk and watercress, then heat through, stirring, and taste for seasoning before serving.

Above: Won Ton soup.

Won Ton Soup

SERVES 4

1 quantity Pork Won Tons (see page 200)

1 tbsp oil

4 spring onions, grated diagonally

1 carrot, cut into fine matchstick strips

1 quantity Chinese-style Stock (see page 53)

100 g (4 oz) broccoli, divided into small florets

salt and freshly ground black pepper

First make the Pork Won Tons as given in the recipe on page 200.

Heat the oil in a large saucepan. Add the spring onions and carrot, and stirfry for 3 minutes. Then pour in the stock and bring to the boil. Reduce the heat, cover the saucepan and simmer for 10 minutes. Add the broccoli and cook for 5 minutes.

Make sure the soup is simmering steadily, then add the Pork Won Tons. Simmer for 5 minutes, stirring them round occasionally, until they are tender and the filling has cooked through. Taste the soup for seasoning and serve.

Bean Curd and Rice Stick Soup

SERVES 4

175 g (6 oz) firm bean curd

2 tbsp sake

2 tbsp Japanese soy sauce

3 spring onions, finely chopped

1 carrot

1 quantity Japanese Stock (see page 53)

100 g (4 oz) ribbon rice sticks

Cut the bean curd into neat diamond shapes and place it in a shallow dish. Sprinkle with the sake, soy sauce and spring onions and set aside to marinate for 1 hour.

Meanwhile, peel the carrot. Use a canelle knife or small pointed knife to cut strips down the length of the carrot (if using a knife, then cut "V" strips into the carrot along its length), then cut it into thin slices.

Place the stock in a saucepan and add the decorative carrot slices. Bring to simmering point, then cook for 5 minutes. Add the rice sticks and cook for a further 10 minutes. Remove the soup from the heat.

Divide the bean curd between serving bowls. Spoon some of the rice sticks and carrots into the bowls, then ladle in the broth. Serve at once.

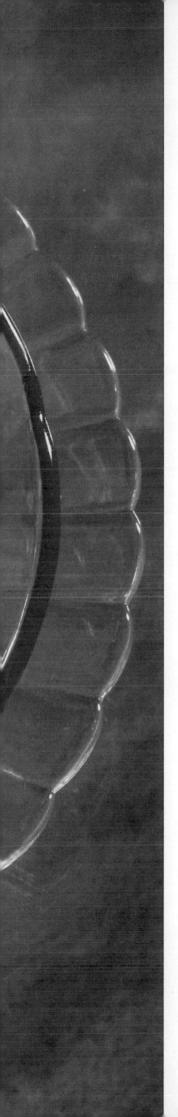

HOTPOTS AND STEWS

The idea behind this chapter is to bring together a range of dishes that are more or less a meal in themselves, with, perhaps, some bread or a salad accompaniment.

Instead of being cooked and served separately, the pasta is added to moist stews or casseroles, then cooked until tender. This does limit the choice of pasta as large or long shapes do not cook successfully in the limited quantity of liquid. Very thick shapes tend to require longer cooking and more water, so thin pasta and small shapes are ideal.

When pasta is added to a liquid already slightly thickened with other ingredients, the cooking time is increased. So, do not be surprised at the length of cooking suggested after the pasta is added to a stew.

If you think this is going to be a collection of meat stews packed with macaroni, then read on and I hope you will change your mind.

Seafarer's Hotpot

SERVES 4

25 g (1 oz) butter

1 garlic clove, crushed

1 onion, chopped

225 g (8 oz) mushrooms, sliced

25 g (1 oz) plain flour

900 ml (1½ pt) fish stock

300 ml (½ pt) dry cider

397 g (14 oz) tin chopped tomatoes

salt and freshly ground black pepper

100 g (4 oz) frozen peas

350 g (12 oz)   pasta shells

675 g (1½ lb) white fish fillet, skinned and cut in chunks

225 g (8 oz) peeled, cooked prawns

4 tbsp chopped fresh parsley

Melt the butter in a large, flameproof casserole or heavy-based saucepan. Add the garlic and onion, then cook, stirring occasionally, for 5 minutes. Add the mushrooms and stir well, then stir in the flour and slowly pour in the stock. Bring to the boil, stirring all the time. Add the cider, tomatoes and salt and pepper to taste. Bring back to the boil, then add the peas and pasta. Reduce the heat so that the sauce simmers. Cover the saucepan and cook gently for about 20 minutes, or until the pasta is tender. Stir occasionally during cooking to prevent the pasta sticking to the pan.

Stir in the fish and cook gently for a further 5 minutes. Then add the prawns and parsley and cook for a further 5 minutes, until the fish is cooked and the prawns are hot. Taste for seasoning, then serve piping hot.

Grecian Lamb Casserole

Orzo or minestra are the small Greek pasta shapes that resemble large rice grains when raw. They absorb the juices in this rich, herby casserole to make a splendid meal. Serve a light, crisp salad as a palate-cleansing side dish.

SERVES 4

1 kg (2¼ lb) stewing lamb (such as best end neck),
   chopped into bite-size pieces

1 tbsp olive oil

2 large onions, chopped

3 garlic cloves, crushed

1 bay leaf

2 tbsp chopped fresh oregano

397 g (14 oz) tin chopped tomatoes

900 ml (1½ pt) water

salt and freshly ground black pepper

225 g (8 oz) orzo

4 tbsp chopped fresh parsley

French bread, to serve

Pre-heat the oven to 180°C/350°F/Gas Mark 4.

Trim any excess fat from the lamb. Heat the oil in a large, flameproof, ovenproof casserole and brown the lamb well all over.

When the pieces of meat have browned, add the onions, garlic, bay leaf and oregano and mix well. Continue to cook for about 5 minutes, to take the raw edge off the onions before adding any liquid.

Pour in the tomatoes and water, then add plenty of salt and some pepper. Heat until the liquid is just simmering. Cover the casserole and bake in the pre-heated oven for 1½ hours, or until the lamb is tender.

Taste the sauce for seasoning, add the orzo and cook for a further 30 minutes, or until the pasta is tender. Serve at once, with plenty of French bread to mop up the delicious juices.

Smoked Fish Hotpot

SERVES 4

2 tbsp olive oil

1 large onion, halved and thinly sliced

1 red pepper, de-seeded and sliced

grated rind of 1 lemon

2 tbsp plain flour

900 ml (1½ pt) fish stock

salt and freshly ground black pepper

225 g (8 oz) pasta spirals

675 g (1½ lb) smoked fish fillet, skinned

25 g (1 oz) butter (optional)

4 eggs, hard-boiled and roughly chopped

Smoked fish tastes really good with pasta. I have used spirals here, but shells or other shapes that cook reasonably quickly may be used.

Heat the olive oil in a flameproof casserole or heavy-based saucepan. Add the onion, pepper and lemon rind. Cook, stirring occasionally, for 10 minutes. Stir in the flour, then slowly pour in the stock. Add salt and pepper and bring to the boil, stirring all the time. Add the pasta, then reduce the heat so that the sauce simmers.

Place the fish on a suitable plate to cover the pan. Top with the butter if using and cover with a saucepan lid or foil. Put the fish on top of the saucepan in place of its lid and simmer gently for 20–30 minutes, or until the pasta is cooked. Stir occasionally to prevent the pasta sticking.

Flake the fish, discarding the skin and any bones. Lightly mix it into the pasta with all the butter from steaming (if used) and the hard-boiled eggs. Taste for seasoning and serve at once.

Mediterranean Medley

SERVES 4

1 aubergine, cubed

salt and freshly ground black pepper

4 tbsp olive oil

8 chicken thighs, skinned

2 garlic cloves, finely chopped

2 tbsp chopped fresh or 1 tbsp dried oregano

2 onions, halved and sliced

1 green pepper, halved, de-seeded and sliced

1 bay leaf

25 g (1 oz) sultanas

300 ml (½ pt) red wine

600 ml (1 pt) chicken stock

397 g (14 oz) tin chopped tomatoes

225 g (8 oz) rigatoni or penne

10 black olives, stoned and halved

4 tbsp pine nuts

4 tbsp chopped fresh parsley

harissa (red chilli condiment) to serve

Place the aubergine in a colander, sprinkle each layer with salt, then leave to stand over a bowl for 30 minutes. Rinse and drain well.

Heat half the olive oil in a large, flameproof casserole or heavy-based saucepan. Fry the pieces of aubergine until lightly browned in parts, but not softened. Use a slotted spoon to remove them from the pan. Add the remaining oil and brown the chicken pieces, then remove them also. Add the garlic, oregano, onions and green pepper to the fat remaining in the pan. Cook, stirring, for 5 minutes.

Stir in the bay leaf and the aubergine cubes, then return the chicken pieces to the saucepan and sprinkle with the sultanas. Pour in the wine, stock and tomatoes. Add salt and pepper, and bring to the boil. Reduce the heat and cover the pan, then cook gently for 30 minutes.

Add the rigatoni or penne, stirring them down into the sauce and displacing the chicken so that they are covered with sauce. Bring back to simmering point and cover the saucepan tightly. Cook gently for a further 20 minutes. Add the olives and continue to cook for about 10 minutes, or until the pasta is cooked.

Meanwhile, place the pine nuts in a small, heavy-based saucepan and cook, shaking the saucepan often, over a medium heat until the pine nuts are lightly browned. Remove from the heat.

Taste the casserole for seasoning. Sprinkle the pine nuts and parsley over and serve with harissa, which may be added to taste by the diners.

Braised Turkey with Fennel

SERVES 4

675 g (1½ lb) boneless turkey breast, cut into chunks

2 tbsp plain flour

salt and freshly ground black pepper

25 g (1 oz) butter

2 fennel bulbs, sliced

1 onion, finely chopped

600 ml (1 pt) dry white wine

600 ml (1 pt) chicken stock

1 fresh bouquet garni

350 g (12 oz) anellini or other pasta rings

150 ml (¼ pt) soured cream

Pre-heat the oven to 180°C/350°F/Gas Mark 4.

Toss the pieces of turkey breast with the flour and plenty of salt and pepper. Melt the butter in a large, flameproof, ovenproof casserole and brown the turkey pieces all over, then add the fennel and onion. Turn the vegetables and turkey together over the heat for about 5 minutes. Then pour in the wine and stock. Add the bouquet garni and anellini and bring to the boil, then remove from the heat.

Stir the pasta and turkey mixture and cover the casserole tightly. Bake for about 40 minutes, until the pasta is cooked and the fennel is tender. Stir in the soured cream and taste for seasoning before serving.

Above: Mediterranean Medley.

Pheasant Galantine with Walnut Cappelletti

This is an ideal dinner party dish. It does take a lot of preparation, but, once this is over, the attention to detail at the last minute is fairly straightforward. Side dishes of red cabbage stirfried with onions and French beans will make a memorable meal.

SERVES 4

1 pheasant, boned (see Cook's Tip right)

225 g (8 oz) venison sausages

100 g (4 oz) cooked ham, finely chopped

2 onions, finely chopped

1 eating apple, peeled, cored and finely chopped

1 tbsp chopped fresh sage

2 tsp chopped fresh thyme

2 tbsp chopped fresh parsley

salt and freshly ground black pepper

25 g (1 oz) butter

100 g (4 oz) rindless smoked bacon, diced

1 small carrot, finely diced

1 celery stick, finely diced

100 g (4 oz) mushrooms, sliced

1 bottle of red wine

2 bay leaves

1 quantity cappelletti with Walnut Stuffing (see page 155)

Lay the pheasant out on a board, skin side down. Skin the venison sausages and place the meat in a bowl. Add the ham, half the chopped onion, the apple, sage, thyme, parsley and plenty of seasoning. Pound the ingredients together with the back of a mixing spoon to thoroughly combine them. Then place the stuffing down the middle of the pheasant. Fold the bird over the stuffing and use a trussing needle with cooking thread or string to sew it up.

Pre-heat the oven to 180°C/350°F/Gas Mark 4.

Melt the butter in a flameproof, ovenproof casserole. Brown the outside of the Pheasant Galantine lightly, then remove it from the saucepan and set aside.

Add the remaining onion, bacon, carrot, celery and mushrooms to the fat in the pan. Cook for 2–3 minutes, then pour in the wine and add the bay leaves. Stir in salt and pepper to taste and heat the wine to just below simmering point. Lower the Pheasant Galantine into the casserole. Cover and bake in the oven for 1½ hours. Turn the Galantine halfway through cooking.

Meanwhile, make the walnut-filled cappelletti as given on pages 155. Just before taking the Pheasant Galantine from the oven, cook the cappelletti in boiling salted water for 2 minutes, so that they are three-quarters cooked, but not quite tender. Drain well.

Carefully lift the Pheasant Galantine from the casserole. Remove the bay leaves from the sauce and taste for seasoning. Tip in the cappelletti. Stir to coat the cappelletti in sauce, then cover the casserole and return it to the oven whilst you carve the Galantine. The cappelletti will finish cooking in the sauce.

COOK'S TIP

A butcher will bone the pheasant if you ask in advance, but if you are doing it yourself, you need a sharp, pointed knife and a pair of kitchen scissors. Place the pheasant on a board, breast side down. Cut through the skin and meat into the bone all along the back of the bird. Then, slide the point of the knife under the meat, close to the bone, down one side. Work all the meat off the carcase, from the middle of the bird down the side as far as the breastbone. Scrape the meat off the leg joints, carefully turning the meat and skin inside out off the bones. Snip the meat off or round the joint ends with scissors. When the meat is free from the bones on one side, turn the board round and work down the other side. Leave the meat attached along the top of the soft breastbone as you work. Finally, carefully cut the meat off the breastbone, taking the merest sliver of bone to avoid puncturing the skin (it is important to keep the skin whole whilst doing this).

Gnocchi-topped Chicken

SERVES 4

1 quantity Semolina Gnocchi (see page 45)

2 tbsp olive oil

4 boneless chicken breasts, skinned

1 onion, halved and thinly sliced

2 garlic cloves, crushed

6 sage leaves, grated

100 g (4 oz) mushrooms, sliced

4 tbsp brandy (optional)

150 ml (¼ pt) red wine

600 ml (1 pt) passata

salt and freshly ground black pepper

100 g (4 oz) lean cooked ham, grated

25 g (1 oz) butter, melted

This makes a delicious supper and it is a great way of turning simple semolina gnocchi into a special dinner party dish. For a formal main course, serve Sautéed Leeks with Spinach and some lightly sautéed courgettes as accompaniments.

Make the Semolina Gnocchi as given on page 49, and cut it into squares or circles.

Preheat the oven to 190°C/315°F/Gas Mark 5.

Heat the olive oil in a flameproof casserole that can be placed in the oven. Brown the chicken pieces all over, then use a slotted spoon to remove them from the pan. Add the onion and garlic, and cook for 5 minutes, stirring occasionally. Add the sage and mushrooms and stir for a few minutes. Pour in the brandy, wine and passata and bring to the boil, stirring. Remove from the heat and taste for seasoning.

Return the chicken pieces to the pan, spooning the sauce over them, and sprinkle the gammon over the top. Arrange the Semolina Gnocchi, overlapping, on top of the chicken, then brush with the butter. Bake in the pre-heated oven for about 40 minutes, until the chicken is cooked through and the Semolina Gnocchi are golden brown and well crusted.

Hotpot of Venison Meatballs

Minced venison is available from supermarkets and butchers. It makes a simple pot of meatballs and pasta, but is rich and delicious.

FOR THE VENISON MEATBALLS (SERVES 4)

1 onion, grated

50 g (2 oz) fresh breadcrumbs

1 garlic clove, crushed

1 tsp ground mace

225 g (8 oz) rindless streaky bacon, finely chopped or minced

450 g (1 lb) minced venison

1 tsp finely chopped fresh rosemary

salt and freshly ground black pepper

1 egg

1 tsp oil

FOR THE SAUCE

1 onion, sliced

1 carrot, halved and sliced

1 celery stick, sliced

1 bay leaf

2 sprigs of sage

1 tbsp plain flour

600 ml (1 pt) chicken stock

600 ml (1 pt) red wine

1 tbsp tomato purée

2 tbsp mushroom ketchup

225 g (8 oz) pasta twists

4 tbsp chopped fresh parsley

First, make the Venison Meatballs. Mix the onion, breadcrumbs, garlic, mace, bacon, venison, rosemary, plenty of salt and pepper, and the egg in a bowl. Pound the ingredients together with the back of a mixing spoon until they are thoroughly combined. Wet your hands, then shape the mixture into 16 meatballs, kneading the meat together firmly so that they are smooth and well bound on the outside. Rinse your hands under cold water frequently to prevent the meat from sticking to them.

Heat the oil in a large, flameproof casserole or heavy-based saucepan. Brown the meatballs all over, then use a slotted spoon to remove them from the saucepan and set aside.

Next, prepare the sauce. Add the onion, carrot, celery, bay leaf and sage to the casserole or saucepan. Cook, stirring occasionally, for 5 minutes. Then stir in the flour and pour in the stock and wine. Add the tomato purée and mushroom ketchup with salt and pepper to taste. Bring to the boil, stirring all the time. Reduce the heat so that the sauce barely simmers and return the meatballs to the casserole or saucepan. Cover and cook gently for 45 minutes.

Add the pasta and continue to cook for a further 30 minutes, stirring once or twice, until the pasta is tender.

Taste for seasoning and stir in the parsley before serving.

Gingered Lamb with Broccoli

Tangy ginger is good with rich lamb and slightly crunchy broccoli completes the meal-in-a-pot. Use any fresh pasta shapes instead of the paglia a fieno.

SERVES 4

2 tbsp olive oil

1 large onion, halved and thinly sliced

25 g (1 oz) fresh root ginger, peeled and finely chopped

750 g (1½ lb) lean, boneless lamb, diced

600 ml (1 pt) medium cider

600 ml (1 pt) chicken stock

1 bay leaf

2 sprigs of rosemary

4 tbsp redcurrant jelly

salt and freshly ground black pepper

350 g (12 oz) fresh paglia e fieno

25 g (1 oz) butter

450 g (1 lb) broccoli

150 ml (¼ pt) soured cream

Above: Gingered lamb with broccoli.

Contemporary Cock-a-leekie

Pasta is the ideal ingredient for bringing this soup-cum-stew of boiled chicken with leeks and prunes right up to date. Select large pasta shapes for this recipe.

SERVES 6

175 g (6 oz) rindless streaky bacon, diced

1½ kg (3 lb) chicken

1 large carrot, sliced

1 large onion, sliced

strip of pared lemon rind

1 fresh bouquet garni

1 blade of mace

salt and freshly ground black pepper

450 g (1 lb) leeks, sliced

450 g (1 lb) lumache

175 g (6 oz) ready-to-eat prunes, stoned and quartered

4 tbsp chopped fresh parsley

Place the bacon in a large, heavy-based saucepan and heat gently until the fat begins to run from the bacon. Then increase the heat and cook until the bacon is lightly browned.

Meanwhile, make sure the chicken is ready for the pot, that its giblets have been removed and it is securely trussed. Brown the bird as best you can on all sides, then turn it so that it lies breast down in the pot. Add the carrot, onion, lemon rind, bouquet garni, blade of mace and plenty of salt and pepper. Pour in water to completely cover the chicken. Bring the water to the boil, skimming off any scum that rises to the surface. Then top up with water if necessary. Reduce the heat so that the water simmers. Cover the saucepan and cook for about 2 hours, turning the chicken over halfway through cooking until the bird is cooked through and tender.

Carefully remove the chicken from the pot, draining the stock into the pan. Add the leeks, pasta and prunes. Bring the soup liquid to the boil, then reduce the heat slightly so that the liquid bubbles at a fast simmer.

Partially cover the saucepan and cook for 15–20 minutes, or until the pasta is tender. Stir occasionally to make sure that the pasta does not stick to the pan.

Meanwhile, discard the skin from the chicken and cut the meat off the carcase, carving it in neat pieces. Taste the pasta mixture for seasoning, then stir in the parsley. Ladle the pasta and leeks into large bowls and top with the chicken.

Beef and Chestnut Stew

Dried chestnuts are available from healthfood shops as well as some delicatessens. They readily absorb the flavour of the rich cooking liquor in this beef stew and their floury texture goes well with the beef and pasta to make a satisfying meal. Serve a light vegetable accompaniment with the stew – some sautéed courgettes, lightly cooked carrots, cauliflower or Brussels sprouts, say.

SERVES 4

100 g (4 oz) dried chestnuts

1 tbsp oil

100 g (4 oz) rindless streaky bacon, diced

1 kg (2¼ lb) lean stewing beef

2 onions, sliced

100 g (4 oz) chestnut mushrooms, sliced

1 fresh bouquet garni

strip of pared orange rind

salt and freshly ground black pepper

600 ml (1 pt) water

600 ml (1 pt) stout

1 tbsp tomato purée

225 g (8 oz) multi-coloured pasta shapes

25 g (1 oz) raisins

Sprigs of parsley and halved orange slices, to garnish

Place the chestnuts in a bowl and cover with cold water. Leave to soak for 4 – 6 hours.

Pre-heat the oven to 160°C/325°F/Gas Mark 3.

Heat the oil in a large, flameproof, ovenproof casserole. Add the bacon and beef and cook, stirring often, until the

beef is sealed and has lightly browned. Add the onions and mushrooms, and continue to cook for a further 5 minutes, or until the onions are beginning to soften slightly and the mushrooms have reduced in volume.

Drain the chestnuts and stir them into the meat mixture. Add the bouquet garni and orange rind with plenty of salt and pepper. Pour in the water, stout and tomato purée and heat until the liquid is just simmering. Cover the saucepan and bake in the pre-heated oven for

3 hours. Stir the stew occasionally during cooking.

Taste the sauce for seasoning. Add the pasta and raisins and cook for a further 20–30 minutes, or until the pasta is tender. Remove the orange rind and bouquet garni before serving or as you ladle out the stew. A garnish of parsley and orange slices may be added to single portions or to one side of the stew if you are serving it for a special meal.

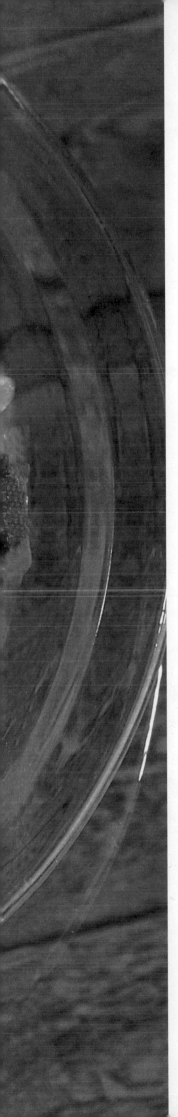

MAIN COURSE SAUCES

For a pasta course or meal to be a success, the sauce and the chosen pasta must work together.

Think in terms of the taste of the sauce and its type, then decide on the pasta accompaniment. Lightly flavoured delicate sauces go well with fine pasta. For example, a thin sauce of prawns would be ruined by serving it with chunky rigatoni or huge shells – it would be rather like cutting door-step slices of bread and butter to serve with the finest, thinnest pieces of smoked salmon. On the other hand, a red-hot chilli and garlic sauce based on a thin mixture of tomato and oil will work just as well with chunky pasta as it will with fine spaghetti as it is strong enough to stand out whatever it is served with. Remember, fine flavour, fine pasta.

The colour and arrangement of pasta with a sauce also deserves forethought. Simply ladling the sauce over the pasta is not always the best option. Instead serve the two alongside each other in shallow bowls, when the sauce is a chunky one, or else offer the pasta separately garnished.

Even if the pasta and the sauce are slightly out of step with each other in terms of flavour, appearance and texture, all the pastas taste good with all the sauces. The only combination to avoid is an oriental pasta with an Italian sauce or vice versa.

Simple Fish Sauce

SERVES

750 g (1½ lb) cod fillet

1 bay leaf

600 ml (1 pt) milk

40 g (1½ oz) butter

1 small onion, finely chopped

1 small carrot, finely diced

40 g (1½ oz) plain flour

225 g (8 oz) button mushrooms, sliced

1 tbsp horseradish sauce (optional)

3 tbsp chopped fresh parsley

1 tbsp chopped capers

salt and freshly ground black pepper

freshly grated Parmesan cheese, to serve

This is an ideal way to cook frozen fish fillets or steaks. Smoked fish can be used instead of plain white fish for a little variety and cooked seafood, such as peeled cooked prawns, can be added to the sauce for extra texture and flavour. Serve the sauce on a bed of tagliatelle verde or on fettuccine flavoured with squid ink. This is a sauce that can be served with any pasta you like.

Place the cod in a saucepan or deep frying pan. Add the bay leaf and pour in the milk. Heat gently until the milk is just coming to simmering point. Then, remove from the heat and leave to cool.

When the fish has cooled, lift it from the milk and flake the flesh off the skin in large pieces. Reserve the milk.

Melt the butter in a saucepan. Add the onion and carrot and stir well. Cover and cook for 15 minutes, until the onion has softened.

Meanwhile, strain the reserved milk.

Stir the flour into the onion mixture, then stir in the milk and bring the sauce to the boil. Add the mushrooms and cook gently, stirring, for 3 minutes. The liquor from the mushrooms will thin the sauce slightly.

Add the horseradish sauce, parsley, capers, salt and pepper to the sauce and taste it to check the seasoning. Then add the fish. Cook gently for 2–3 minutes, until the fish is hot. Serve at once, offering freshly grated Parmesan cheese with the sauce and pasta.

Fresh Tuna Sauce

A fresh green chilli and some lime juice add satisfying piquancy to this sauce, which has an avocado and soured cream topping. Serve it with shells or other small pasta shapes.

SERVES 4

450 g (1 lb) fresh tuna steak, skinned and
   cut into 2.5 cm (1 in) cubes
4 tbsp olive oil
grated rind and juice of 1 lime
50 g (2 oz) tin anchovy fillets
2 garlic cloves, crushed
1 green chilli, de-seeded and chopped
   (see Cook's Tip, page 80)
1 tbsp chopped fresh oregano
1 onion, finely chopped
1 red pepper, de-seeded and chopped
2 x 397 g (14 oz) tins Chopped tomatoes
100 g (4 oz) mushrooms, sliced
salt and freshly ground black pepper
2 avocados
150 ml (¼ pt) soured cream
2 tbsp chopped fresh coriander

Place the tuna steak in a dish. Pour the olive oil, lime rind and juice over, then cover and leave to marinate for 2–4 hours.

Drain the oil from the anchovies into a saucepan, setting the anchovies aside. Add the garlic, chilli, oregano, onion and pepper. Cook, stirring, for 10 minutes.

Then, add the tuna, with the marinade, the tomatoes and mushrooms. Chop the anchovies and stir them into the sauce with salt and pepper to taste. Heat until just simmering, cover and cook gently for 40 minutes.

When the fish is cooked, quarter the avocados, remove the stone and peel, then slice the flesh across into pieces.

Ladle the sauce over a bed of freshly cooked pasta, then swirl with soured cream and sprinkle with chopped coriander. Finally top with the avocado and serve at once.

Clam Sauce

Clam sauce is a traditional accompaniment for spaghetti. Clams vary enormously in size and it is not always possible to get the small ones that are about the size of large cockles or mussel shells, so if you can only get big clams, chop them up once cooked.

SERVES 4

1 kg (2 lb) fresh clams
4 tbsp olive oil
1 large onion, finely chopped
3 garlic cloves, crushed
1 kg (2¼ lb) tomatoes, peeled, de-seeded and diced
½ tsp sugar
salt and freshly ground black pepper
6 tbsp chopped fresh parsley
freshly grated Parmesan cheese, to serve

Clean the clams and cook them following the instructions in the Cook's Tip and first step of the method on page 126. Strain the cooking liquid through fine muslin, then boil it, uncovered, until it has reduced to 300 ml (½ pt). Remove the clams from their shells, reserving a few in their shells for garnishing if you like, and set aside.

Heat the olive oil in a saucepan. Add the onion and garlic and cook gently for 10 minutes.

Then, stir in the tomatoes, sugar, plenty of seasoning and the cookery liquor from the clams. Bring to the boil, reduce the heat and simmer the sauce, uncovered, for 30 minutes.

Add the clams and parsley to the sauce. Taste for seasoning, then pour it over freshly cooked spaghetti and toss together well before serving. Garnish with any reserved clams and offer Parmesan cheese with the sauce.

Seafood Sauce

You can vary the seafood used in this sauce according to what is available and personal taste, using the ingredients list below as a guide for your own variations.

SERVES 4

450 g (1 lb) fresh mussels

450 g (1 lb) fresh cockles or small clams (optional)

300 ml (½ pt) water

2 tbsp olive oil

1 garlic clove, crushed

1 onion, chopped

2 celery sticks, thinly sliced

1 carrot, diced

100 g (4 oz) mushrooms, sliced

25 g (1 oz) plain flour

300 ml (½ pt) light red wine

1 tbsp tomato purée

salt and freshly ground black pepper

4 squid sacs, sliced (see Cook's Tip, page 204)

450 g (1 lb) white fish fillet, skinned and cut into chunks

8–12 uncooked Mediterranean prawns

8 fresh scallops, shelled and sliced

freshly grated Parmesan cheese, to serve

Clean the mussels and cockles or clams, if using (see Cook's Tip below). Place them in a large saucepan and pour in the water. Bring the water to the boil, then reduce the heat so that the water simmers and cover the pan. Cook, shaking the pan occasionally, for about 10 minutes, or until all the shells have opened (discard any that do not open). Reserve a few mussels in their shells for garnishing, if you like, then remove the other mussels and cockles or clams from their shells and set aside.

Strain the cooking liquid through muslin and boil it to reduce it to about 300 ml∕½ pt, if necessary. Set this aside.

Heat the olive oil in a saucepan. Add the garlic, onion, celery and carrot. Stir well, cover the pan and cook gently for 20 minutes, shaking the pan occasionally, until the vegetables are tender, but not browned.

Add the mushrooms and stir in the flour. Slowly pour in the strained cooking liquor and wine. Bring to the boil, stirring, and add the tomato purée. Stir in salt and freshly ground black pepper to taste. Add the squid to the sauce, cover and simmer gently for 15 minutes.

Then, add the white fish and continue to cook, covered, for 10 minutes. Next, add the prawns and cook for 5 minutes. Add the scallops and poach gently for 5 minutes. Lastly, add the cooked mussels and cockles or clams. Heat for a few minutes without simmering or boiling. Taste for seasoning and serve. Offer freshly grated Parmesan cheese with the sauce and pasta and garnish with the reserved mussels in their shells, if liked.

COOK'S TIP

This is how to clean and cook live mussels, clams and cockles.

Thoroughly scrub the shells and scrape off any barnacles. Discard any open or broken shells which do not close when tapped sharply.

Traditionally, shellfish require purging by leaving them to stand in cold water so that they egest any sand from their shells. Leave the shellfish to soak overnight in a large bucket of cold water with a handful of oatmeal added, leaving the bucket in a cold place.

Next day, drain and rinse the shellfish. Remove the "beards" from the mussels – the group of fine, black hairs that protrude from the shells. Pull them away sharply.

The two important points to remember are, first, to discard opened uncooked shellfish that do not shut when tapped and, second, to discard any shells that do not open during cooking. In both cases, there is a risk of poisoning as these shellfish are dead and may contain toxins.

Lobster and Spinach Topping

SERVES 4

2 small, cooked lobsters
  (about 450 g (1 lb) each)

50 g (2 oz) butter

1 small onion, finely chopped

1 kg (2¼ lb) fresh spinach, trimmed,
  washed and left wet

salt and freshly ground black pepper

225 g (8 oz) oyster mushrooms,
  halved if large

squeeze of lemon juice

150 ml (¼ pt) fromage frais

2 tbsp freshly grated Parmesan cheese

lemon wedges, to serve (optional)

This is a good way in which to use the small ready cooked lobsters that are readily available from supermarkets and also sold frozen.

Twist off the lobster claws and legs. Crack the claws with nut crackers and use a meat skewer to pick out all the meat. Break the legs at the joints and pick out all the meat. Lay one of the lobsters on a board on its back. Use a sharp, pointed knife to cut through the shell along the tail, underneath the firm bright shell which overlaps the jointed section. Do this along both sides so that you can pull off the softer area of shell covering the tail meat. Lift out the tail meat in one piece, then slice it.

Melt half the butter in a large saucepan. Add the onion and cook, stirring often, for about 10 minutes, or until it has softened but not browned.

Add the wet spinach, cover the pan and steam it for about 7 minutes, or until it has reduced and is tender. Stir well, then add salt and pepper to taste. Keep hot over a low heat.

Melt the remaining butter in a large frying pan and add the lobster meat with the oyster mushrooms. Sprinkle in salt and pepper. Cook, turning the mushrooms and lobster gently, until both are piping hot. Add a squeeze of lemon juice, the fromage frais and the Parmesan. Stir well, then remove the pan from the heat to prevent the fromage frais curdling.

Give the spinach a stir, then tip it on to a bed of freshly cooked pasta. Top with the lobster and mushrooms and serve at once with lemon wedges to squeeze over the lobster, if liked.

Smoked Haddock and Egg Sauce

SERVES 4

600 ml (1 pt) Béchamel Sauce (page 56)

675 g (1½ lb) smoked haddock fillet,
  skinned and cut into chunks

4 tbsp chopped fresh parsley

4 eggs, hard-boiled and chopped

100 g (4 oz) button mushrooms,
  thinly sliced

a little lemon juice

salt and freshly ground black pepper

This is good with pasta verde, such as tagliatelle, or shells. It also makes a flavoursome filling for layered pasta dishes, such as lasagne.

Make the Béchamel Sauce as given on page 56, but without adding any salt and pepper.

Stir the smoked haddock into the sauce and simmer it very gently for about 5 minutes or until the pieces of fish are just cooked.

Stir in the parsley, eggs, mushrooms and a squeeze of lemon juice. Then add seasoning to taste. Heat gently for about 3 minutes before serving.

Above: Lobster and spinach topping.

Swordfish and Tomato Sauce

Firm swordfish steak makes a satisfying sauce to serve with any type of pasta. Halibut, tuna or monkfish may be substituted if preferred and, indeed, any other thick fillets of white fish will also taste good in the sauce, but cod or haddock fillets should be poached for a shorter period to avoid overcooking them. The sauce may also be layered with lasagne and topped with Béchamel Sauce (see page 56), then baked.

SERVES 4

750 g (1½ lb) swordfish steak, cut into chunks

1 tbsp chopped fresh marjoram

3 tbsp chopped fresh parsley

3 tbsp olive oil

1 garlic clove, crushed

1 onion, finely chopped

1 green pepper, de-seeded and chopped

600 ml (1 pt) passata

150 ml (¼ pt) dry white wine

salt and freshly ground black pepper

225 g (8 oz) cooked fresh or frozen peas

grated rind of ½ a lemon

freshly grated Parmesan cheese, to serve

Place the swordfish in a bowl. Sprinkle the marjoram, parsley, olive oil and garlic over. Cover and leave to marinate for 2–4 hours.

Drain the oil from the fish into a saucepan. Add the onion and pepper, then cook, stirring often, for 15 minutes, or until the onion has softened, but not browned.

Stir in the passata and wine and add seasoning to taste. Add the swordfish, with the herbs, and heat gently until the sauce is just about to simmer. Cover the pan and cook gently for 20 minutes, or until the fish has cooked.

Add the peas and lemon rind and taste the sauce for seasoning. Cook gently for a further 5 minutes, or until the peas are hot. Serve with freshly grated Parmesan.

Cucumber and Prawn Sauce

A light sauce to make a summery meal. Shells, tagliatelle, spaghetti, spirals or cappelletti all come to mind as being suitable, which indicates that almost any type of pasta will go with this sauce.

SERVES 4

15 g (½ oz) butter

1 small onion, finely chopped

1 cucumber, peeled and diced

150 ml (¼ pt) dry white wine

salt and freshly ground black pepper

450 g (1 lb) peeled, cooked prawns,
  defrosted and well-drained if frozen

300 ml (½ pt) Greek yoghurt

4 tbsp freshly grated Parmesan cheese

3 tbsp chopped fresh dill

whole prawns and cucumber slices, to garnish (optional)

Melt the butter in a saucepan. Add the onion and stir well. Cover and cook for 5 minutes. Stir in the cucumber, cover again and cook for a further 5 minutes. Add the wine and heat until it is simmering, then cover the pan and simmer for a further 15 minutes, or until the cucumber is tender.

Add salt and pepper to taste to the cucumber, then stir in the prawns. Stir in the yoghurt and cheese. Heat the mixture gently, stirring all the time (if the yoghurt reaches simmering point, it will curdle, so take care to remove it from the heat as soon as the mixture is pleasantly hot enough to eat). Serve immediately, tossed with piping hot, freshly cooked pasta, and garnish with prawns and cucumber, if liked.

Chicken Supreme

SERVES 4

1 tbsp oil

25 g (1 oz) butter

1 small onion, chopped

3 boneless chicken breasts,
  skinned and diced

40 g (1½ oz) plain flour

150 ml (¼ pt) dry white wine

450 ml (¾ pt) chicken stock

1 bouquet garni

350 g (12 oz) small button mushrooms

salt and freshly ground black pepper

300 ml (½ pt) single cream

2 tbsp chopped fresh parsley

This is an old favourite, but it is a sauce that goes so well with almost any type of pasta that I never tire of it. Serve it with a bowl of tagliatelle verde and a side salad for an informal supper party or toss the sauce with pasta shapes for a weekday supper. As the sauce itself is pale, it looks particularly good if ladled over multi-coloured pasta shapes. The sauce can be multiplied up to serve a crowd, and it freezes well before the cream is added.

Heat the oil and butter in a flameproof casserole. Add the onion and cook, stirring occasionally, for 10 minutes.

Add the chicken and brown the pieces lightly all over. Stir in the flour, then cook for 2 minutes before slowly pouring in the wine and stock. Add the bouquet garni, bring the sauce to the boil and reduce the heat so that it is just simmering.

Stir the mushrooms into the sauce (which is very thick at this stage) and add salt and pepper to taste. Cover the casserole tightly and cook the sauce gently for 20 minutes. The liquid that the mushrooms yield during cookery will thin the sauce slightly.

Stir the cream into the sauce and heat it through gently, then add the parsley and discard the bouquet garni before serving the sauce.

Turkey with Flageolet Beans and Pesto

SERVES 4

450 g(1 lb) skinned, boneless turkey breast, cut into thin strips

3 tbsp flour

salt and freshly ground black pepper

grated rind of 1 lemon

1 tbsp olive oil

25 g (1 oz) butter

4 spring onions, chopped

225 g (8 oz) mushrooms, sliced

425 g (15 oz) tin flageolet beans, drained

½ quantity Pesto (see page 67), to serve

A simple, sautéed mixture to toss with tagliatelle, spaghetti or any other of the long pasta shapes. Spoon the Pesto over individual portions of the pasta mixture.

Dust the turkey with the flour, salt, pepper and the lemon rind. Heat the oil and butter in a large frying pan. Add the turkey and cook, turning the strips occasionally, until they are golden brown.

Add the spring onions, mushrooms and beans and continue to cook for 2–3 minutes, or until all the ingredients are hot.

Toss the cooked turkey mixture with your chosen cooked pasta and serve topped with Pesto to taste.

Duck with Sweet Ginger Sauce

SERVES 4

4 boneless duck breasts, skinned

1 tbsp cornflour

salt and freshly ground black pepper

2 tbsp oil

1 onion, halved and thinly sliced

1 bay leaf

1 sprig of thyme

450 ml (¾ pt) dry cider

3 pieces preserved stem ginger, chopped

1 tbsp syrup from preserved ginger jar

This is good with linguine, spaghetti or bucatini. Serve with the crisp Good Green Salad with some fresh orange segments mixed in.

Slice the duck breasts and toss them with the cornflour and salt and pepper.

Heat the oil in a large frying pan. Add the onion, bay leaf and thyme. Stir for about 5 minutes to start cooking the onion, then add the duck and cook, turning and stirring the pieces, until lightly browned in parts.

Stir in the cider, ginger and ginger syrup. Bring to the boil, then reduce the heat and simmer the sauce, uncovered, for 30 minutes. Taste for seasoning before serving.

Above: Turkey with Flageolet beans and pesto.

Above: Venison with dried peaches.

Venison with Dried Peaches

A rich, dark meat sauce to serve with Spätzle (see page 46) or Potato Gnocchi (see page 42), as well as any of the chunkier pasta shapes. Tagliatelle, fettuccine, ziti or mafaldine are also good choices if you want to offer pasta and a meat sauce separately, with a vegetable accompaniment.

SERVES 4

750 g (1½ lb) stewing venison, trimmed of any fat and cubed

8 juniper berries, crushed

2 garlic cloves, crushed

1 bay leaf

1 sprig of thyme

salt and freshly ground black pepper

a little grated nutmeg

1 bottle of red wine

2 tbsp dried porcini or boletus mushrooms, sliced

1 tbsp olive oil

350 g (12 oz) rindless streaky bacon, diced

450 g (1 lb) shallots or pickling onions, peeled

3 tbsp flour

100 g (4 oz) dried peaches, roughly chopped

4 tbsp redcurrant jelly

3 tbsp chopped fresh parsley

Place the venison in a bowl. Add the juniper berries, garlic, bay leaf, thyme, salt and pepper, nutmeg and wine. Mix well, then cover and leave the meat to marinate for 24 hours.

Place the dried porcini or boletus in a mug or small bowl and pour in enough hot water to cover them. Set aside to soak for 30 minutes and pre-heat the oven to 160°C/325°F/Gas Mark 3.

Drain the porcini or boletus, reserving the soaking liquid. Cut the porcini slices into small pieces. Strain the liquid through fine muslin to remove any grit.

Drain the meat well, reserving the marinade.

Heat the oil in a large, heavy-based frying pan, add the bacon and cook until the fat runs from it, stirring occasionally. Add the shallots or pickling onions and cook until lightly browned all over, then use a slotted spoon to transfer them to an ovenproof casserole. Brown the venison in the fat remaining in the pan, then stir in the flour and the marinade. Stir until the sauce boils, then transfer the meat and sauce to the casserole.

Stir the porcini or boletus, their soaking liquid and the dried peaches into the venison mixture. Cover tightly and bake in the pre-heated oven for about 3 hours, or until the meat is very tender. Stir twice during cooking.

Stir in the redcurrant jelly until it has melted, add the chopped parsley, and taste for seasoning before serving.

Venison Stroganof

A variation on the traditional recipe using beef, this is rich and delicious with tagliatelle or paglia e fieno.

SERVES 4

750 g (1½ lb) venison steak

2 tbsp plain flour

salt and freshly ground black pepper

25 g (1 oz) butter

1 large onion, halved and thinly sliced

225 g (8 oz) mushrooms, thinly sliced

4 tbsp brandy

300 ml (½ pt) red wine

6 tbsp chopped fresh parsley

150 ml (¼ pt) soured cream

Cut the venison across the grain into fine strips. Toss these with the flour and plenty of seasoning.

Melt the butter in a large frying pan. Brown the venison in the butter, then add the onion and mushrooms and continue cooking, stirring often, for about 15 minutes, or until the onion has softened slightly.

Warm the brandy in a small saucepan. Ignite it and pour it over the venison mixture. When the flames have died, add the wine and bring to the boil, stirring. Simmer the sauce gently for 5 minutes. Remove the pan from the heat, stir in the parsley, swirl in the soured cream, then serve at once.

Meatballs

Meatballs in tomato sauce are a classic topping for pasta. Serve them with spaghetti, tagliatelle, perciatelli or other long pasta. For slightly easier eating, ladle the mixture over short pasta shapes.

SERVES 4

450 g (1 lb) minced beef

1 onion, finely chopped

4 tbsp grated Parmesan cheese

grated rind of 1 lemon

50 g (2 oz) rindless bacon, very finely chopped or minced

25 g (1 oz) fresh breadcrumbs

1 tsp grated nutmeg

salt and freshly ground black pepper

1 large egg

1 tsp olive oil

1 quantity Light Fresh Tomato Sauce (see page 55) or
   Rich Tomato Sauce (see page 54)

4 tbsp chopped fresh parsley

1 large garlic clove, finely chopped (optional)

Mix the minced beef, onion, Parmesan, half the lemon rind, the bacon, breadcrumbs, nutmeg, salt and pepper to taste and the egg. Pound the mixture with the back of a mixing spoon until the ingredients are thoroughly combined. Alternatively, the ingredients may be kneaded together by hand.

To shape the meatballs, use a tsp to pick up lumps of mixture. Wet your hands, then press and mould the mixture into a small, smooth ball. Repeat with the remaining mixture, which makes 20 meatballs about the size of walnuts.

Heat the oil in a large, deep, lidded frying pan or flameproof casserole and fry the meatballs for 15–20 minutes, turning and rolling them carefully with one or two spoons to make them a neat, round shape.

When the meatballs have browned all over, add the tomato sauce and bring to the boil. Reduce the heat, cover and simmer with the meatballs for 30 minutes, stirring and turning them once during this time.

Mix the remaining lemon rind with the parsley and garlic, if using. Ladle the meatballs over the pasta base and sprinkle with the parsley mixture. Serve at once.

Goulash

Spätzle or potato gnocchi are ideal accompaniments for a hearty goulash, but tagliatelle or mafaldine are often the favoured side dishes for a supper party menu.

SERVES 4

750 g (1½ lb) stewing beef, cubed

2 tbsp mild paprika

2 tbsp plain flour

salt and freshly ground black pepper

2 tbsp oil

2 garlic cloves, crushed

2 large onions, halved and thinly sliced

1 red pepper, de-seeded and diced

1 kg (2¼ lb) tomatoes, peeled (see Cook's Tip, page 72),
   de-seeded and chopped

1 tsp sugar

300 ml (½ pt) beef stock

150 ml (¼ pt) soured cream, to serve (optional)

Toss the beef with the paprika, flour and plenty of salt and pepper. Heat the oil in a flameproof casserole and brown the meat all over, use a slotted spoon to remove it to a plate.

Add the garlic, onions and red pepper, and cook, stirring, for 10 minutes. Return the meat and add the tomatoes. Stir in the sugar and stock. Bring to the boil, then reduce the heat so that the mixture simmers. Cover tightly and cook gently for 2½–3 hours, or until the meat is tender.

Stir the goulash occasionally during cooking. Taste for seasoning at the end of cooking. Soured cream may be served with the goulash if liked.

Right: Classic meatballs with Penne.

Hot Beef Sauce

SERVES

675 g (1½ lb) rump steak

4 garlic cloves, crushed

2 green chillies, de-seeded and diced (Cook's Tip, page 90)

2 tbsp ground coriander

grated rind and juice of 1 lime

salt and freshly ground black pepper

2 tbsp oil

2 large onions, halved and thinly sliced

1 red pepper, halved, de-seeded and thinly sliced

397 g (14 oz) tin chopped tomatoes

2 avocados

1 papaya

4 tbsp chopped fresh coriander

150 ml (¼ pt) soured cream

Cut the steak across the grain into fine strips. Mix these with the garlic, chillies, ground coriander, grated lime rind and juice. Add plenty of seasoning and set aside to marinate for several hours or overnight.

Heat the oil in a large frying pan. Fry the steak, reserving the lime juice from marinating, until it is lightly browned. Add the onions and pepper, then continue to cook for about 20 minutes, or until the onion has softened.

Add the reserved lime juice and tomatoes and bring to the boil, stirring. Taste for seasoning.

Cut the avocados into quarters, remove their stones and peel them, then slice each section across into small pieces. Halve the papaya, scoop out the seeds and peel the fruit. Cut the pieces of papaya in half lengthways, then across into pieces of a similar size to the avocado.

Mix the avocado, papaya and coriander with the beef. Taste the mixture for seasoning, then serve it on a bed of cooked pasta. Top with soured cream, or offer this separately, and serve at once.

Rich Ragoût

A rich sauce of the Bolognese type, this may be served with spaghetti or long pasta.

SERVES 4

25 g (1 oz) dried mushrooms (ceps or porcini are good)

150 ml (¼ pt) hot water

2 tbsp olive oil

450 g (1 lb) stewing beef, finely diced

225 g (8 oz) lean boneless pork, finely diced

225 g (8 oz) chicken livers, chopped

2 garlic cloves, crushed

2 onions, chopped

1 green pepper, de-seeded and diced

1 bay leaf

1 tbsp chopped fresh oregano

1 tbsp chopped fresh thyme

4 tbsp brandy

600 ml (1 pt) robust red wine

300 ml (½ pt) passata

salt and freshly ground black pepper

225 g (8 oz) mushrooms, chopped

freshly grated Parmesan cheese, to serve

Soak the mushrooms in the water for 30 minutes. Then drain them well and chop them. Strain the soaking liquor through muslin to remove grit from the mushrooms and set aside.

Heat the oil in a large, flameproof casserole or heavy-based saucepan. Add the beef, pork and chicken livers and cook, stirring, until the meats are sealed. Stir in the garlic, onions and pepper, then cook for a further 10 minutes.

Add the bay leaf, oregano and thyme. Pour in the brandy, wine, passata and strained soaking water. Add the prepared dried mushrooms and plenty of seasoning. Bring just to boiling point, stirring, then reduce the heat and cover the casserole or pan. Simmer for 2½ hours, or until the meat is extremely tender. Stir occasionally to ensure that the meat does not stick to the bottom of the pan.

Add the mushrooms and cook uncovered for 30 minutes. Taste and adjust the seasoning before serving with Parmesan cheese.

Piquant Diced Lamb

SERVES 4

675 g (1½ lb) lean, boneless lamb, diced

1–2 fresh green chillies, de-seeded and
  chopped (see Cook's Tip, page 90)

2 garlic cloves, crushed

salt and freshly ground black pepper

grated rind and juice of 1 orange

1 tbsp chopped fresh oregano

1 tbsp ground coriander

2 tbsp olive oil

1 large onion, chopped

1 red pepper, de-seeded and diced

2 tbsp plain flour

600 ml (1 pt) lamb or chicken stock

Fresh chillies bring this lamb mixture to life. It is delicious with substantial pasta shapes, such as long mafaldine or pappardelle, or chunky rigatoni, cicatelli di San Severo or lumache.

Mix the lamb with the chillies, garlic, plenty of salt and pepper, the orange rind, oregano and coriander. Cover and leave to marinate for at least 2–3 hours or overnight.

Heat the oil in a flameproof casserole and brown the meat. Then, add the onion and pepper and cook, stirring, for 5 minutes.

Stir in the flour, then pour in the stock and orange juice. Bring just to the boil, then reduce the heat and cover the pan. Simmer the sauce very gently for 1 hour. Taste for seasoning before serving.

Above: Gammon and beetroot sauce.

Gammon and Olive Dressing

This delicious mixture is chunky, so it goes well with short, fairly large pasta shapes. Wide, long shapes, such as tagliatelle verde or mafaldine, are also suitable accompaniments.

SERVES 4

2 tbsp olive oil

1 large onion, thinly sliced

1 garlic clove, crushed

2 large sprigs of thyme

1 bay leaf

2 large sprigs oregano or marjoram

2 large sage leaves, grated

350 g (12 oz)   lean, rindless gammon, diced

100 g (4 oz) mushrooms, sliced

450 g (1 lb) tomatoes, peeled and roughly chopped

9 black olives, stoned

4 tbsp pale cream or dry sherry

salt and freshly ground black pepper

freshly grated Parmesan cheese, to serve

Heat the olive oil in a large, flameproof casserole. Add the onion, garlic, thyme, bay leaf, oregano or marjoram and sage. Stir well, cover and cook, stirring occasionally, for 15 minutes.

Add the gammon and cook until the pieces have lightly browned in parts, turning and stirring now and again to prevent them sticking.

Stir in the mushrooms, tomatoes, olives and sherry. Add a little pepper to taste and heat until the mixture is steadily bubbling. Cover tightly and simmer for 5 minutes, not boiling the mixture too rapidly (when the dressing is cooked, the tomatoes should be more or less broken down, but not completely reduced to a pulp).

Taste the sauce for seasoning before serving (it is best not to add salt at the earlier stage as the gammon may be quite salty). Ladle the sauce over the pasta and serve with Parmesan and extra black pepper, if liked.

Gammon and Beetroot Sauce

SERVES 4

2 tbsp olive oil

350 g (12 oz)   lean, rindless gammon, diced

1 large or 2 medium onions, chopped

2 garlic cloves, crushed

5 cm (2 in) strip of pared orange rind

1 carrot, diced

1 bay leaf

12 sage leaves, grated

1 tbsp flour

300 ml (½ pt) red wine

150 ml (¼ pt) water

juice of 1 orange

salt and freshly ground black pepper

350 g (12 oz)   cooked beetroot (see Cook's Tip below), diced

Flavoursome gammon tastes terrific with slightly sweet beetroot and tangy orange. If you want to serve the sauce with long, thin pasta, such as spaghetti, then dice the gammon and vegetables quite small so that they are easy to eat.

Heat the oil in a flameproof casserole or heavy-based saucepan. Add the gammon, onion, garlic, orange rind, carrot, bay leaf and sage. Stir well, then cover and cook for 15 minutes.

Stir in the flour, cook for about 1 minute, then pour in the wine, water and orange juice. Bring to the boil, stirring, then reduce the heat, cover and simmer for 15 minutes. Add salt and pepper to taste and stir in the beetroot. Stir for 1–2 minutes, or until the beetroot is hot, before serving.

COOK'S TIP
Vacuum-packed cooked beetroot is a good alternative to freshly boiled beetroot in this recipe. Avoid beetroot preserved with any acid or vinegar, though.

Amatriciana Sauce

Serve this thin sauce, pepped up with chilli, with spaghetti, bucatini or any slim pasta.

SERVES 4

4 tbsp olive oil

2 red chillies, de-seeded and chopped
  (see Cook's Tip, page 90)

1 red pepper, de-seeded and chopped

1 bay leaf

1 onion, chopped

2 garlic cloves, chopped

225 g (8 oz) rindless bacon, diced

1 kg (2¼ lb) tomatoes, peeled, de-seeded and chopped

1 tsp sugar

salt and freshly ground black pepper

freshly grated pecorino or Parmesan cheese, to serve

Heat the oil in a saucepan. Add the chillies, pepper, bay leaf, onion, garlic and bacon. Fry the mixture for 15 minutes, then add the tomatoes, sugar and plenty of seasoning. Heat until the tomatoes are bubbling merrily, then cover the pan tightly and cook for about 45 minutes, stirring occasionally, until the sauce is thick and rich.

Taste the sauce for seasoning, then serve with pasta and offer pecorino or Parmesan cheese separately.

Chorizo with Chickpeas

A rich passata-based sauce, this brings spicy Spanish sausage and nutty chickpeas together. This is another sauce that will work well with almost any type of pasta, from elbow macaroni to ziti.

SERVES 4

2 tbsp olive oil

1 onion, chopped

2 garlic cloves, crushed

1 celery stick, diced

1 green pepper, de-seeded and diced

225 g (8 oz) black pudding, diced

225 g (8 oz) mushrooms, sliced

2 x 439 g (15 oz) tins chickpeas

450 ml (¾ pt) passata

salt and freshly ground black pepper

lots of chopped fresh parsley

150 ml (¼ pt) soured cream and/or freshly grated Parmesan cheese, to serve (optional)

Heat the olive oil in a saucepan. Add the onion, garlic, celery and green pepper. Cook, stirring often, for 10 minutes.

Stir in the black pudding, mushrooms, chickpeas with the liquid from the tins, passata and salt and pepper. Bring to the boil, reduce the heat and cover the pan. Then simmer the mixture for 15 minutes.

Taste for seasoning and stir in lots of chopped fresh parsley just before serving. Offer soured cream and/or Parmesan cheese with the sauce, if liked. seasoning before serving.

Boscaiola Sauce

SERVES 4

4 tbsp olive oil

350 g (12 oz) chestnut mushrooms, sliced

2 garlic cloves, crushed

1 bay leaf

350 ml (12 fl oz) passata

100 g (4 oz) Parma ham or cooked
  ham, diced

salt and freshly ground black pepper

This "woodcutter's sauce" goes well with any short pasta shapes, such as penne, rigatoni, spirals or bows. If available, porcini-flavoured pasta in novelty mushroom shapes may be served as a base for this sauce.

Heat the olive oil in a large saucepan. Add the mushrooms, garlic and bay leaf, then cook, stirring occasionally, for 10 minutes.

Stir in the passata, gammon and salt and pepper to taste. Bring to simmering point, stirring, then cover the pan tightly and simmer the sauce for a further 10 minutes. Taste for seasoning before serving.

Liver with Peppers and Pine Nuts

SERVES 4

4 tbsp pine nuts

450 g (1 lb) lambs' or calves' liver,
  cut into thin strips

2 tbsp flour

salt and freshly ground black pepper

25 g (1 oz) butter

2 tbsp olive oil

225 g (8 oz) rindless bacon,
  cut into thin strips

1 large onion, halved and thinly sliced

1 green pepper, de-seeded and sliced

1 red pepper, de-seeded and sliced

6 sage leaves, grated

4 tbsp brandy

150 ml (¼ pt) soured cream

4 large sprigs of basil, grated

Serve this cream-dressed liver and pepper mixture on a bed of tagliatelle or toss it with slim pasta shapes, such as spirals or bows.

Dry roast the pine nuts in a small, heavy-based saucepan over a low to medium heat until they are lightly browned. Shake the pan often to prevent the pine nuts overbrowning on one side. Set aside.

Dust the liver with the flour and plenty of seasoning. Heat the butter and olive oil, then fry the liver, turning often, until just lightly browned in parts, firm and cooked. Use a slotted spoon to remove the liver from the pan and set it aside.

Add the bacon, onion, green and red peppers, and sage to the fat remaining in the pan. Cook, stirring, for about 15 minutes, or until the bacon and vegetables are just cooked.

Return the liver to the pan, stirring it gently with the vegetables, and pour in the brandy. Add a little salt and pepper, if necessary, then heat the liver through for about 2 minutes.

Swirl the soured cream into the liver, then turn it out on to a bed of cooked pasta. Sprinkle with the basil and pine nuts and serve at once.

Creamed Eggs with Smoked Salmon

SERVES 4

100 g (4 oz) smoked salmon offcuts

4 tbsp snipped chives

8 eggs

150 ml (¼ pt) single cream

salt and freshly ground black pepper

50 g (2 oz) butter

Good old scrambled eggs turn up trumps again, but this time with the help of some smoked salmon. The important point to remember when scrambling eggs for serving with pasta is that they should be cooked until just creamy, then the pasta should be tossed with them. If they are cooked until set, then, by the time the pasta is mixed in, the eggs will be overcooked.

Cut the smoked salmon pieces into slim strips and mix them with the chives. Beat the eggs with the cream, adding salt and pepper to taste.

Melt the butter in a saucepan over a gentle heat (do not heat it too fiercely or the eggs will begin to set as soon as they are added to the pan). Pour in the egg mixture and whisk it constantly over a low to medium heat until they begin to thicken.

Stir in the smoked salmon, chives and freshly cooked pasta. Serve at once.

Above: Poached eggs with creamed watercress.

Poached Eggs with Creamed Watercress

SERVES 4

50 g (2 oz) butter

2 bunches watercress, leaves only, chopped

2 spring onions, finely chopped

300 ml (½ pt) single cream

salt and freshly ground black pepper

freshly grated nutmeg

a little vinegar

8 fresh eggs

sprigs of watercress, to garnish

freshly grated Parmesan cheese, to serve

Melt the butter in a saucepan. Add the watercress and spring onions. Stir over a low heat for 5 minutes, then add the cream with salt, pepper and nutmeg to taste. Set aside over a low heat.

Prepare a frying pan or saucepan of water for poaching the eggs. Add salt and a splash of vinegar, then bring the water to a steady simmer. Crack the eggs into a saucer one at a time, swirl the water gently and slide in the egg. Continue adding the eggs, swirling the water in different areas of the pan, until all are added. Poach the eggs until cooked to taste (about 3 minutes for a set white and soft yolk). Use a slotted spoon to remove the eggs from the pan and trim their edges with a knife or kitchen scissors.

Toss freshly cooked pasta with the hot watercress cream, then transfer to heated serving plates or a suitable dish and top with the eggs. Garnish with sprigs of watercress and serve with Parmesan.

Puffed Eggs on Pasta

This is definitely not a recipe for healthy eating, but, if you have sampled – and enjoyed – deep-fried eggs, then it makes a simple supper treat. Have tagliatelle, vermicelli, mafaldine or spaghetti piping hot ready to toss with the sauce and top with the eggs. Poached or soft-boiled eggs may be served instead of deep-fried eggs.

SERVES 4

2 tbsp olive oil

1 small onion, finely chopped

1 garlic clove, crushed

1 red pepper, de-seeded and diced

1 green pepper, de-seeded and diced

225 g (8 oz) tomatoes, peeled, de-seeded and diced

salt and freshly ground black pepper

4 tbsp chopped fresh parsley

4 eggs

oil, for deep frying

Heat the olive oil in a saucepan. Add the onion, garlic, red and green peppers. Stir well, then cover the pan and cook for 20 minutes, or until the vegetables have softened. Stir in the tomatoes with plenty of seasoning and cook for a further 5 minutes. Add the parsley and toss the mixture with freshly cooked pasta. Turn into a serving dish and keep hot.

Heat sufficient oil to deep-fry the eggs to 180°C/350°F /Gas Mark 4 or until a cube of day-old bread browns in 30 seconds. Crack an egg on to a saucer, then slide it into the hot oil. Stand well back as you do this and work from the side of the pan rather than above it as the oil does spit. Use a slotted spoon to gently ease the egg off the bottom of the pan, if necessary, after a few seconds. It will float to the surface when cooked. Lift the egg with a slotted spoon at this point and allow all the oil to drain off before transferring the egg to the pasta.

Cook all the eggs in the same way – they only take a few seconds to cook and it is possible to cook two at a time. Serve the pasta topped with the eggs, immediately.

Eggs with Stilton and Beans

SERVES 4

225 g (8 oz) haricot vert or French beans,
  cut into short lengths

salt and freshly ground black pepper

25 g (1 oz) butter

2 spring onions, chopped

2 tbsp chopped fresh tarragon or chervil

2 tbsp chopped fresh parsley

4 tbsp dry white wine or cider

6 eggs, hard-boiled and roughly chopped

175 g (6 oz) blue Stilton cheese, crumbled or chopped

Add the beans to boiling salted water and bring back to the boil. Cook for 1 minute, then drain them. Melt the butter in a saucepan. Add the spring onions and beans and cook for 2–3 minutes, stirring. Stir in the tarragon or chervil, parsley and wine or cider. Bring to the boil, then remove the saucepan from the heat. Add the eggs and Stilton with salt and freshly ground black pepper to taste. Stir the mixture lightly, then immediately mix it into freshly cooked pasta before the cheese melts. Serve at once.

Fondue with Pasta

This may not be conventional, but it is a good idea for serving rich cheese fondue as starchy pasta tastes excellent with it. In the past, I had often served a pasta salad as an accompaniment for a cheese fondue, so moving on one step further, to offering pasta for dipping, made good sense.

FOR THE FONDUE (SERVES 4)

225 g (8 oz) Caerphilly or Lancashire cheese,
  grated or finely chopped

225 g (8 oz) Gruyère or Emmental cheese, grated

3 tbsp plain flour

salt and freshly ground black pepper

¼ tsp ground mace

150 ml (¼ pt) dry white wine

4 tbsp brandy

1 garlic clove, crushed

2 tbsp snipped chives

FOODS TO DIP

(See Cook's Tip below)

celery, cut into thick slices

dessert apples, cored and cut into chunks

one or more of the following types of pasta:

  Potato Gnocchi (see page 42)

  cappelletti filled with Walnut Stuffing (pages 155)

  tortellini filled with Mushroom Stuffing (pages 154)

  Uszka (see page 173)

25–50 g (1–2 oz) butter, melted

Mix the Caerphilly or Lancashire with the Gruyère or Emmenthal, flour, salt and pepper to taste and mace. Heat the wine, brandy and garlic in a fondue pot until it is just about to simmer. Then, gradually add the cheese mixture, stirring all the time and allowing each addition to melt before adding any more. Do not allow the wine base to simmer as the cheese is being added or the fondue will curdle. Continue stirring over a low to medium heat until the fondue is smooth and thick, then stir in the chives.

Cook the chosen pasta just before serving the fondue and toss it in the melted butter, then place it on heated serving dishes. Arrange the celery and apples on serving dishes.

Stand the pot of fondue over a spirit burner. Provide long-handled forks for diners to spear and dip the pasta, celery and apple into the fondue.

COOK'S TIP

Deep-fried filled pasta, such as ravioli or cappelletti, are excellent for dipping. Cook the pasta as normal in boiling water, then drain well and toss in flour. Deep-fry for a few seconds until crisp and golden, then drain well on kitchen paper.

Above: Goats' cheese with grapes and bows.

Blue Cheese and Cucumber Sauce

SERVES 4

1 tbsp olive oil

1 bay leaf

2 garlic cloves, crushed

1 cucumber, peeled and diced

150 ml (¼ pt) dry cider

350 g (¾ oz) Danish blue cheese, diced

2 tbsp plain flour

4 spring onions, finely chopped

4 tbsp single cream

freshly ground black pepper

Heat the olive oil in a saucepan. Add the bay leaf, garlic and cucumber. Stir well, then cover the saucepan and cook for 20 minutes, shaking the saucepan occasionally. Pour in the cider and heat until just about to simmer.

Reduce the heat to the lowest setting. Gradually add the cheese, stirring until each addition has melted before adding the next. Cook until the sauce has thickened and is just at simmering point.

Stir in the spring onions and cream, and add pepper to taste. Serve at once.

Goats' Cheese with Grapes and Bows

SERVES 4

3 tbsp olive oil

2 garlic cloves, crushed

1 onion, halved and thinly sliced

16 black olives, stoned and thickly sliced

225 g (8 oz) seedless green grapes, halved

175 g (6 oz) soft goats' cheese

This will serve six as a first course. Otherwise, hungry diners may find the portions slightly small for a hearty main meal, but it is ideal for an average appetite and lunch or supper. The flat shape of bows is ideal for this sauce, but you can use any other pasta shapes, if you like.

Heat the oil in a saucepan. Add the garlic and onion, and cook, stirring, for 10 minutes, or until the onion has softened but not browned (at this stage, leave the saucepan over a very low heat if the pasta is not well on the way to being cooked).

Stir the olives and grapes into the onion and cook for 2–3 minutes, until really hot. Quickly stir in the goats' cheese, then remove the saucepan from the heat and toss the sauce with hot, freshly drained pasta. Serve at once.

Garlic Cheese with Sun-dried Tomatoes

SERVES 4

8 sun-dried tomatoes

200 ml (⅓ pt) full-bodied red wine

1 small onion, finely chopped

2 tbsp chopped fresh oregano

2 bay leaves

salt and freshly ground black pepper

4 tbsp olive oil

225 g (8 oz) garlic-flavoured Tei fi cheese, cut into cubes (see Cook's Tip below)

2 pickled walnuts, chopped

4 tbsp chopped fresh parsley

Use a pair of kitchen scissors to snip the sun-dried tomatoes into small pieces. Place them in a small saucepan with the wine, onion, oregano, bay leaves and salt and pepper to taste. Heat gently until simmering. Then, cover the saucepan and cook for 5 minutes. Remove from the heat and leave to stand for 2 hours.

Add the olive oil, cheese and walnuts to the tomato mixture, stir well and leave to marinate overnight. To serve, strain the liquid from the cheese mixture into a large saucepan. Bring to the boil and boil hard for 3 minutes, whisking occasionally. Pour this hot dressing over freshly cooked pasta. Add the strained cheese and tomato mixture, and the parsley. Toss well and serve at once.

COOK'S TIP

Teifi cheese is a firm, moist cheese rather like Gouda in texture. It is readily available from delicatessens, both plain, and with a variety of flavouring ingredients added, including garlic. Gouda may be substituted, in which case 3 chopped garlic cloves should be added to the tomato and wine mixture. Alternatively, try Gapron or Gaperon, the strong French, dome-shaped peppered cheese that is heavily laced with garlic.

Dolcelatte Dressing with Fennel and Olives

SERVES 4

1 fennel bulb, diced

juice of 1 lemon

2 tbsp olive oil

1 garlic clove, crushed

12 green olives, stoned and sliced

1 tbsp chopped capers

salt and freshly ground black pepper

cayenne pepper

3 tbsp chopped fresh parsley

350 g (¾ oz) Dolcelatte cheese, diced

Toss the fennel with the lemon juice. Heat the oil in a saucepan. Add the fennel and garlic and cook for about 5 minutes, until the fennel is lightly cooked but still crunchy.

Stir in the olives, capers, salt and pepper to taste, a little cayenne and the parsley. Remove the saucepan from the heat and mix in the Dolcelatte. Then pour the mixture over a bowl of freshly cooked pasta and mix well. Serve at once.

Above: Garlic cheese with sun-dried tomatoes.

Arrabiatta Sauce

A hot tomato sauce, spiced with chillies, this is, literally translated, an "angry" sauce. Authentically, it is served with penne (all' Arrabiatta), but it goes well with any pasta.

SERVES 4

3 tbsp olive oil

1 large onion, chopped

2 red or green chillies, de-seeded and chopped (or more i f you like; see Cook's Tip, page 80)

2 garlic cloves, crushed

2 celery sticks, chopped

1 carrot, chopped

1 bay leaf

600 ml (1 pt) passata

150 ml (¼ pt) stock (chicken or vegetable)

salt and freshly ground black pepper

1 tsp sugar

Heat the oil in a saucepan, add the onion, chillies, garlic, celery, carrot and bay leaf. Stir well, then cover the saucepan and cook for 15 minutes, shaking the saucepan occasionally.

Stir in the passata and stock with plenty of salt and pepper. Add the sugar and bring to the boil. Reduce the heat and cover the saucepan, then simmer the sauce gently for 30 minutes. Taste for seasoning before serving.

Ratatouille

Ratatouille and pasta are natural partners, but they are not often served together.

SERVES 4

1 large aubergine, cut into chunks

salt and freshly ground black pepper

150 ml (¼ pt) olive oil

2 garlic cloves, crushed

1 bay leaf

1 large onion, halved and thinly sliced

1 large green pepper, de-seeded and diced

1 large red pepper, de-seeded and diced

225 g (8 oz) courgettes, sliced

1 kg (2¼ lb) tomatoes, peeled, de-seeded and quartered

2 tbsp chopped fresh marjoram

6 tbsp chopped fresh parsley

freshly grated pecorino or Parmesan cheese, to serve

Place the aubergine in a colander, sprinkling each layer of chunks with salt. Stand the colander over a bowl and leave the aubergine to drain for 30 minutes. Then rinse and dry it well.

Heat the olive oil in a large, flameproof casserole. Add the aubergine and cook, stirring for 3–5 minutes, until the pieces are lightly cooked, but not softened. Add the garlic, bay leaf, onion, peppers and courgettes. Stir well, add salt and pepper to taste and then mix in the tomatoes and marjoram. Mix well and heat until the mixture is just bubbling. Cover and cook for about 50 minutes, until the vegetables have softened to a thickened, flavoursome sauce.

Taste the ratatouille for seasoning and stir in the parsley just before serving. Offer plenty of freshly grated pecorino or Parmesan with the Ratatouille and, pasta.

Puttanesca Sauce

SERVES 4

50 g (2 oz) tin anchovy fillets

2 tbsp olive oil

1 onion, chopped

1 green chilli, de-seeded and chopped
  (see Cook's Tip, page 80)

1 large garlic clove, crushed

2 tbsp capers, chopped

2 x 397 g (14 oz) tins chopped tomatoes

16 black olives, stoned and sliced

salt and freshly ground black pepper

A thin, perky sauce, flavoured with a hint of chilli, this is traditionally served with spaghetti. It is thin and smooth, so ideal for any long, slim pasta, but it is just as delicious with any shapes you happen to have, especially as it is a great standby for using storecupboard ingredients.

Drain the oil from the anchovies into a saucepan. Add the olive oil. Heat the oils, then add the onion, chilli and garlic. Cook, stirring, for 10 minutes.

Meanwhile, chap the anchovy fillets. Add them to the saucepan with the capers, tomatoes and olives. Sprinkle in a little salt and pepper to taste, bring just to the boil, then cover the saucepan and reduce the heat. Simmer the sauce for 15 minutes.

Fennel and Almond Sauce

This is ideal for coating pasta that is served as a side dish, for example, as an accompaniment for roast lamb or grilled meat or poultry.

SERVES 4

2 fennel bulbs, halved

100 g (4 oz) blanched almonds

300 ml (½ pt) chicken or vegetable stock

150 ml (¼ pt) dry white wine

salt and freshly ground black pepper

1 bay leaf

25 g (1 oz) butter

1 small onion, chopped

25 g (1 oz) plain flour

100 ml (4 fl oz) single cream

25 g (1 oz) flaked almonds, toasted, to serve

Cut the fennel bulbs in half lengthways. Place them in a saucepan with the blanched almonds. Add the stock, wine, salt and pepper to taste and the bay leaf. Heat until simmering, then cover and cook for about 45 minutes, or until the fennel is tender right through. Leave it to cool slightly.

Lift the fennel from the liquid with a slotted spoon. Slice and reserve two halves, then roughly chop the remaining pair and purée them with the almonds and cooking liquid. Press the purée through a fine sieve.

Rinse out the saucepan, then melt the butter in it. Add the onion and cook, stirring, until it is well softened but has not browned. Stir in the flour, then gradually stir in the fennel purée and bring to the boil. Simmer for 3 minutes. Add the sliced fennel and stir in the cream. Taste for seasoning and heat gently without boiling. Pour the sauce over the chosen cooked pasta and sprinkle with the toasted almonds before serving.

Carbonara-style Leeks with Horseradish

This was one of those "the larder is bare"-type suppers that started as a good idea, that I despaired of as I mixed it together, then bounced back to give the tastebuds a real treat when we sat down to eat! The pasta should be freshly cooked, ready for stirring into the sauce, which will not stay in good spirit if it is kept waiting.

SERVES 4

50 g (2 oz) butter

450 g (1 lb) leeks, sliced

8 eggs

3 tbsp creamed horseradish

4 tbsp single cream

salt and freshly ground black pepper

tbsp freshly grated Parmesan cheese

Melt the butter in a large saucepan. Add the leeks, stir well, then cover the saucepan and cook for 15 minutes or until the leeks are tender and have reduced.

Meanwhile, beat the eggs with the horseradish and cream, adding plenty of salt and pepper. Stir the egg mixture into the leeks and continue to stir over a low to medium heat until the eggs begin to set and the mixture becomes creamy.

Stir in the pasta immediately and cook for a few seconds. Do not continue cooking until the eggs set or the sauce will curdle. Taste for seasoning and serve at once.

Spicy Okra and Mango

SERVES 4

225 g (8 oz) small, young okra

4 tsp ground coriander

1 large firm mango

3 tbsp olive oil

1 large onion, chopped

1 large red pepper, de-seeded, halved
lengthways and sliced

2 garlic cloves, crushed

2 green chillies, de-seeded and chopped
  (see Cook's Tip, page 80)

4 tsp chopped fresh oregano

salt and freshly ground black pepper

1 lime, cut into wedges, to serve

I felt inclined to serve this with fairly substantial fresh pasta shapes fresh Potato Gnocchi (see page 42), for example – or the dried types, which tend to be a bit thicker when cooked, such as gli strozzapreti, cicatelli di San Severo, rigatoni or lumache.

The okra must be small, firm, bright in colour and unblemished. Old fibrous or large okra will not cook successfully. Trim the stalk ends and points off the pods, then slice them thinly and place in a bowl. Add the coriander and toss well.

The mango should be just ripe, but still firm (fruit that is soft or too sweet will not complement the okra). Peel the mango, then slice the flesh off the large, flat central stone. Cut the slices into small pieces.

Heat the oil in a saucepan. Add the onion, pepper, garlic, chillies and oregano, then cook, stirring occasionally, for 10 minutes. Stir in the okra and cook over a fairly high heat for about 3–5 minutes, until the okra slices are slightly browned in part and just tender. Stir in the mango, taste for seasoning and serve. Toss the okra mixture with the pasta, then arrange lime wedges around the edge of the dish so that their juice may be squeezed over to taste.

Above: Turnip and pepper sauce.

Turnip and Pepper Sauce

Turnips are a very underrated vegetable. Their slightly peppery flavour is extremely good with sweet red and yellow peppers, and the rather "dry" flavour of Emmental marries the two well. Ensure that the vegetables are finely cut and the sauce is a perfectly suitable topping for long pasta, such as spaghetti, bucatini or the finest capellini.

SERVES 4

225 g (8 oz) small turnips
juice of ½ a lemon
2 large red peppers
2 large yellow peppers
300 ml (½ pt) dry cider
50 g (2 oz) butter
2 tbsp plain flour
175 g (6 oz) Emmental cheese, finely grated
salt and freshly ground black pepper

Peel and thinly slice the turnips. Then cut the slices into fine matchsticks. Place in a bowl, sprinkle with the lemon juice and cover with cold water.

Char and skin the peppers. Halve and de-seed them, cut them in half widthways before slicing them into fine strips.

Drain the turnips and place them in a saucepan. Pour in the cider and bring to the boil. Reduce the heat, cover the saucepan and simmer until the turnip matchsticks are just tender (about 5 minutes). Add the pepper strips and simmer for a further 2 minutes. Remove from the heat.

Melt half the butter in a small saucepan. Stir in the flour, then strain the cooking liquid from the turnip and peppers into the saucepan. Whisk the sauce until smooth and boiling. Drain the vegetables in a fine sieve over the saucepan to ensure all the cider is added to the sauce, then return the vegetables to their empty cooking saucepan, add the remaining butter. Put the saucepan over the lowest heat to melt the butter and cover to keep the vegetables hot.

Stir the Emmental and salt and pepper to taste into the sauce, then heat gently until the cheese has completely melted. Pour the sauce over the chosen pasta, then toss the peppers and turnips in. Serve immediately.

Dark Mushroom Sauce

This thin, well-flavoured sauce is good with thin, long pasta shapes, such as spaghetti, bucatini, perciatelli, tagliatelle or fettuccine.

SERVES 4

3 tbsp olive oil
25 g (1 oz) butter
1 onion, finely chopped
1 garlic clove, crushed
450 g (1 lb) open cap mushrooms, sliced
3 pickled walnuts, chopped
3 tbsp mushroom ketchup
8 tbsp dry sherry
12 black olives, stoned and thinly sliced
salt and freshly ground black pepper
lots of chopped fresh parsley
freshly grated Parmesan cheese, to serve

Heat the oil and butter. Add the onion and garlic and cook for 5 minutes. Add the mushrooms and stir well. Continue to cook, stirring until the mushrooms have reduced in volume. Then simmer the mushrooms in their own liquor until it begins to reduce. Increase the heat to evaporate the liquid, stirring to prevent the mushrooms sticking. The mushrooms are ready when they are moist, but not sitting in liquid.

Add the pickled walnuts, mushroom ketchup, sherry, olives and salt and pepper to taste. Simmer gently for 5 minutes, stirring often. Taste for seasoning and stir in plenty of parsley. Toss the mushrooms with the chosen pasta and serve with plenty of freshly grated Parmesan.

Creamed Celeriac with Baby Spinach and Dill

Celeriac is a versatile vegetable, with a mild celery-like flavour. Baby spinach leaves are a real boon: they are sold ready for cookery in many large supermarkets and they have a delicious flavour. This simple mixture is perfect for tossing into linguine, spaghetti or tagliatelle. It also goes well with other slim shapes, such as short twists or spirals, but I would not serve it with really chunky shapes.

SERVES 4

1 kg (2¼ lb) celeriac

salt and freshly ground black pepper

50 g (2 oz) butter

1 leek, thinly sliced

225 g (8 oz) baby spinach leaves, washed

100 g (4 oz) cream cheese

4 tbsp chopped fresh dill

6 tbsp freshly grated pecorino or Parmesan cheese

Peel the celeriac, then cut it into fairly thin slices. Cut the slices into slim sticks, then cut these into 2.5–5 cm (1–2 in) lengths. Blanch the celeriac strips in boiling salted water for 2 minutes, then drain well.

Melt the butter in a large saucepan. Add the leek, stir well and cover the saucepan. Cook for 10 minutes, until the leek is reduced and tender. Stir in the celeriac with salt and pepper to taste. Add the spinach and mix well. Cover the saucepan and cook for 5 minutes, or until the spinach has wilted and the vegetables are just cooked.

Stir in the cream cheese until it has melted to make a sauce, then remove the saucepan from the heat. Mix in the dill and pecorino or Parmesan cheese. Taste for seasoning and serve at once on a bed of freshly cooked pasta.

Artichoke Bottoms with Parma Ham and Peas

This is made using tinned artichoke bottoms, but, for a very special treat, you could boil fresh artichokes, then trim them down to the tender bottoms and use those (you will need 6 fresh artichokes if you intend using fresh vegetables).

SERVES 4

2 x 425 g (15 oz) tins artichoke bottoms, drained

1 tbsp olive oil

25 g (1 oz) butter

100 g (4 oz) Parma ham, cut into short, thin strips

1 small onion, halved and thinly sliced

1 small sprig of rosemary

1 tbsp plain flour

300 ml (½ pt) chicken stock

450 g (1 lb) fresh peas, shelled

salt and freshly ground black pepper

Slice the artichoke bottoms and set them aside. Heat the olive oil and butter in a saucepan. Add the ham and cook, stirring, for 5 minutes. Then add the onion and rosemary and cook until the onion has softened but not browned.

Stir in the flour, then gradually pour in the stock and bring to the boil. Add the peas with a little salt and pepper to taste. Reduce the heat so that the sauce simmers, then cover the saucepan and simmer for about 15 minutes, or until the peas are tender.

Stir the artichoke bottoms into the sauce and heat them through for 3 minutes. Taste for seasoning and remove the rosemary before serving.

Broad Beans with Bacon

SERVES 4

450 g (1 lb) rindless streaky bacon, diced

2 garlic cloves, crushed

450 g (1 lb) young broad beans

salt and freshly ground black pepper

50 g (2 oz) butter

3 tbsp chopped fresh parsley

4 sprigs of basil, grated

freshly grated Parmesan or pecorino,
  to serve

Fresh, young broad beans are delicious with pasta. Simply toss them with freshly cooked pasta shapes, adding hot melted butter and freshly ground black pepper to make a delicious meal. This version, with bacon and basil, works well with small or short pasta shapes.

Heat the bacon in a heavy-based frying pan over a low to medium heat until the fat runs from it. Then add the garlic and continue cooking, stirring occasionally, until the pieces are well cooked and slightly crisp

Meanwhile, cook the broad beans in boiling salted water for 5–10 minutes, depending on how large and old they are (small, young beans will be ready very quickly; older ones will take about 10 minutes). Drain the beans and toss them with the bacon. Add seasoning to taste, remove the pan from the heat and add the butter.

Toss the bacon and beans with the chosen pasta, scraping all the butter from the pan. Toss in the parsley and basil and serve at once. Offer freshly grated Parmesan or pecorino cheese with the pasta.

Vegetable Medley

SERVES 4

SERVES 4

175 g (6 oz) cauliflower, divided into small florets

salt and freshly ground black pepper

2 tbsp olive oil

25 g (1 oz) butter

1 onion, chopped

175 g (6 oz) young carrots, quartered lengthways and thinly sliced

225 g (8 oz) young courgettes, very lightly peeled (see Cook's Tip right) and thinly sliced

100 g (4 oz) closed cap mushrooms, sliced

1 large, leafy sprig of tarragon, chopped

grated rind of ½ a lemon

squeeze of lemon juice

I scribbled a large "yum" at the end of my testing notes for this sauce. Serve the sweated, mixed vegetables with shells, spirals or pasta shapes rather than with long, thin pasta.

Cook the cauliflower in boiling salted water for about 3 minutes, until lightly cooked. Drain well.

Heat the olive oil and butter in a large saucepan. Add the onion, carrots and cauliflower, stir well, then cover the saucepan and cook for 10 minutes. Shake the saucepan occasionally to prevent the vegetables sticking.

Add the courgettes, mushrooms, tarragon, lemon rind and juice. Stir well, cover the saucepan again and cook for a further 2–3 minutes, or until the courgettes are bright green and tender, but with a bit of bite and full of flavour. Taste for seasoning before serving.

COOK'S TIP

If you use a sharp potato peeler to remove very fine slices of peel down the length of the courgettes, the outside of the vegetables becomes bright green and the flavour when cooked is excellent.

Patty Pan and Avocado Topping

SERVES 4–6

50 g (2 oz) butter

2 onions, sliced

1 carrot, halved and thinly sliced

1 sprig of tarragon

450 g (1 lb) patty pan squash,
 halved horizontally

salt and freshly ground black pepper

4 avocados

juice of ½ lemon

8 large sprigs of dill, chopped

Small, yellow patty pan squash are complemented by the avocado in this sautéed mixture, which makes a colourful, light first course, or light lunch or supper dish. Halve the quantities if the mixture is served as topping for a first-course portion of pasta. Fresh pasta shapes are the best base for this topping.

Melt the butter in a large saucepan. Add the onions, carrot and tarragon. Stir well, cover and cook for about 15 minutes, or until the onions have softened.

Stir in the patty pan, salt and pepper to taste, and cover the saucepan, then continue to cook for a further 15 minutes, stirring once or twice, until the squash are tender but not too soft.

Halve the avocados, remove their stones and cut them into quarters lengthways. Peel each segment of avocado and slice it widthways. Sprinkle with the lemon juice. Stir the avocado into the patty pan mixture, add the dill and mix well. Then taste for seasoning before serving. Toss the vegetables into a large bowl of pasta or spoon them on top of single dishes of pasta.

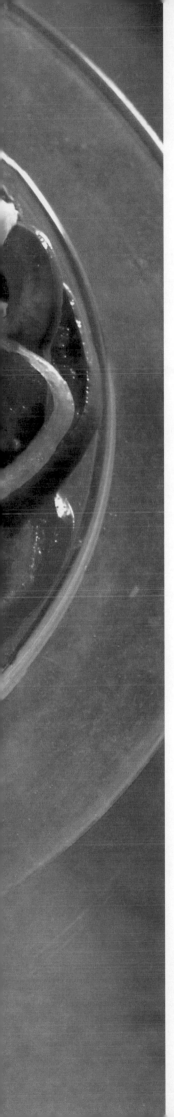

STUFFED AND FILLED PASTA

This section includes a combination of stuffed pasta shapes that are filled before cooking and other dishes that combine cooked pasta with a filling before baking or grilling.

For success, allow plenty of time for making small, fairly fiddly pasta shapes. Once you are into the swing of making and shaping them, though, it is surprising how many you can turn out in a relatively short period of time (for this reason it is often worth making a large batch of filling and dough, then freezing the shapes for future use).

To freeze filled pasta, spread them out on a tray lined with cling film and open freeze them. Pack them into bags when they are firm, then you can remove as many shapes as required and add them straight to a saucepan of boiling water.

A tip for speeding up the process, if you do not want to make the dough but fancy trying single fillings, is to buy fresh lasagne and use small cutters to stamp out circles or make miniature sheets of ravioli. Making extra-large ravioli is also a good way of speeding up the process of stuffing pasta.

I have used this term to describe pasta that is filled with a stuffing before cooking – shapes such as ravioli and tortellini. There is a wide variety of fillings that can be used to make different shapes. The following section includes the techniques and tips for filling and cooking pasta shapes so that you can select your own stuffing. In some of the recipes that follow, there are instructions for using a particular filling and a complementary sauce or dressing, but otherwise the general information given applies.

As well as making small shapes, there is no reason for not making larger squares, but serving fewer of them. They may not look quite so attractive, but they will taste as good. The only point to remember is not to make very large shapes with a solid, raw filling that requires lengthy boiling. If you are making large, filled shapes, the stuffing should be cooked so that it heats through quickly, otherwise the pasta will be overboiled before the stuffing is cooked.

The stuffing recipes are sufficient for filling a half quantity of the Rich Egg Pasta Dough (see page 40) or two thirds of the Pasta Dough (also see page 40), making 72 tortellini or 36 normal-sized ravioli.

Remember that the stuffing should be full-flavoured and well-seasoned so that it stands out in the cooked pasta. The flavour of very delicate or underseasoned stuffings can be completely lost once they are encased in pasta and served with a sauce.

Making Stuffed Circles, Round Ravioli or Cappelletti

Make ½ quantity Rich Egg Pasta Dough (see page 40) or ⅔ quantity Pasta Dough (also see page 40).

Roll out half the pasta dough to form a 30 cm (12 in) square. Stamp out forty, 4 cm (1½ inch) circles, dipping the cutter in flour occasionally to prevent it sticking to the dough.

Use half the stuffing on 20 of the circles. Brush the remaining circles with a little beaten egg. Then sandwich the stuffing between the pasta circles, pinching their edges together neatly. Repeat with the remaining dough and stuffing.

Making Square Ravioli

Make ½ quantity Rich Egg Pasta Dough (see page 40) or ⅔ quantity Pasta Dough (also see page 40).

Roll out half the pasta dough until it is slightly larger than a 30 cm (12 in) square, then trim the edges neatly.

Dot six small mounds of stuffing, spacing them evenly along the top of the dough. Then dot another five mounds evenly spaced at right angles to this row down one end of the dough. Using these as a guide to keep the mounds of stuffing evenly spaced in neat lines, place six lines of stuffing mounds on the dough, working from the top down towards the bottom edge.

Cover the stuffing and dough loosely with cling film to prevent it drying out as you roll out the covering. Roll out the remaining pasta dough until it is slightly larger than a 30 cm (12 in) square.

Brush the pasta between the mounds of stuffing with beaten egg. Then carefully lay the second sheet of dough over the top.

Working from one edge of the dough, press the dough together along the edge, then seal it neatly between the mounds of dough. Continue pressing the dough together until all the spaces between the stuffing are sealed. It is important to work methodically in one direction otherwise you can trap air pockets.

Use a pastry wheel or knife to cut between the stuffing, right along the middle of the sealed paths of dough.

Filling and Shaping Tortellini

Make ½ quantity Rich Egg Pasta Dough (see page 40) or ⅔ quantity Pasta Dough (also see page 40).

Cut the pasta dough in half. Roll out one portion into a 30 cm (12 in) square. Cut the dough into 5 cm (2 in) wide strips. Then cut these across in the opposite direction to make 5 cm (2 in) squares.

Work on about a quarter of the squares at a time, keeping the others covered loosely with cling film to prevent the pasta drying out. Brush the squares with egg and place a little of the filling in the middle. Just less than ½ tsp (not a measuring spoon, but a cutlery tsp) of filling is sufficient for each square.

Fold the pasta diagonally over the filling and pinch the edges together to make a triangle, then curl the long side round a finger tip and pinch the points together to shape each tortellini.

Repeat, using the remaining pasta to make a total of 72 tortellini.

Cooking Stuffed Pasta

Add the pasta to salted water that is just boiling. It must not be bubbling too rapidly as this may cause some delicate shapes to open before the pasta seals firmly round the edge, but do not let the water go off the boil.

Small shapes with a cooked filling will cook in about 3 minutes, whilst some shapes filled with raw meat require longer boiling, up to 15 minutes.

Large stuffed pasta shapes can be cooked by first boiling them, then coating them with a sauce and baking. This ensures that the filling is cooked through without over-boiling the pasta case.

Note about the Recipes

The following recipes for a delicious array of stuffings make enough to fill about 72 tortellini, 36 ravioli or 8 cannelloni, unless otherwise stated.

Above: Folding the pasta dough over the filling.

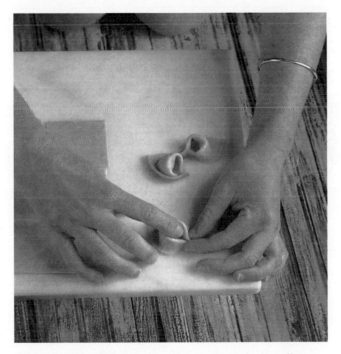

Above: Pinching the points together to shape the Tortellini.

Creamed Chicken Stuffing

This is easier to handle than a stuffing made from uncooked chicken and it also has the advantage of cooking quickly. Mascarpone gives a particularly rich result, but cream may be substituted for it.

INGREDIENTS

225 g (8 oz) skinned, boneless chicken breast,
  very finely chopped or minced
1 spring onion, very finely chopped
25 g (1 oz) fresh white breadcrumbs
2 tbsp chopped fresh parsley
1 tbsp chopped fresh sage or tarragon
freshly grated nutmeg
salt and freshly ground black pepper
1 tbsp dry sherry
4 tbsp mascarpone

Mix the chicken with the onion, breadcrumbs, parsley, sage or tarragon, a little nutmeg and plenty of salt and pepper (it is easier to mix all the ingredients in this way, and to ensure they are thoroughly combined, before the moist ingredients are added).

Stir in the sherry and pound the mascarpone with the mixture until thoroughly combined. The mixture will be quite dry, but this makes it easy to handle and the mascarpone melts during cooking to moisten the filling.

Pumpkin and Leek Stuffing

If fresh pumpkin is not available, use the tinned pumpkin, drained, or make the mixture using cooked and mashed swede instead – the flavour is different but just as good.

INGREDIENTS

25 g (1 oz) butter
175 g (6 oz) leek, finely chopped
225 g (8 oz) cooked pumpkin, mashed
50 g (2 oz) fresh white breadcrumbs
salt and freshly ground black pepper
50 g (2 oz) Emmental or Gruyère cheese, finely grated

Melt the butter in a saucepan. Add the leek and cook, stirring occasionally, until the leek has reduced and is tender. Remove the saucepan from the heat. Stir in the pumpkin, breadcrumbs and salt and pepper, then set the mixture aside until cool, if necessary. Finally, mix in the cheese.

Smoked Mackerel and Lemon Stuffing

INGREDIENTS

25 g (1 oz) fresh white breadcrumbs
2 tbsp milk
75 g (3 oz) skinned and boned smoked mackerel fillet
grated rind of ½ a lemon
2 cocktail gherkins, finely chopped
1 tsp chopped fresh oregano
2 tinned anchovy fillets, finely chopped or mashed
salt and freshly ground black pepper

Place the breadcrumbs in a small bowl. Sprinkle the milk over and set aside for 10 minutes. Flake the fish into the breadcrumbs and mash both together until thoroughly mixed. Mix in the lemon rind, gherkins, oregano, anchovy fillets and salt and pepper to taste.

Beef Stuffing

INGREDIENTS

25 g (1 oz) butter

1 small onion, very finely chopped
  or grated

1 garlic clove, crushed

1 tsp chopped fresh oregano

½ tsp chopped fresh thyme

¼ tsp ground mace

225 g (8 oz) lean minced steak

salt and freshly ground black pepper

25 g (1 oz) fresh breadcrumbs

1 tsp tomato purée

1 egg, beaten

Melt the butter in a saucepan. Add the onion and garlic and cook, stirring, for 2–3 minutes. Remove from the heat. Stir in the oregano, thyme and mace. Then add the steak, plenty of salt and pepper and the breadcrumbs. Pound the ingredients together well, then add the tomato purée and about half the egg (reserve the remainder for brushing the pasta dough). Mix the ingredients thoroughly so that the seasonings and flavourings are evenly distributed and the mixture is well bound together.

Mushroom Stuffing

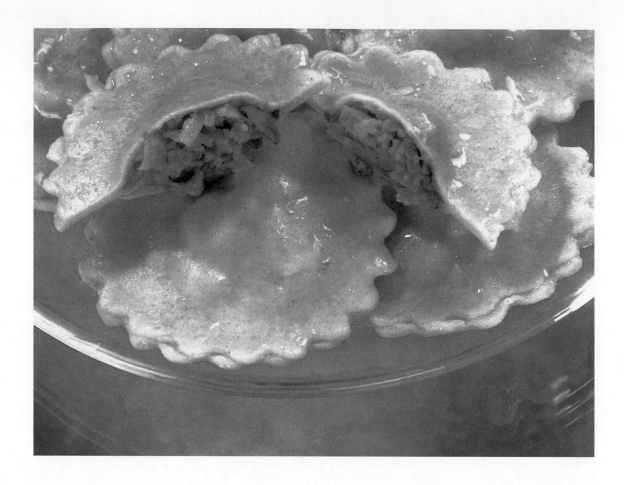

INGREDIENTS

25 g (1 oz) butter

50 g (2 oz) onion, finely chopped

100 g (4 oz) closed cap mushrooms,
  finely chopped

50 g (2 oz) wholemeal breadcrumbs

salt and freshly ground black pepper

1 tbsp mushroom ketchup

Melt the butter in a saucepan. Add the onion and cook, stirring, for 2 minutes. Add the mushrooms and continue to cook for a further 5 minutes, stirring occasionally.

Remove the saucepan from the heat, add the breadcrumbs and plenty of salt and pepper, then stir in the ketchup. Remember to season the mixture well so that the flavour stands out once the pasta dough is filled.

Walnut Stuffing

INGREDIENTS

75 g (3 oz) walnuts

40 g (1½ oz) fresh wholemeal breadcrumbs

25 g (1 oz) onion, finely chopped

2 tsp chopped fresh tarragon

salt and freshly ground black pepper

5 tsp single cream

Grind the walnuts in a food processor or liquidiser or by putting them through a small mouli grater. Mix the nuts with the breadcrumbs, onion, tarragon and plenty of salt and pepper. Stir in the cream to bind the mixture together.

Ham and Cheese Stuffing

INGREDIENTS

50 g (2 oz) cooked ham, finely chopped or minced

50 g (2 oz) mature Cheddar cheese, finely grated

25 g (1 oz) fresh breadcrumbs

4 sage leaves, chopped

salt and freshly ground black pepper

a little grated nutmeg

1 tbsp dry sherry

1 tbsp cream or milk

A food processor is ideal for preparing the gammon and cheese. Mix both together, add the breadcrumbs, sage, salt and pepper and a little nutmeg. Stir in the sherry and cream or milk, then pound the mixture with the back of a spoon until the ingredients are thoroughly combined.

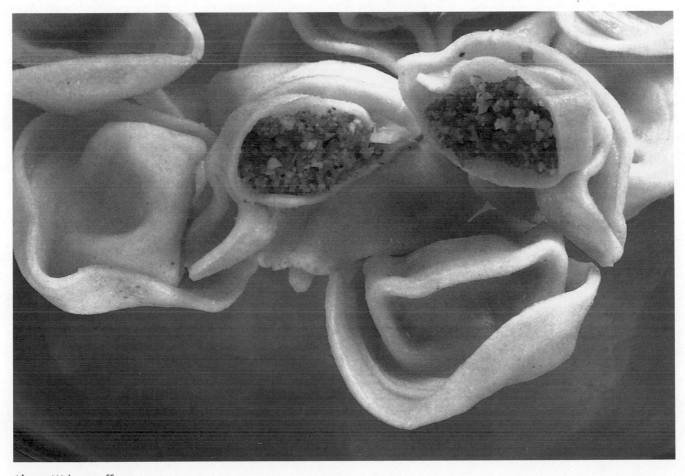

Above: Walnut stuffing.

Above: Salmon-stuffed shells with fresh chives.

Salmon-stuffed Shells

Look out for very large pasta shells in good delicatessens or Italian grocers. If you cannot find them, then substitute large lumache.

SERVES 4

250 g (9 oz) salmon fillet, skinned

150 ml (¼ pt) water .

150 ml (¼ pt) dry white wine

25 g (1 oz) butter

1 small onion, finely chopped

25 g (1 oz) plain flour

225 g (8 oz) closed cap mushrooms, sliced

150 ml (¼ pt) single cream

6 tbsp freshly grated Parmesan cheese

salt and freshly ground black pepper

175 g (6 oz) ricotta cheese

50 g (2 oz) fresh breadcrumbs

2 tbsp chopped fresh parsley

2 tbsp snipped chives

12–16 large pasta shells

sprigs of herbs, to garnish

Lay the salmon in a saucepan. Add the water and wine. Heat until just simmering, then remove the saucepan from the heat and leave to stand for 15 minutes. Drain and flake the fish, reserving the liquid, but discarding any bones.
Pre-heat the oven to 190°C/375°F/Gas Mark 5.

Melt the butter in a small saucepan. Add the onion and cook for 10 minutes, stirring, until it has softened. Stir in the flour, then add the cooking liquor from the salmon and the mushrooms. Bring to the boil, stirring, and simmer gently for 3 minutes. Mix in the cream, 2 tbsp of the Parmesan and salt and pepper to taste. Pour the mushrooms and the sauce into an ovenproof gratin dish.

Mix the salmon with the ricotta, breadcrumbs, parsley, chives and salt and pepper to taste.

Cook the pasta shells in boiling salted water for about 12 minutes, or until tender. Drain well and rinse under cold water, then drain again.

Fill the shells with the salmon mixture. Arrange them on top of the sauce and sprinkle the remaining Parmesan over them. Bake in the pre-heated oven for about 20 minutes, or until they are hot and have browned. Serve at once, garnished with sprigs of herbs.

Spinach and Ricotta Stuffing

INGREDIENTS

175 g (6 oz) fresh spinach

100 g (4 oz) ricotta cheese

4 tbsp freshly grated Parmesan or pecorino cheese

1 spring onion, very finely chopped

1 tbsp chopped fresh parsley

1 tbsp chopped fresh oregano

freshly grated nutmeg

salt and freshly ground black pepper

25 g (1 oz) fresh white breadcrumbs

Trim the stalks from the spinach, then wash the leaves well and place in a saucepan, leaving the leaves quite wet. Cover the saucepan tightly and cook for 5 minutes over a fairly high heat, shaking the saucepan often. The spinach is cooked when it is limp and just tender.

Drain the spinach in a fine sieve, pressing out all the liquid with the back of a spoon. Chop the spinach finely – preferably in a food processor. Mix the ricotta, Parmesan or pecorino (for a milder flavour), spring onion, parsley and oregano into the spinach. Add a little nutmeg and salt and pepper, then mix in the breadcrumbs. Cover and leave to stand for 5 minutes before using.

Stuffed Lumache

Lumache ("snails") comes in a variety of sizes and the very large ones are intended for filling with a stuffing. Here, they are nestled together on a bed of vegetables before being browned in the oven.

FOR THE LUMACHE (SERVES 4)

25 g (1 oz) butter

1 onion, finely chopped

100 g (4 oz) mushrooms, finely chopped

50 g (2 oz) breadcrumbs

salt and freshly ground black pepper

1 tbsp chopped fresh oregano

225 g (8 oz) ricotta cheese

1 bunch of watercress, leaves only, finely chopped

freshly grated nutmeg

16 large lumache

300 ml (½ pt) Béchamel Sauce (see page 56)

4 tbsp freshly grated Parmesan cheese

FOR THE VEGETABLE BASE

2 tbsp olive oil

1 large onion, halved and thinly sliced

1 garlic clove, crushed

1 green pepper, de-seeded, halved and thinly sliced

1 red pepper, de-seeded, halved and thinly sliced

2 medium courgettes, thinly sliced

6 tomatoes, peeled, de-seeded and quartered

First, prepare the stuffing for the lumache. Melt the butter in a saucepan. Add the onion and cook, stirring, for 5 minutes. Then add the mushrooms and continue to cook, stirring occasionally, for a further 10 minutes. Mix in the breadcrumbs, salt and pepper to taste and oregano. Then, add the ricotta cheese and watercress. Season with a little grated nutmeg to taste and set aside. Pre-heat the oven to 200°C/400°F/Gas Mark 6.

Cook the lumache in boiling salted water for about 12 minutes, or until tender. Drain well, rinse under cold water and drain again so they do not close up.

Meanwhile, prepare the Béchamel Sauce (page 56).

Next, prepare the vegetable base. Heat the oil in a frying pan. Add the onion, garlic and peppers. Cook for 15 minutes, or until the onion has softened. Stir in the courgettes and cook for 2 minutes, then add the tomatoes with salt and pepper to taste. Cook for 2–3 minutes, to soften the tomatoes, then turn the mixture into an ovenproof dish or four single gratin dishes.

Fill the lumache with the mushroom mixture. Then arrange them on the vegetable base. Spoon a little Béchamel Sauce over the top of each stuffed lumache and sprinkle with a little Parmesan. Bake for about 15 minutes or until the top has browned.

Rich Pork and Beef Stuffing

This is a popular filling for pasta as the combination of pork and beef, enriched with chicken livers, gives pasta an excellent flavour.

INGREDIENTS

1 tbsp olive oil

1 small onion, finely chopped

2 garlic cloves, crushed

25 g (1 oz) chicken livers, finely chopped

1 tsp ground coriander

1 tsp chopped fresh marjoram

2 tbsp chopped fresh parsley

100 g (4 oz) lean minced pork

100 g (4 oz) lean minced steak

25 g (1 oz) fresh white breadcrumbs

2 tbsp brandy

salt and ground black pepper

Heat the olive oil in a small saucepan. Add the onion and garlic. Cook, stirring, for 2–3 minutes. Stir in the chicken livers and cook for about a minute, or until just set. Remove the saucepan from the heat.

Stir in the coriander, marjoram and parsley. Mix the pork and steak in a bowl and stir in the onion and chicken liver mixture. Pound the ingredients until thoroughly combined. Then pound in the breadcrumbs, brandy and plenty of salt and pepper.

Above: Stuffed lumache.

Chicken and Spinach Roulade

FOR THE ROULADE (SERVES 4)

¼ quantity Rich Egg Pasta Dough (see page 40)

225 g (8 oz) frozen spinach, defrosted and drained

1 onion, very finely chopped

1 garlic clove, crushed

100 g (4 oz) skinned, boneless, cooked chicken breast,
  finely chopped or minced

225 g (8 oz) ricotta cheese

1 egg, beaten

25 g (1 oz) fresh breadcrumbs

salt and freshly ground black pepper

FOR THE TOPPING

1 tbsp single cream or milk

2 fresh basil sprigs, finely grated

3 tbsp fresh white breadcrumbs

2 tbsp freshly grated Parmesan cheese

TO GARNISH AND SERVE

2–3 tomatoes, sliced, to garnish

sprigs of basil, to garnish

Rich Tomato Sauce (see page 54) or Mushroom Sauce
  (also see page 58), to serve

First, make the pasta dough as given on page 40.

Mix the spinach, onion, garlic, chicken and half the ricotta cheese. Stir in most of the egg (reserving a little to use to seal the pasta dough later), then mix in the breadcrumbs and add salt and pepper to taste.

Cut a large sheet of cookery foil measuring about 86 X 41 cm (34 X 16 in). Fold the foil in half widthways so it measures roughly 43 X 41 cm (17 X 16 in) and grease it lightly. Roll out the pasta to form a rectangle 33 X 25 cm (13 X 10 in). Spread the spinach and chicken filling over it, leaving an uncovered border of about 3 cm (½ in) round the edge. Fold the two narrow pasta edges and the long edge nearest to you over the filling. Brush the top of the folded pasta edges with beaten egg, then roll up the pasta and filling, like a Swiss roll, towards the unfolded

pasta edge. Roll the pasta gently, to avoid squeezing out the filling.

Brush the unfolded edge with egg and make sure the join is well sealed, pressing the edge neatly with the end of a round-bladed knife. Then, dust the roulade with flour and gently roll it on to the prepared foil, placing the join underneath. Make sure the ends are neat, then lift the roulade on the foil into a deep roasting tin. If you have a fish kettle, then it is ideal for cooking the roulade.

Pour boiling water from the kettle around the roulade to just cover it. Add salt to the water, then cover the roasting tin tightly with foil or put a lid on the fish kettle. Simmer the roulade for 1 hour, turning it over halfway through cooking, if necessary, should the water not be deep enough to cover it.

Meanwhile, prepare the topping. Mix the remaining ricotta cheese with the single cream or milk and basil. Stir in salt and pepper to taste. Have a large, shallow gratin dish ready for the roulade (for example a lasagne dish or oval fish dish). Lift the roulade from the water (see Cook's Tip below) and place it in the dish. Spread the ricotta mixture over the top. Mix the breadcrumbs and Parmesan together, then sprinkle this over. Brown the topping under a hot grill. Garnish with sliced tomatoes and basil. Serve at once, cutting the roulade into thick slices and offering either the Rich Tomato Sauce or Mushroom Sauce as an accompaniment.

COOK'S TIP

If you have cooked the roulade in a roasting tin, the best way to drain it is to pour off some of the water from the tin first, then lift the roulade on the foil, otherwise it tends to float aside slightly.

Pheasant Cappelletti with Dried Morels and Oyster Mushrooms

This dish elevates pasta to the dinner party menu. Serve a salad of Frisée with Dates, Olives and Onions (see page 316) or Braised Fennel (see page 314) as a classy side dish to accompany the ravioli. Use the carcase from the pheasant to make the stock for the mushroom sauce in this recipe.

SERVES 4–6

½ quantity Rich Egg Pasta Dough (see page 40)

1 quantity Pheasant and Bacon Stuffing (see page 195)

40–50 g (1½– 2 oz) dried morels

300 ml (½ pt) pheasant or chicken stock

50 g (2 oz) butter

1 small onion, finely chopped

1 bay leaf

25 g (1 oz) plain flour

300 ml (½ pt) dry white wine

salt and freshly ground black pepper

150 ml (¼ pt) single cream

4 sprigs of basil, finely grated

450 g (1 lb) oyster mushrooms

sprigs of basil, to garnish

First, make the pasta and the pheasant stuffing as given on pages 44, 190 and 195.

Roll out half the pasta dough to form a 30 cm (12 in) square. Stamp out forty 4 cm (1½ in) circles, dipping the cutter in flour occasionally to prevent it sticking to the dough.

Place a little pheasant stuffing on 20 of the circles. Brush the remaining circles with a little beaten egg. Then sandwich the stuffing between the pasta circles, pinching their edges together neatly. Repeat with the remaining dough and stuffing.

Make the sauce before cooking the pasta. Rinse the morels once or twice, then place them in a bowl. Heat the stock until it is just hot and pour it over the morels, then cover the bowl and set the morels aside to soak for 20 minutes or until softened.

Meanwhile, melt half the butter in a saucepan, add the onion and bay leaf and stir well. Cover the saucepan and leave to cook for 15 minutes.

Drain the morels and strain the stock through fine muslin to remove any grit. Set the morels aside. Stir the flour into the onion, then add the strained stock and wine, stirring all the time. Add a little salt and pepper, and bring the sauce to the boil. Reduce the heat and cover the saucepan, then simmer for 15 minutes. Add the morels, cover the saucepan and cook for a further 5 minutes.

Cook the Pheasant Cappelletti in plenty of boiling salted water for 3–4 minutes. Stir the cream and basil into the sauce, taste for seasoning and warm the sauce for a few seconds without boiling it, then remove the saucepan from the heat and , leave, covered, on one side. Drain the cappelletti and turn them into a serving dish. Pour the sauce over and mix lightly.

Melt the remaining butter in a large frying saucepan. Add the oyster mushrooms and season them well. Toss them over a high heat for 2 minutes, then arrange the mushrooms and their cooking juices around the Pheasant Cappelletti. Garnish with sprigs of basil and serve at once.

PHEASANT CAPPELLETTI VARIATIONS

If the budget does not stretch to buying dried morels, the pasta and its oyster mushroom accompaniment may be served with Red or White Wine Sauce (see page56) or Light Tomato Sauce (see page 55). Alternatively, toss the freshly cooked pasta with truffle butter, serve with the sautéed oyster mushrooms and sprinkle with grated basil instead of making a sauce.

Ham and Cheese Ravioli with Broccoli and Leeks

SERVES 4

½ quantity Rich Egg Pasta dough (see page 40)

1 quantity gammon and Cheese Stuffing (see page 197)

1 egg, beaten

225 g (8 oz) broccoli, divided into small florets

salt and freshly ground black pepper

2 tbsp olive oil

25 g (1 oz) butter (optional)

450 g (1 lb) leeks, sliced

First, make the pasta dough as given on page 40 and set it aside to rest whilst you make the filling (see page 197).

Roll out half the pasta dough until it is slightly larger than a 30 cm (12 in) square, then trim the edges neatly. Dot six small mounds of stuffing, spacing them evenly, along the top edge of the dough. Then dot another five mounds, spacing them evenly too, at right angles to the first row, down one side of the dough. Using these as a guide to keep the mounds of stuffing evenly spaced in neat lines, place six lines of stuffing mounds on the dough, working from the top edge down towards the bottom edge.

Cover the stuffing and dough loosely with cling film to prevent it drying out as you roll out the covering. Roll out the remaining pasta dough until it is slightly larger than a 30 cm (12 in) square. Brush the pasta between the mounds of stuffing with beaten egg. Then carefully lay the second sheet of dough over the top. Working from one edge of the dough, press the dough together along the edge, then seal it neatly between the mounds of dough. Continue pressing the dough together until all the spaces between the stuffing are sealed. It is important to work methodically in one direction otherwise you can trap air pockets.

Use a pastry wheel or knife to cut between the mounds of stuffing, right along the middles of the sealed paths of dough, to form the ravioli. Prepare the broccoli and leek mixture before cooking the pasta, but have a large saucepan of boiling salted water ready for cooking it.

Cook the broccoli in boiling salted water for 3 minutes, then drain well. Heat the oil and butter, if using, in a large saucepan. Add the leeks and stir well. Cover the saucepan and cook, shaking the saucepan occasionally, for about 15 minutes, or until the leeks have reduced and are tender. Stir in salt and pepper to taste and add the broccoli. Leave to cook gently whilst boiling the pasta.

Cook the ravioli in the boiling water for about 3 minutes, then drain it well and turn it into a large serving dish. Pour the leek and broccoli mixture over, together with all the liquid from the saucepan, and mix together lightly. Serve at once.

Gammon Parcels

These are satisfying and flavoursome, so a Good Green Salad or some simply cooked vegetables are suitable accompaniments.

SERVES 4

¼ quantity Rich Egg Pasta Dough (see page 40)

225 g (8 oz) lean, rindless gammon steak, cut into four equal pieces

1 tbsp olive oil

75 g (3 oz) mushrooms, roughly chopped

4 cocktail gherkins, chopped

75 g (3 oz) courgette, grated

salt and freshly ground black pepper

1 egg, beaten

a little butter

4 ripe tomatoes (preferably plum tomatoes), sliced

150 g (5 oz) mozzarella cheese, thinly sliced

First, make the pasta as given on page 40, then set it aside to rest as you prepare the filling.

The gammon pieces should be fairly even in size, if not, beat the smaller piece(s) out slightly with a steak mallet or rolling pin. Heat the oil in a frying pan and cook the gammon pieces until browned on both

sides and just cooked. Then drain them well and set aside.

Brown the mushrooms in the remaining juices, then remove from the heat and stir in the gherkins, courgette and salt and pepper. Leave to cool.

Roll out the pasta until it is slightly larger than a 30 cm (12 in) square. Trim the edges neatly, then cut it into four 15 cm (6 in) squares. Place a quarter of the vegetable mixture on each square and top with a piece of gammon. Brush the edges of the pasta dough with beaten egg, then fold the corners of the pasta over the gammon, like an envelope, sealing it in. Carefully pinch and smooth the joins in the pasta.

Cook the pasta parcels in boiling salted water for 5 minutes. Use a slotted spoon to remove them from the saucepan and place in a buttered gratin dish or single serving dishes that can go under the grill. Top the gammon parcels with sliced tomatoes and mozzarella cheese and grill until golden, then serve at once.

GAMMON PARCEL VARIATIONS

The filling in the gammon parcels makes them quite moist, but, if you like, instead of the tomato and mozzarella topping, a coating sauce can be poured over the parcels. Rich Tomato Sauce, Mushroom Sauce, or Cheese Sauce (see page 54) would all work well. Mozzarella cheese may be placed on the sauced parcels and browned under the grill, if liked.

Beef Cannelloni

FOR THE BEEF CANNELLONI (SERVES 4)

12 cannelloni tubes

salt and freshly ground black pepper

2 tbsp olive oil

1 onion, finely chopped

2 garlic cloves, crushed

1 tbsp chopped fresh oregano

225 g (8 oz) chicken livers, chopped

100 g (4 oz) rindless bacon, finely chopped or minced

350 g (12 oz) minced steak

6 black olives, stoned and chopped

3 tbsp mushroom ketchup

50 g (2 oz) fresh breadcrumbs

4 tbsp brandy

1 quantity Rich Tomato Sauce (see page 54)

FOR THE TOPPING

150 g (5 oz) mozzarella cheese, chopped

2 tbsp freshly grated Parmesan cheese

4 tbsp dried white breadcrumbs

Cook the cannelloni in boiling salted water for 6 minutes, or until tender. Drain and rinse under cold running water to keep the tubes open, then drain and lay them out on a clean teatowel to dry.

Pre-heat the oven to 160°C/320°F/Gas Mark 3. Use a little of the oil to lightly grease an ovenproof dish.

Heat the remaining oil in a small saucepan. Add the onion and garlic, then cook, stirring, for 5 minutes. Stir in the oregano and chicken livers and cook for 2 minutes, then remove from the heat.

Mix the bacon and steak with the olives, mushroom ketchup, breadcrumbs and brandy. Add the chicken liver mixture and salt and pepper to taste, then pound the ingredients together until they are thoroughly combined. Pipe or spoon the filling into the cannelloni tubes, then lay them in the prepared dish.

Pour the Rich Tomato Sauce over, cover with foil and bake in the pre-heated oven for 45 minutes.

Meanwhile, mix the mozzarella, Parmesan and breadcrumbs for the topping.

Remove the foil and sprinkle the cheese mixture over the cannelloni. Return it to the oven, increase the temperature to 180°C/350°F/Gas Mark 4 and bake for a further 40—45 minutes, or until the topping is crisp and golden and the Beef Cannelloni are cooked through.

Turkey Cannelloni with Lemon Sauce

This is a good way in which to transform the leftovers of a roast turkey into a tempting meal. Instead of using bought tubes, try making fresh pasta, as here. Alternatively, for results of a similar standard, buy fresh lasagne and use it to roll round the filling. The prepared cannelloni, coated in sauce, may be frozen for up to 3 months.

SERVES 6

½ quantity Rich Egg Pasta Dough flavoured with herbs (see pages 40-41)

a little butter, for greasing

1 quantity Béchamel Sauce (see page 56)

450 g (1 lb) cooked turkey, finely chopped or minced

100 g (4 oz) button mushrooms, chopped

100 g (4 oz) fresh white breadcrumbs

3 tbsp snipped chives

1 tbsp chopped fresh tarragon

2 tbsp chopped fresh parsley

grated rind of 1 lemon

50 g (2 oz) mild Cheddar cheese, grated

Make the pasta dough as given on page 40 and divide it in half. Roll out one half to form a square that is slightly larger than 30 cm (12 in). Trim the edges and cut the pasta into nine 10 cm (4 in) squares. Repeat with the remaining pasta dough, then cook the squares in plenty of boiling salted water for 3 minutes. Drain well, rinse under cold water and lay out on a clean teatowel.

Pre-heat the oven to 180°C/350°F/Gas Mark 4 and grease an ovenproof dish with a little butter.

Make the Béchamel Sauce as given on page 56.

Mix the turkey with the mushrooms, half the

breadcrumbs, the chives, tarragon, parsley and salt and pepper to taste. Stir in a little of the sauce – just enough to bind the ingredients into a firm mixture. Divide the mixture in half. Roughly mould half the mixture into a cylinder shape on a plate and mark it into nine equal portions.

Cut off a portion of stuffing, roll it into a sausage and place it on a piece of pasta, then roll up the pasta to form cannelloni. Place in the prepared ovenproof dish. Repeat this process with the remaining sheets of pasta and portions of stuffing.

Stir the lemon rind into the remaining Béchamel Sauce and taste it for seasoning before pouring it over the cannelloni. Mix the remaining breadcrumbs with the cheese. Sprinkle this over the sauce and bake in the oven for about 30 minutes, or until the topping is crisp and the cannelloni have heated through.

Walnut Tortellini Tossed with Cucumber and Stilton

SERVES 4–6

½ quantity Rich Egg Pasta dough (see page 40)

1 quantity Walnut Stuffing (see page 155)

1 egg, beaten

2 tbsp olive oil

50 g (2 oz) butter

½ cucumber, very lightly peeled (see opposite) and diced

4 tbsp snipped chives

salt and freshly ground black pepper

4 tbsp dry white vermouth or dry white wine

175 g (6 oz) blue Stilton cheese, crumbled

sprigs of tarragon, to garnish (optional)

Make the pasta and the stuffing as given on pages 40 and 155.

Cut the pasta dough in half. Roll out one portion to form a 30 cm (12 in) square. Cut the dough into 5 cm (2 in) wide strips. Then cut these across in the opposite direction to make 5 cm (2 in) squares.

Work on about a quarter of the squares at a time, keeping the others covered loosely with cling film to prevent the pasta drying out. Brush the squares with egg and place a little of the filling in the middle – just less than ½ tsp (not a measuring spoon, but a cutlery tsp) of filling is sufficient for each square. Fold the pasta diagonally over the filling and pinch the edges together to make a triangle, then curl the long side round a finger tip and pinch the points together to shape each tortellini (see page 150). Repeat using the remaining pasta to make a total of 72 tortellini.

Once the tortellini are shaped, prepare the Cucumber and Stilton dressing. Heat the olive oil and butter together. The cucumber should be so finely peeled that only the very outer layer of skin is removed, leaving the outside of the vegetable quite green. Add the cucumber to the butter and oil and cook, stirring, for 5 minutes. Stir in the chives, salt and pepper to taste and vermouth or wine. Heat until the mixture is just simmering, then cover the saucepan and leave it over the lowest setting until the pasta is ready.

Cook the tortellini in boiling salted water for 3–5 minutes. Drain well and transfer to a heated serving dish. If you have to cook the pasta in batches, then spoon a little liquid from the cucumber over the first batch, keep it covered and hot until successive batches are cooked.

Toss the cucumber and its liquid and the Stilton with the cooked tortellini and serve at once. Garnishing the tortellini with sprigs of tarragon indicates the flavour of the Walnut Stuffing.

A SALAD-STYLE STARTER
Prepare a half quantity of the tortellini and serve them on a generous base of frisée and watercress salad with a little rocket if available. Then spoon over the Cucumber and Stilton dressing and serve at once. The hot tortellini is delicious with the cold salad.

Baked Spinach and Ricotta Cannelloni

If you want to serve this as a first course, then halve the quantities or increase the number of portions to eight.

SERVES 4
double quantity Spinach and Ricotta Stuffing (see page 157)
16 cannelloni tubes
salt and freshly ground black pepper
2 tbsp olive oil
1 large onion, chopped
1 garlic clove, crushed
2 x 397 g (14 oz) tins chopped tomatoes
2 tbsp tomato purée
3 tbsp chopped fresh parsley
150 g (5 oz) mozzarella cheese, chopped
4 tbsp freshly grated Parmesan cheese

First, make the stuffing as given on page 157.

Cook the cannelloni in boiling salted water for 6 minutes, then drain well. Rinse the tubes under cold running water to open them, then set them out on a clean teatowel to dry.

Pre-heat the oven at 180°C/350°F/Gas Mark 4 and brush an ovenproof dish lightly with a little of the oil.

Heat the remaining oil in a saucepan, add the onion and garlic and cook, stirring, for about 15 minutes, or until slightly softened.

Stir in the tomatoes, tomato purée, parsley and salt and pepper to taste. Bring to the boil and simmer for 5 minutes.

Meanwhile, put the Spinach and Ricotta Stuffing into a piping bag fitted with a plain nozzle and fill the cannelloni tubes, placing them in the prepared dish as you do so.

Pour the tomato sauce over the cannelloni. Mix the mozzarella and Parmesan, then sprinkle this over the top of the cannelloni and bake in the pre-heated oven for 20–30 minutes, or until the sauce is bubbling and the topping has browned and cooked through.

Feta Circles with Walnut Oil and Olives

These are just delicious! I have included a variety of alternative serving suggestions below as they are quite versatile.

SERVES 4

½ quantity Rich Egg Pasta dough (see page 40)

150 g (5 oz) feta cheese

1 egg, beaten

salt and freshly ground black pepper

2 tbsp sunflower oil

25 g (1 oz) butter

6 spring onions, finely chopped

12 black olives, stoned and thinly sliced

3 tbsp walnut oil

2 tbsp chopped fresh parsley

First, make the pasta dough as given on page 40.

Cut the cheese into 5 mm (¼ in) cubes.

ALTERNATIVE DRESSINGS AND SAUCES

FETA CIRCLES WITH TOMATO SAUCE

Toss the pasta with Light Tomato Sauce (see page 54) or Rich Tomato Sauce (see page 55)

FETA CIRCLES WITH PUTTANESCA SAUCE

Puttanesca Sauce (see page 139) complements the cheese

BUTTERY FETA CIRCLES

Garlic Butter (see page 62) or Lemon Anchovy Butter (see page 63) are good with the pasta.

FETA CIRCLES WITH A LIGHT DRESSING

For a less-rich dressing, try Light Tomato Sauce (see page 55) or Greek Yoghurt Topping (see page 71).

FETA CIRCLES WITH OLIVE DRESSINGS

Mixed Olive and Pepper Topping (see page 77) or Anchovy and Olive Paste (see page 76) are ideal for lightly coating the cheese pasta.

Roll out half the pasta dough to form a 30 cm (12 in) square. Stamp out forty 4 cm (1½ in) circles, dipping the cutter in flour occasionally to prevent it sticking to the dough.

Place cubes of cheese on 20 of the circles. Brush the remaining circles with a little beaten egg. Then sandwich the cheese between the pasta circles, pinching their edges together neatly. Repeat with the remaining dough and cheese.

Cook the pasta circles in plenty of boiling salted water for 3 minutes.

Meanwhile, heat the sunflower oil and butter, add the spring onions and olives, and stir over low heat for 2–3 minutes to lightly cook the onions.

Drain the cooked pasta and turn it into a warmed serving dish. Stir the walnut oil and parsley into the spring onion and olive mixture, pour this dressing over the pasta, scraping every last drop from the saucepan. Toss well and serve at once.

DIFFERENT CHEESE FILLINGS

Feta cheese may be replaced with a full-flavoured alternative, such as a blue cheese (Dolcelatte, Gorgonzola, Stilton or Danish blue), garlic-flavoured cheese or Windsor red. Many of the flavoured cheeses go well, as long as they are fairly powerful. For example, try Teifi cheese flavoured with cumin seeds – mmm!

Uszka

Uszka are small, tortellini-type pasta filled with a dried mushroom mixture. To be completely authentic, these Polish dumplings would need to be made slightly smaller than here, but they are a bit easier to make this size. They are a classic accompaniment for bortsch (beetroot soup) and, if you want to serve them in soup, then cut the pasta into 7 strips, then across into 49 squares and make tiny, filled pasta appropriate to soup.

DRIED MUSHROOMS
Polish dried wild mushrooms are threaded on long strings and hung to dry. You will find the authentic ingredients hanging in Polish delicatessens; however, dried porcini or ceps may be substituted. Do not use Chinese dried mushrooms (shiitake) as they have a quite different, strong flavour.

SERVES 4 – 6
½ quantity Rich Egg Pasta Dough (see page 40)
5 large dried mushrooms (see note)
25 g (1 oz) butter
1 onion, very finely chopped
75 g (3 oz) fresh white breadcrumbs
salt and freshly ground black pepper
1 egg, beaten
75 g (3 oz) butter, to serve

First, make the pasta dough as given on page 40 and set aside whilst you prepare the filling. Place the mushrooms in a small saucepan and add enough water to cover them. Bring to the boil, then reduce the heat and cover the saucepan. Simmer the mushrooms for about 5 minutes, or until they are tender. Drain the mushrooms, reserving the liquid. Rinse the saucepan out, then strain the liquid back into it through a sieve lined with muslin (this removes any grit that has come from the mushrooms). Boil the liquid until it has reduced to about 2 tbsp, then set it aside.

Chop the mushrooms finely, discarding any tough stalk ends. Melt the butter in a saucepan, add the onion and cook, stirring often, for 10 minutes. Mix the mushrooms, onion and breadcrumbs. Add salt and pepper to taste, then stir in the reduced cooking liquor.

Cut the pasta dough in half. Roll out one portion to form a 30 cm (12 in) square. Cut the dough into 5 cm (2 in) wide strips. Then cut these across in the opposite direction to make 5 cm (2 in) squares.

Cook the Uszka in boiling salted water for 3–4 minutes. Drain and toss with melted butter.

SERVING SUGGESTIONS

USZKA WITH CHIVES AND TARRAGON
Add 4 tbsp snipped chives and 2 tbsp chopped fresh tarragon to the melted butter for serving.

USZKA WITH HORSERADISH CREAM AND BEETROOT
Mix 2 tbsp horseradish sauce into 300 ml (½ pt) soured cream. Add 3 tbsp chopped fresh dill and a little salt and pepper to taste. Toss the freshly cooked Uszka with a knob of melted butter and the horseradish cream. Top each portion with cooked beetroot cut into fine matchsticks and serve at once.

USZKA WITH BEETROOT AND SPRING ONIONS
Coarsely grate 100 g (4 oz) cooked beetroot and finely chop 4 spring onions. Cook the vegetables together in half the melted butter. Toss the Uszka in the remaining butter, then spoon the beetroot mixture on top.

CREAMY USZKA
Make a Béchamel Sauce (see page 56) and stir in 2–4 tbsp horseradish sauce, to taste. Toss the Uszka with the sauce, adding 4 tbsp chopped dill.
Serve garnished with sprigs of dill and offer a grated mild cheese with the Uszka, such as Lancashire or Caerphilly.

Pierogi

These are the Polish equivalent of the Italian ravioli family of filled pasta. You can use any leftover cooked pork or beef as a filling instead of the smoked pork given in the ingredients below. Cottage cheese, stiffened with breadcrumbs, is another suitable filling.

SERVES 4–6
FOR THE DOUGH

225 g (8 oz) plain flour

½ tsp salt

1 egg

5 tbsp water

1 egg, beaten

FOR THE PORK AND SAUERKRAUT FILLING

1 tbsp oil

1 small onion, finely chopped

1 garlic clove, crushed

50 g (2 oz) sauerkraut, finely chopped

175 g (6 oz) smoked pork, minced

salt and freshly ground black pepper

TO SERVE

50 g (2 oz) butter

225 g (8 oz) rindless streaky bacon

First, make the dough. Place the flour in a bowl. Mix in the salt and make a well in the middle of the flour. Beat the egg with the water, pour it into the well in the flour, then gradually mix in the flour to make a firm dough. Knead the dough on a lightly floured surface until smooth.

Wrap the dough in a polythene bag and set it aside to rest whilst you prepare the filling.

Heat the oil in a small saucepan. Add the onion and garlic, then cook, stirring, for about 10 minutes, until the onion has softened but not browned. Add the sauerkraut and pork. Remove the saucepan from the heat. Stir in salt and pepper to taste, then pound the mixture until it binds together.

Work with a quarter of the dough and a quarter of the filling at a time. Take the first quarter of dough and roll it out thinly on a lightly floured work surface, into a round measuring roughly 25–30 cm (10–12 in) in diameter. Use a 6 cm (2½ in) round cutter to stamp out circles.

Take the first quarter of the filling mixture and spoon small amounts of it on to each of the circles. Brush the edges of the circles with beaten egg, then fold one side over the filling to make little pasty-like shapes. Pinch the edges to seal them together and flute them attractively. Place the filled Pierogi on a floured platter. Repeat this process for each of the remaining quarters of dough and filling.

When the Pierogi are made, melt the butter and fry the bacon. Add the Pierogi to boiling salted water and cook at a steady, but not too fast, boil for about 4 minutes. Drain and serve tossed with the butter and bacon.

Fruit Pierozki

MAKES ABOUT 32
FOR THE DOUGH

175 g (6 oz) plain flour

pinch of salt

1 egg, beaten

3 tbsp water

FOR THE FILLING

about 225 g (8 oz) fresh fruit, such as cherries, plums,
  apricots or blueberries

icing sugar, to dredge

soured cream, to serve

Place the flour in a bowl and mix in the salt. Make a well in the middle, then add the egg and water. Mix in the flour to form a dough, then knead well until smooth.

Prepare the fruit according to type: stone cherries, halve and stone plums and apricots, rinse and dry blueberries.

Roll out the dough into a circle on a lightly floured surface until it is roughly 40 cm (16 in) across. Then

stamp out 6 cm (2½ in) rounds. Place a piece of fruit on each round and brush the edges of the dough lightly with water. Then fold the dough round the fruit and pinch the edges to seal them well.

Cook the Pierozki in boiling water for about 3 minutes, then drain well and serve dredged with icing sugar, with soured cream as an accompaniment.

Above: Apricot and almond gems.

Apricot and Almond Gems

I cannot decide how many of these should be served to make up a portion – I would find four an ample portion, but my partner will happily eat six...The almonds in the middle of the apricots were his idea.

MAKES 36
FOR THE APRICOT AND ALMOND GEMS
½ quantity Rich Egg Pasta Dough (see page 40)
36 blanched almonds
36 ready-to-eat dried apricots
1 egg, beaten
flour, for dredging
oil, for frying
caster sugar, for dredging
whipped cream, to serve

FOR THE SAUCE
225 g (8 oz) apricot jam
200 ml (7 fl oz) dry sherry
First, make the pasta dough as given on page 40.

Place an almond in the middle of each apricot.

Roll out half the dough until it is slightly larger than 30 cm (12 in) square. Stamp out neat lines of 5 cm (2 in) diameter circles, making 36 in all.

Place an almond-filled apricot on each of 18 of the circles. Brush the edges of the circles with egg, then cover with the remaining 18 circles. Pinch the dough neatly round the apricot to seal it in firmly. Repeat with the remaining apricots and dough.

Cook the pasta in boiling salted water for 3 minutes, then drain thoroughly and dredge with flour.

Heat sufficient oil to deep-fry the pasta to 180°C/350°F/Gas Mark 4 and fry the pasta for a few seconds until it is crisp and golden. Drain well on kitchen paper and dredge at once with caster sugar.

Make the sauce. Simply boil the jam with the sherry.

Serve the sauce with the Apricot Gems, spooning a little on the side of each plate, and offer whipped cream.

Blackcurrant Circles

SERVES 4–6
175 g (6 oz) fresh blackcurrants, topped and tailed
50 g (2 oz) sugar
50 g (2 oz) Amaretti biscuits, crushed
½ quantity Rich Egg Pasta Dough (see page 40)
1 egg, beaten
icing sugar, for dredging
whipped cream, to serve
bunches of blackcurrants, to decorate

Place the blackcurrants in a saucepan with the sugar. Heat gently until the juice runs from the fruit, then, simmer, stirring occasionally, until the fruit are soft. Remove from the heat and stir in the crushed Amaretti biscuits. Leave to cool, then chill.

Meanwhile, make the pasta dough as given on page 40.

Roll out half the dough to form a square roughly 30 cm (12 in) on each side. Stamp out about 36 5 cm (2 in) circles. Place a little blackcurrant filling on half the circles (about 18), using half the filling altogether. Brush the remaining circles with egg and cover them with the blackcurrant filling. Pinch the edges to seal them well. Repeat with the remaining dough and filling.

Cook the pasta in boiling water for 3–4 minutes, then drain them well. Serve at once, on hot plates, dredged with icing sugar and topped with whipped cream. Decorate with bunches of blackcurrants.

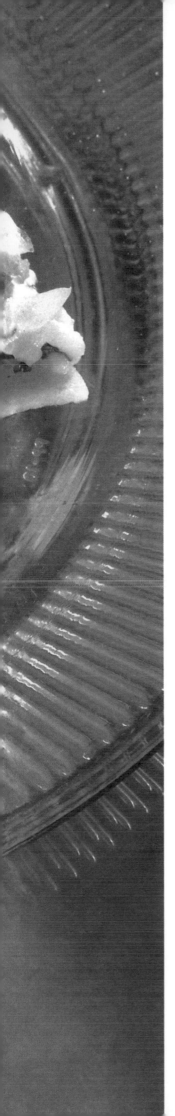

BAKED PASTA DISHES

From the old favourite lasagne to a few ways to vary the traditional approach to stuffing vegetables, this chapter includes dishes that are part of everyone's repertoire with others to surprise guests or add a new note to everyday meals.

As well as layering and baking lasagne, remember that any pasta shape will work in the same way.

Bows or butterflies make excellent flat layers between sauces, for example, and macaroni and soup pasta are also good for making smooth layers. Tagliatelle and the chunkier or rounded shapes tend to make uneven layers with bubbling-hot tops and golden-crusted peaks.

So, do as you will with these recipes, mixing and matching the sauces, pastas and topping for a variety of effects.

Making Perfect Lasagne

The majority of the lasagne available in supermarkets is of the "no-need-to-pre-cook" type. The quality of this type of pasta varies significantly. Some brands look suspect, the colour of pale cardboard, with a textured, fibrous appearance and fork marks or holes all over. Then there are other types that look just like ordinary dried pasta.

I have tried a few types with very mixed results. One batch of pasta completely ruined what started out as a decent sauce, whilst another type was surprisingly OK, but not special. The result of my testing was that the dried pasta, which is boiled before being layered, and fresh lasagne were by far the best.

Here are some practical notes on the different types and on constructing a good lasagne.

Using No Need to Pre-Cook Lasagne

Look out for pasta that has the appearance of ordinary dried pasta, then experiment with different brands to see whether there is one you like.

I find that this type of lasagne only suitable for layering with very moist sauces. Bolognese sauce is usually sufficiently liquid, but if you have reduced it to a thick richness, add more tinned tomatoes as the pasta absorbs a significant amount of liquid. For comparatively dry fillings, such as a mixture of spinach and ricotta, the pasta should be boiled until tender first. Also, there must be plenty of room in your baking dish for a good covering of sauce on top of the pasta, otherwise the surface dries up quickly during cooking.

I obtained best results with this type of pasta by selecting a good brand, which looked like ordinary pasta, and boiling it for about 6–8 minutes in lightly salted water, until just tender. In essence, I treated it as "quick-cook" pasta rather than as a "ready-to-use" pasta.

Dried Lasagne

This is the next best alternative to fresh lasagne, but it is very difficult to obtain because supermarkets stock the types that do not need pre-cooking. Some delicatessens or specialist Italian grocers, however, keep a supply of dried pasta that has to be boiled before layering it with sauce.

The lasagne expands on boiling, so you do not need quite as much of this type as you do of the no-need-to-precook types.

Fresh Lasagne

Readily available, this is the better choice. Cook the sheets in plenty of boiling salted water until just tender (about 3 minutes, or according to the instructions on the packet), then drain and use with any sauce you like.

Boiling Lasagne

Follow the steps below to pre-cook lasagne successfully.
1 Lower the sheets, one at a time, into a large saucepan of boiling salted water. Stir them as soon as they are in the saucepan to prevent them sticking together.
2 Boil until tender (how long this will take varies according to type).
3 Lay out a couple of clean teatowels. Drain the pasta in a colander, then rinse it with cold running water, separating the sheets.
4 Lay the sheets out on the teatowels and mop their tops with kitchen paper.

THE CHOICE OF DISH
I think this is the most difficult aspect of making lasagne! Look out for a straight-sided rectangular dish that is slightly deeper than the usual gratin dishes. A good kitchen shop will usually offer one or two suitable dishes. The other practical possibility is to use a traditional, deep-sided roasting tin.

Lasagne al Forno

SERVES 6–8

1 quantity Bolognese Sauce (see page 57)

½ quantities Béchamel Sauce
  (see page 56)

about 8–10 sheets lasagne (see page 37)

salt and freshly ground black pepper

a little butter, for greasing

25 g (1 oz) fresh white breadcrumbs

4 tbsp freshly grated Parmesan cheese

50 g (2 oz) mozzarella cheese,
  finely chopped

Baked lasagne, layered with meat and topped with Béchamel Sauce is an international favourite. A Good Green Salad has to be the inseparable accompaniment for this dish.

Pre-heat the oven to 180°C/350°F/Gas Mark 4 and grease a large, rectangular ovenproof dish of about 30–38 X 20 cm (12–15 X 8 inches). Make the Bolognese and Béchamel Sauces as given on pages 57 and 56.

Cook the lasagne in plenty of boiling salted water according to the instructions on the packet or allow 3 minutes for fresh pasta. Drain well and rinse it under cold water, then lay the sheets out on a clean teatowel to dry.

Spread some of the Bolognese Sauce in the bottom of the prepared dish, then dot some of the Béchamel Sauce over it. Top with a layer of pasta. Continue layering the Bolognese Sauce, Béchamel Sauce and pasta, ending with a layer of pasta and with a good quantity of Béchamel Sauce left. Pour this over the top to coat the pasta completely.

Mix the breadcrumbs, Parmesan and mozzarella, then sprinkle this over the top of the lasagne. Bake in the pre-heated oven for 45–50 minutes, or until the topping is crisp and golden and the layers are bubbling hot.

Prawn Lasagne Pots

SERVES 4

4 sheets fresh lasagne

salt and freshly ground black pepper

50 g (2 oz) butter

2 garlic cloves, finely chopped

225 g (8 oz) peeled, cooked prawns

50 g (2 oz) button mushrooms,
  thinly sliced

3 tbsp chopped fresh parsley

4 tbsp freshly grated Parmesan cheese

4 tbsp single cream

2 tbsp dried white breadcrumbs

sprigs of parsley and lemon, quartered
  and sliced, to garnish

Circles of lasagne conceal buttery garlic prawns and mushrooms. The pasta absorbs the juices to make a well-balanced first course.

Pre-heat the oven to 200°C/400°F/Gas Mark 6.

Cook the lasagne in boiling salted water for 4 minutes, or until tender. Drain and rinse under cold water, then lay the sheets on a clean teatowel to dry. Using a ramekin dish as a guide, cut out two circles of pasta from each sheet.

Melt the butter in a small saucepan. Add the garlic cloves and cook gently for 2 minutes. Remove the saucepan from the heat and mix in the prawns, mushrooms and parsley with salt and pepper to taste.

Place a spoonful of the prawn mixture in the bottom of each of four ramekin dishes. Top with a circle of pasta, then share the remaining prawn mixture among the ramekins. Cover with another circle of pasta and press down firmly. Sprinkle the cheese over the pasta, then trickle the cream over and finally sprinkle with breadcrumbs.

Stand the ramekins on a baking tray and cook for 10–15 minutes, until browned on top and hot. Garnish with parsley and lemon and serve at once.

Smoked Haddock Lasagne

SERVES 6

a little butter, for greasing

about 8–10 sheets lasagne (see page 33)

double quantity Béchamel Sauce
  (see page 56)

750 g (1½ lb) smoked haddock fillets,
  skinned and cut into chunks

4 eggs, hard-boiled and roughly chopped

4 tbsp chopped fresh parsley

grated rind of ½ a lemon

salt and freshly ground black pepper

75 g (3 oz) mature Cheddar cheese, grated

3 tbsp dried white breadcrumbs

Pre-heat the oven to 180°C/350°F/Gas Mark 4. Grease a large, rectangular, ovenproof dish with butter.

Cook the lasagne in plenty of boiling salted water according to the instructions on the packet or allow 3minutes for fresh pasta. Drain well and rinse it under cold water, then lay the sheets out on a clean teatowel.

Make the Béchamel Sauce as given on page 56.

Mix the haddock, eggs, parsley, lemon rind and a little salt and pepper together in a bowl. Place about a third of the fish mixture in the dish, then coat with some of the sauce (just under a quarter of the total volume) and top with lasagne. Layer the remaining fish, sauce and lasagne, ending with a layer of lasagne and reserving enough sauce to coat it.

Add 50 g (2 oz) of the cheese to the remaining sauce, then pour it over the top of the lasagne. Mix the remaining cheese with the breadcrumbs and sprinkle the mixture over the top of the sauce. Bake in the pre-heated oven for about 45 minutes, or until the topping is golden brown and the sauce is bubbling hot.

Hidden Oysters

SERVES 4

12 oysters

1 tbsp lemon juice

salt and freshly ground black pepper

50 g (2 oz) butter, melted and cooled

50 g (2 oz) soup pasta

200 ml (1/3 pt) Béchamel Sauce
  (see page 56)

2 tbsp freshly grated Parmesan cheese

2 tbsp chopped fresh parsley

lemon slices and sprigs of parsley, to
  garnish (optional)

The browned topping of creamy pasta conceals lightly cooked oysters. Serve thin rye bread and butter with this first course.

Shuck the oysters, saving their liquor, then place both in a bowl. Add the lemon juice and a little salt and pepper. Divide the oysters between four ovenproof shell dishes or single gratin dishes. Spoon the butter over and set aside on a baking tray.

Pre-heat the oven to 200°C/400°F/Gas Mark 6.

Cook the pasta in plenty of boiling salted water for about 10 minutes, or until tender, then drain well.

Meanwhile, make the Béchamel Sauce as given on page 56.

Mix the pasta with the Béchamel Sauce, then add the Parmesan and parsley with salt and pepper if necessary. Spoon pasta mixture over the oysters, then bake in the pre-heated oven for about 20 minutes, or until the pasta mixture has browned and the oysters cooked. Serve at once, garnished, if liked, with slices of lemon and sprigs of parsley.

Pork and Pasta Peppers

SERVES 4

100 g (4 oz) soup pasta

salt and freshly ground black pepper

4 red or green peppers

2 tbsp olive oil

1 onion, finely chopped

1 celery stick, chopped

1 garlic clove, crushed

225 g (8 oz) minced pork

1 tbsp chopped fresh oregano

397 g (14 oz) tin chopped tomatoes

1 tbsp tomato purée

150 g (5 oz) mozzarella cheese, cut into four slices

Pre-heat the oven to 180°C/350°F/Gas Mark 4.

Cook the pasta in boiling salted water for about 7 minutes, or until tender. Drain well.

Meanwhile, cut the tops off the peppers and scoop out the seeds and core. Rinse and drain well, reserving the lids.

Heat the oil in a frying pan. Add the onion, celery, garlic and pork. Cook, stirring, until the onion has softened and the meat lightly browned. Stir in the oregano, tomatoes, tomato purée and salt and pepper. Remove from the heat and mix in the pasta.

Stand the peppers in an ovenproof dish, cutting the merest sliver off their bases, if necessary, to make them stand upright. Spoon the meat and pasta mixture into the peppers, cover the dish and bake in the pre-heated oven for 40 minutes.

Place a slice of mozzarella on top of each pepper, then replace their tops. Cover loosely with foil and bake for a further 20 minutes.

Soufflé-topped Pasta

This can also be cooked in single soufflé or gratin dishes, when it actually looks better, but it tastes just as good when it is baked in one large dish.

SERVES 4

175 g (6 oz) orecchiette

1 large leek, sliced

salt and freshly ground black pepper

2 courgettes, thinly sliced

100 g (4 oz) mushrooms, sliced

½ quantity Rich Tomato Sauce (see page 54)

8 tbsp freshly grated Parmesan cheese

3 eggs, separated

75 g (3 oz) Cheddar cheese, grated

3 tbsp plain flour

3 tbsp milk

Pre-heat the oven to 190°C/375°F/Gas Mark 5.

Cook the orecchiette and leek together in boiling salted water for about 15 minutes, or until tender. Add the courgettes for the last minute before draining the pasta, to blanch them lightly. Drain the pasta mixture well.

Meanwhile, make the Rich Tomato Sauce as given on page 54.

Turn the pasta mixture into a casserole or deep, ovenproof dish. Mix in the mushrooms, Rich Tomato Sauce, salt and pepper, and half the Parmesan. Smooth the top of the pasta mixture level.

Mix the egg yolks, Cheddar, remaining Parmesan and flour, then beat in the milk. Pound the mixture thoroughly and add a little salt and pepper. Whisk the egg whites until stiff and fold them into the cheese mixture. Spread this over the top of the pasta and bake for 30 minutes, or until the topping has risen and browned. Serve at once.

Pasta-filled Aubergines

SERVES 4

2 large aubergines 675 g (1½ lb)

salt and freshly ground black pepper

100 g (4 oz) soup pasta

50 g (2 oz) butter

1 onion, finely chopped

50 g (2 oz) button mushrooms, chopped

8 tbsp single cream

8 tbsp grated Parmesan cheese

2 tbsp chopped fresh parsley

2 closed cap mushrooms, sliced, a little lemon juice and a few sprigs of parsley,
   to garnish

The shells are not eaten, so be sure to scoop out all the soft middle of the aubergine. A side salad of tomatoes, olives and croutons on a leafy base is ideal with this creamy pasta filling.

Cut the aubergines in half lengthways and scoop out the flesh. Reserve the shells, placing them in a gratin dish.

Cut the flesh into chunks and place it in a colander, sprinkling the layers with salt. Set aside over a bowl for 20 minutes, then rinse well and pat dry. Chop the aubergine flesh finely.

Cook the pasta in boiling salted water for about 7 minutes or according to the instructions on the packet until just tender. Melt the butter in a saucepan and add the onion. Cook, stirring, for 5 minutes. Then add the chopped aubergine and mushrooms and continue to cook for about 15–20 minutes, or until the vegetables are cooked.

Stir in the pasta, cream, Parmesan and parsley with salt and pepper to taste. Divide this mixture between the aubergine shells, spooning it into them neatly. Cook under a hot grill until they are golden on top.

Quickly toss the mushroom slices in lemon juice, top the aubergines with the mushroom slices and sprigs of parsley, then serve at once.

Seafood Lasagne

SERVES 6

FOR THE LASAGNE

a little butter, for greasing

about 8–10 sheets lasagne (see page 33)

1 quantity White Wine Sauce (see page 56)

10 fresh scallops, shelled and sliced

225 g (8 oz) cooked, shelled mussels

225 g (8 oz) peeled, cooked prawns, defrosted and
  drained if frozen

450 g (1 lb) salmon fillet, skinned and cut into chunks

2 tbsp chopped fresh parsley

2 tbsp chopped fresh dill (optional)

salt and freshly ground black pepper

FOR THE TOPPING

1 tbsp plain flour

150 ml (¼ pt) milk

2 eggs

300 ml (½ pt) single cream

4 tbsp freshly grated Parmesan cheese

Pre-heat the oven to 180°C/350°/Gas Mark 4. Grease a large, rectangular, ovenproof dish with butter.

Cook the lasagne in plenty of boiling salted water according to the instructions on the packet or allow 3 minutes for fresh pasta. Drain well and rinse it under cold water, then lay the sheets out on a clean teatowel to dry.

Make the White Wine Sauce as given on page 56 and remove from the heat. Stir in the scallops, mussels, prawns, salmon, parsley, dill and salt and pepper to taste. Layer the seafood mixture and lasagne in the dish, starting with seafood and ending with pasta.

To make the topping, place the flour in a large bowl and gradually whisk in the milk. Whisk in the eggs, then, when they are thoroughly combined, lightly whisk in the cream and Parmesan with a little salt and pepper to taste. Pour this mixture over the top of the lasagne and bake in the pre-heated oven for about 40 minutes, or until it has set and browned.

Turkey and Chestnut Lasagne

Look out for vacuum-packed tinned chestnuts and shrink-wrapped packets of cooked chestnuts in supermarkets and delicatessens. The shrink-wrapped packets 225 g (8 oz) are sometimes displayed near the fresh vegetables and are certainly available round Christmas time, so it is worth stocking up as they have a long shelf-life

SERVES 6

a little oil, for greasing

about 8–10 sheets lasagne (see page 33).

salt and freshly ground black pepper

double quantity Béchamel Sauce (see page 56)

100 g (4 oz) lean rindless bacon

6 spring onions, chopped

450 g (1 lb) cooked turkey, diced

225 g (8 oz) cooked, peeled chestnuts (see left)

2 tbsp chopped fresh sage

2 tbsp chopped fresh parsley

50 g (2 oz) Cheddar cheese, grated

Pre-heat the oven to 180°C/350°F/Gas Mark 4. Grease a large, rectangular, ovenproof dish with a little oil.

Cook the lasagne in plenty of boiling salted water according to the instructions on the packet or allow 3 minutes for fresh pasta. Drain well and rinse it under cold water, then lay the sheets out on a clean teatowel. Make the Béchamel Sauce as given on page 56.

Place the bacon in a large, heavy-based saucepan and cook gently until the fat runs, then stir in the spring onions and cook for 2 minutes.

Cook's TIP

If you want to make a less rich topping, then use low-fat plain yoghurt instead of the cream.

Remove the saucepan from the heat and pour in half the Béchamel Sauce. Stir in the turkey, chestnuts, sage and parsley. Taste for seasoning, then layer this sauce and the lasagne in the dish, starting with the sauce and ending with the pasta.

Stir the cheese into the remaining Béchamel Sauce and pour it over the top of the lasagne. Bake the lasagne for about 45 minutes, until browned.

Above: Turkey and Chestnut Lasagne.

Mushroom Ring

SERVES 4–6

FOR THE PASTA

225 g (8 oz) lasagne verdi or half white lasagne

salt and freshly ground black pepper

2 tbsp olive oil

2 large onions, finely chopped

2 garlic cloves, crushed

450 g (1 lb) mushrooms, chopped

50 g (2 oz) fresh breadcrumbs

350 g (12 oz) ricotta cheese, sieved

2 tbsp chopped fresh sage

2 tbsp chopped fresh parsley

1 egg

FOR THE FILLING

50 g (2 oz) butter or 2 tbsp olive oil

350 g (12 oz) tomatoes, peeled, de-seeded and quartered

2 tbsp snipped chives

Pre-heat the oven to 180°C/350°F/Gas Mark 4 and use a little of the oil to grease a 1¼ l (2 pt) ring tin or mould.

First, cook the lasagne in plenty of boiling salted water according to the instructions on the packet or allow 3 minutes for fresh pasta. Drain and rinse under cold water,then lay the sheets out on a clean teatowel to dry.

Heat the remaining oil in a large saucepan. Add the onions and garlic and cook, stirring occasionally, for 10 minutes. Add the mushrooms and cook for about 15 minutes, or until they are well reduced. Boil off the excess liquid, then remove the saucepan from the heat.

Stir in the breadcrumbs, ricotta cheese, salt and pepper to taste, the sage, parsley and egg. Line the ring tin with pasta, using alternate pieces of green and white if you are using two colours. Leave the excess pasta overhanging the edge of the tin. Fill with the mushroom mixture, then fold the excess pasta over the top. Cover with greased foil and bake in the pre-heated oven for 1 hour. Leave to stand for 15 minutes.

Meanwhile, melt the butter or heat the oil for the filling in a large frying pan. Quickly sauté the tomatoes for a couple of minutes. Add salt and pepper to taste and the chives. Slide a knife between the pasta and the tin or mould to loosen it, then cover with a flat platter and invert the ring. Remove the tin or mould and fill the middle of the ring with the tomatoes. Serve at once.

Peperonata Pasta Round

SERVES 6–8

¼ quantity Rich Egg Pasta Dough (see page 40)

salt and freshly ground black pepper

4 tbsp olive oil

2 large onions, finely chopped

2 red peppers, de-seeded and chopped

2 green peppers, de-seeded and chopped

2 garlic cloves, crushed

1 tbsp chopped fresh oregano

450 g (1 lb) tomatoes, peeled and sliced

4 tbsp chopped fresh parsley

300 g (10 oz) mozzarella cheese, thinly sliced

1 quantity Béchamel Sauce (see page 56)

3 tbsp freshly grated Parmesan cheese

3 tbsp dried white breadcrumbs

Make the pasta dough as given on page 40. Cut the pasta dough in half, then roll out each half to form a large round. Use a 25 cm (10 in) round baking dish to cut out a circle of pasta to fit the dish. Repeat with the remaining dough.

Cook both circles in a large saucepan of boiling salted water for 3–4 minutes. Drain the pasta and rinse it under cold running water, then open out the circles and lay them on a clean teatowel to dry.

Pre-heat the oven to 180°C/350°F/Gas Mark 4.

Grease the dish with a little of the oil, then heat the remainder in a saucepan. Add the onions, peppers and garlic. Mix well, cover the saucepan and cook gently for 20 minutes, or until the vegetables have softened but not browned.

Meanwhile, make the Béchamel Sauce as given on page 56.

Stir the oregano and salt and pepper to taste into the vegetable mixture.

Lay the first pasta round in the dish. Spoon half the pepper mixture into the dish. Top with half the tomatoes, then sprinkle with half the parsley. Lay half the mozzarella slices on top and dot with a little of the Béchamel Sauce, placing the occasional spoonful here and there on top of the cheese. Sprinkle with a little salt and pepper. Then lay the second pasta round on top.

Repeat the layers with the remaining mixture, reserving most of the Béchamel Sauce to cover the top of the lasagne. Stir the Parmesan cheese into the remaining Béchamel Sauce and pour it over the lasagne. Then bake in the pre heated oven for about 45 minutes, or until it has browned on top and is bubbling hot throughout. Leave to stand for 10 minutes, then serve.

Above: Peperonata Pasta Round

Spinach Lasagne

I have added sautéed leeks to the grated spinach filling for this popular lasagne combination. It is great for vegetarians and confirmed carnivores alike.

SERVES 4

about 8–10 sheets lasagne (see page 33)

salt and freshly ground black pepper

2 tbsp olive oil

225 g (8 oz) leeks, thinly sliced

2 garlic cloves, crushed

600 ml (1 pt) Béchamel Sauce (see page 56)

1 kg (2¼ lb) fresh baby spinach leaves, washed and grated

450 g (1 lb) ricotta cheese, sieved

freshly grated nutmeg

6 tbsp freshly grated Parmesan cheese

Pre-heat the oven to 180°C/350°F/Gas Mark 4. Grease a large, rectangular, ovenproof dish with a little of the oil. Cook the lasagne in plenty of boiling salted water according to the instructions on the packet or allow 3 minutes for fresh pasta. Drain well and rinse it under cold water, then lay the sheets out on a clean teatowel to dry.

Heat the remaining oil in a large saucepan. Add the leeks and garlic, then cook, stirring often, for about 15 minutes, or until the leeks are tender.

Meanwhile, make the Béchamel Sauce as given on page 56.

Mix the spinach with the leeks and garlic, cover the saucepan tightly and cook for about 5 minutes, or until the spinach has become limp and is just tender. Remove the saucepan from the heat. Mix in the ricotta with salt and pepper to taste and a little nutmeg.

Layer the spinach mixture and lasagne in the dish, starting with spinach mixture and ending with lasagne. Stir the Parmesan into the Béchamel Sauce and pour this over the lasagne. Bake in the pre-heated oven for about 45 minutes, or until the top has browned and is bubbling.

Bacon and Artichoke Lasagne

This is rich and very tasty, with an unusual tarragon sauce for a topping.

SERVES 6

FOR THE LASAGNE

2 x 285 g (10 oz) jars seasoned artichokes in olive oil

100 g (4 oz) lean rindless bacon, diced

1 onion, halved and sliced

1 red chilli, de-seeded and chopped (see Cook's Tip, page 80)

1 leek, sliced

2 garlic cloves, crushed

1 tbsp plain flour

397 g (14 oz) tin chopped tomatoes

50 g (2 oz) tin anchovy fillets, drained and chopped

salt and freshly ground black pepper

about 175 g (6 oz) lasagne (see page 33)

FOR THE TARRAGON SAUCE

25 g (1 oz) butter

25 g (1 oz) plain flour

450 ml (¾ pt) milk

1 tbsp chopped fresh tarragon

50 g (2 oz) mature Cheddar cheese, grated

Pre-heat the oven to 180°C/350°F/Gas Mark 4.

Now make the lasagne. Drain the oil from one of the jars of artichokes into a large saucepan. Drain the second jar, saving the oil, but it is not required for this recipe. Heat the oil in the saucepan, add the bacon, onion, chilli, leek and garlic. Stir well, then cover the saucepan and cook for 15 minutes.

Stir in the flour, then add the tomatoes, anchovy fillets and the artichokes. Add salt and pepper to taste and bring to the boil. Set aside.

Cook the lasagne in plenty of boiling salted water according to the instructions on the packet or allow 3 minutes for fresh pasta. Drain and rinse under cold water, then lay out on a clean teatowel to dry.

Layer the artichoke sauce and cooked lasagne in a large, rectangular, ovenproof dish, starting with the sauce and ending with lasagne.

Next, make the tarragon sauce. Melt the butter in a saucepan. Stir in the flour, then stir in the milk and bring to the boil. Add the tarragon, cheese and salt and pepper to taste, and stir over a low heat until the cheese has melted.

Pour the tarragon sauce over the lasagne and bake in the pre-heated oven for about 45 minutes, or until it is bubbling hot and golden brown.

Below: Bacon and Artichoke Lasagne

Swede Terrine

SERVES 6

450 g (1 lb) swede, peeled and cubed

salt and freshly ground black pepper

50 g (2 oz) butter

1 small onion, finely chopped

100 g (4 oz) mature Cheddar cheese, grated

50 g (2 oz) slightly dry white breadcrumbs

3 large eggs, beaten

175 g (6 oz) elbow macaroni

75 g (3 oz) mascarpone

3 tbsp plain flour

3 tbsp freshly grated Parmesan cheese

This was a slightly wild card idea that turned out to be a great success. The macaroni formed a lovely crusty base and top and the swede mixture was light and well-flavoured. You do need to use a good non-stick saucepan or non-stick baking parchment, though. A crisp salad of frisée and very finely sliced carrot or Grated Courgette and Basil Salad are ideal accompaniments.

Pre-heat the oven to 180°C/350°F/Gas Mark 4. Grease a 1 kg (2 lb) loaf tin using half of the butter. If the tin is not a good non-stick one, then line its base with non-stick baking parchment.

Cook the swede in boiling salted water for about 10 minutes, or until tender.

Meanwhile, melt the remaining butter in a saucepan and add the onion. Cook, stirring, for 5 minutes.

Drain the swede and mash it thoroughly until smooth, then stir in the onion, cheese and breadcrumbs with salt and pepper to taste. Cool slightly before mixing in 2 of the eggs.

Cook the macaroni in boiling salted water until tender — about 7 minutes, or according to the instructions on the packet.

Drain the macaroni and mix the mascarpone into it. Stir in the flour, Parmesan and salt and pepper to taste. Spread half the macaroni mixture in the base of the tin. Top with the swede mixture, smoothing this evenly over the macaroni, then spread the remaining macaroni mixture on top.

Bake the terrine in the pre-heated oven for 1 hour, or until it feels firm and the top has browned lightly. Slide a flat-bladed knife between the mixture and the tin, then invert the tin on to a flat serving platter. Remove the lining paper, if used, and serve cut into thick slices.

Chicken and Vegetable Lasagne

SERVES 6

3 tbsp olive oil

about 8–10 sheets lasagne (see page 33)

salt and freshly ground black pepper

1 garlic clove, crushed

1 large onion, chopped

4 celery sticks, sliced

1 carrot, diced

4 boneless chicken breasts, skinned
  and diced

100 g (4 oz) mushrooms, sliced

2 x 397 g (14 oz) tins chopped tomatoes

150 ml (¼ pt) water

1 bay leaf

2 tbsp chopped fresh or
  1 tbsp dried oregano

100 g (4 oz) French beans, cut into
  short lengths

100 g (4 oz) frozen peas

1 quantity Béchamel Sauce (see page 56)

150 g (5 oz) mozzarella cheese, chopped

Pre-heat the oven to 180°C/350°F/Gas Mark 4. Grease a large, rectangular, ovenproof dish with a little of the oil.

Cook the lasagne in plenty of boiling salted water according to the instructions on the packet or allow 3 minutes for fresh pasta. Drain well and rinse them under cold water, then lay the sheets out on a clean teatowel to dry.

Heat the remaining oil in a large saucepan. Add the garlic, onion, celery, carrot and chicken. Stir well and fry the mixture until the onion has softened. Add the tomatoes, water, bay leaf, oregano and plenty of salt and pepper. Heat until simmering, then cover the saucepan and simmer for 15 minutes.

Meanwhile, make the Béchamel Sauce as given on page 56.

Stir the beans and peas into the vegetable and chicken mixture and simmer, covered, for a further 5 minutes.

Layer the vegetable and chicken sauce and pasta in the prepared dish, starting with sauce and ending with lasagne. Cover with the Béchamel Sauce, then sprinkle the mozzarella over the top. Bake in the pre-heated oven for 40–50 minutes, or until the topping is golden and the lasagne is bubbling hot.

ORIENTAL SPECIALITIES

The range of pasta products, cookery styles and ingredients used in the orient is enormous. There are, however, similarities that run through the veins of Chinese, Japanese, Malaysian, Singaporean and Thai cookery which I have included here.

This chapter offers some traditional noodle dishes along with interpretations of the themes and flavours that are characteristic of the countries. There are occasional specialist ingredients, for which you may have to travel, but only as far as. A specialist shop in a large town or city. Once you have made the trip, many of the dry ingredients keep for years and some fresh foods can be frozen.

Dim sum are a feature of this chapter. These Chinese snacks date back to the tenth century – perhaps these are the early forms of pasta that Marco Polo found he just could not leave behind.

Leave behind. Dim sum are traditionally served as part of a tea meal, with Chinese tea served as a refresher throughout. You will be able to buy them throughout the day in an authentic Chinese café and they are ideal when shopping gets to be too much and you need a little reviver.

My Hong Kong tourist guide tells me that dim sum literally means "to touch the heart", but it is a light snack in modern terms. They certainly made a lasting impression on me – I hope you enjoy them, too.

Chinese Dim Sum

Dim sum are snacks, traditionally served in tea houses as a form of daytime refreshment and sustenance. Chinese restaurants usually serve dim sum from lunchtime through until the early evening; however, some specialise in these popular dishes and make a feature of providing quite a number of dim sum throughout the day, including main meal times. These may include a wide variety of foods, such as barbecued spare ribs and so on, served in small quantities, but it is the dumplings, won ton and spring rolls that have made dim sum internationally famous.

Using Bamboo Steamers

Piping hot steamed dim sum are served directly from the bamboo steamers in which they are cooked. Bamboo steamers come in a variety of sizes, from as small as 10 cm (4 in) in diameter to wide containers that fit over woks.

These large steamers are stacked on a wok and a lid is placed over the top layer to keep in the steam. The lattice of bamboo slats inside the steamer is greased well and the small dumplings or other dim sum are placed directly on it. However, it is more hygienic and there is less danger of the dim sum sticking if the dim sum are placed on a flat, greased plate. The plate should fit inside the steamer with plenty of space to spare round the sides so that the steam can rise through the layers. Alternatively, the perforated foil technique described below may be used.

Using a Steamer on a Saucepan

Steamers that are graduated in size to fit on top of a saucepan do not afford as much space for cooking dim sum as the bamboo type. The dim sum can be placed directly on the greased steamer, however when cooking a large batch they are difficult to lift off.

A greased plate may be used but this must allow space around the side for the steam to rise through the layers.

A practical method is to cut a double thickness of heavy cookery foil to fit in the base of the steamer. Puncture it all over to allow the steam through, then grease it well. Place the dim sum on the foil and place them in the steamer. Another method used for larger steamed buns is to place a small square of non-stick paper under each bun. As the focus here is on pasta, you will not find recipes for these, but this method can be adopted for the dim sum given here, but it is rather time-consuming, placing each dumpling on a tiny square of paper.

Keep the Pot Boiling

Make sure the water is boiling vigorously so that there is plenty of steam to cook the dim sum. There must also be sufficient water in the wok or saucepan to boil for the complete cooking time. If you are cooking dim sum in batches, you may need to keep a kettle of boiling water nearby to top up the saucepan under the steamer.

Garnishing Oriental Style

Colourful vegetable garnishes are used in oriental cookery. You will need a small, fine-pointed knife with a sharp blade. Special knives with very small, narrow blades for intricate cutting are sold quite cheaply in hardware shops or good-quality carving knives and tools are available from good cookshops and catering suppliers.

Remember that if you plan on cooking a range of dishes or selection of dim sum, then you really must prepare the garnishes well in advance – make them the day before and chill them overnight. Spring onion curls are described on page 256, but here are a few additional ideas for presentation.

Radish Roses

Make small, crescent-shaped cuts down into the sides of the radish in a row around the base. The cuts should loosen a thin peeling of red skin. Then work around, making a second series of cuts above the first row, this time cutting the crescents so that the first starts in the middle of one on the lower row and ends in the middle of the next one. Continue cutting into the radish, building up the layers of petals all round the outside of the vegetable, right up to the top. Place in iced water until the "petals" separate from the radish to open out like a flower – the thinner the cuts, the quicker the flower opens, but it takes at least 30 minutes and they should be left for about an hour – leaving them longer makes the flower open more fully!

Stamping out Carrot Shapes

Thinly slice large carrots and cook in boiling water for 3–4 minutes, then drain well. Use aspic cutters to stamp out a shape from each slice.

Carrot Flowers

Use a canelle knife to pare strips off the length of a carrot, cutting evenly spaced channels around the vegetable. Slice the carrot and blanch in boiling water for 2 minutes.

Chilli Curls

To make chilli curls, use a small, sharp knife to cut a fresh chilli into fine strips lengthways, working from the stalk end towards the point, and leaving all the strips attached at the stalk. Rinse out the seeds and scrape out the middle of the chilli as you work. Place the chilli in a bowl of iced water for at least 30 minutes, or until the strips curl.

Cucumber Curls

Cut 20 cm (4 in) lengths of cucumber. Peel the cucumber, then use a vegetable peeler to pare off thin slices down the length of the cucumber. Curl the long slices around loosely in an informal, ringlet-like arrangement.

Cucumber – Skin Shapes

Cut off thin lengths of cucumber skin and use aspic cutters to stamp out shapes. Alternatively, use a fine-pointed knife to cut out leaves freehand. Cut fine veins out of the skin.

Prawn Har Kow

Once you get into the swing of shaping and filling these little dumplings, they are fun to prepare. If you become extremely adept at making them, then you may want to progress to making tiny, bite-sized dumplings, in which case the quantities given will make between 35 and 40 dumplings.

MAKES 24
FOR THE DUMPLINGS
a little oil

175 g (6 oz) peeled, cooked prawns

1 spring onion, very finely chopped

2 tbsp very finely chopped celery

2 tbsp very finely chopped tinned bamboo shoots

1 tbsp light soy sauce

2 tsp cornflour

1 egg, beaten

1 quantity Dim Sum Dough (see page 49)

cornflour, for rolling out

FOR THE DIPPING SAUCE
1 garlic clove, finely chopped

6 tbsp soy sauce

2 tbsp dry sherry

TO GARNISH
spring onion curls (see Cook's Tip 199)

whole cooked prawns

Prepare a steamer using a little oil (see page 254).

First, make the dumplings. Mince the prawns or chop them very finely in a food processor. Alternatively, chop them finely by hand, then pound them with the back of a mixing spoon or in a mortar with a pestle until they form a coarse paste. Add the spring onion, celery, bamboo shoots, soy sauce and cornflour. Mix the ingredients thoroughly, adding a tsp of the beaten egg if necessary to bind them together.

Make the Dim Sum Dough as given on page 49, then divide the dough in half, and mark each half into 12 equal portions. Cut off one portion and keep the rest of the dough covered. Press out the dough into a circle, then roll it or press it out into a circle measuring about 5–7½ cm (2–3 in) in diameter on a work surface lightly dusted with cornflour.

Place a little of the prawn mixture in the middle of the circle of dough and brush the edge of the dough with a little egg. Fold the dough over the filling to form a shape like a miniature pasty. Pinch the edges of the dough together fluting them decoratively. Place in the prepared steamer. Continue shaping and filling the Har Kow, using all the dough and filling.

Steam the Har Kow dumplings over boiling water for about 10 minutes, or until the dough is cooked, firm and glossy.

Meanwhile prepare the dipping sauce. Mix the garlic, soy sauce and sherry together, then divide it between four small dishes.

Serve the freshly cooked Har Kow garnished with spring onion curls and whole cooked prawns.

Crispy Won Ton Noodles

SERVES 6–8
1 quantity Won Ton Dough, made with baking powder (see page 48)

oil, for frying

Cut the dough in half and roll out one portion thinly on a surface dusted with cornflour. Dust the top of the dough with cornflour, then roll it up loosely. Cut the roll of dough into 5 mm (¼ in) wide slices, then shake them out to make narrow noodles.

Heat sufficient oil to deep-fry the noodles to 190°C/375°F/Gas Mark 5 or until a cube of day-old bread browns in about 30 seconds. Deep-fry the noodles, a handful at a time, until they have puffed up and are crisp and golden. Drain well on kitchen paper.

Above: Prawn Har Kow.

COOK'S TIP

To make spring onion curls, cut the green part of the trimmed onions into fine strips, leaving them attached at the root end. Place in a bowl of iced water for at least 30 minutes. The finely cut green part of the onion will curl during soaking. Drain well before using.

Sweet-and-Sour Pork Won Tons

SERVES 4

about 175 g (6 oz) lean boneless pork

pinch of five spice powder

1 tsp sesame oil

1 garlic clove, finely chopped

1 tbsp soy sauce

18 squares Won Ton Dough made with
    baking powder (see page 48) or ready-
    made wrappers

1 egg, beaten

1 quantity Sweet-and-sour Sauce
    (see page 58)

oil for deep frying

These are delicious – one of my (many) favourite Chinese dishes!

Cut the pork into 18 small, neat pieces, no bigger than 1 cm (½ in) cubes. Place the cubes of meat in a bowl and sprinkle with a good pinch of five spice powder, the sesame oil, garlic and soy sauce. Leave to marinate for a few hours or overnight, allowing plenty of time for the meat to become well-flavoured with garlic and spice.

Brush the middle of a square of Won Ton Dough or a wrapper with a little egg and place a piece of meat on it. Then gather the dough around the meat to make a tiny bundle with frilly edges. Fill and shape all the Won Tons in the same way, then make the Sweet-and-sour Sauce as given on page 63.

Heat sufficient oil to deep-fry the Won Tons to 190°C/375°F/Gas Mark 5 or until a cube of day-old bread browns in about 30 seconds. Fry the Won Tons, a few at a time, until they have puffed up, are golden and cooked through. Drain well on kitchen paper. Transfer to a serving platter and spoon the Sweet-and-sour Sauce over, then serve immediately.

Crispy Won Ton Parcels

MAKES 16

1 tbsp oil

1 tsp sesame oil

1 garlic clove, finely chopped

2 spring onions, finely chopped

2 tbsp chopped vegetables (bamboo shoots, water chestnuts, carrot, celery or a mixture, according to availability)

25 g (1 oz) beansprouts

225 g (8 oz) minced pork

salt

1 quantity Won Ton Dough made with baking powder (see page 48)

cornflour, for dusting

1 egg white

oil, for frying

These are an adaptation of spring rolls.

Heat the oil and sesame oil in a small saucepan. Add the garlic, spring onions and vegetables and cook for 2 minutes. Add the beansprouts, stir well, then remove the saucepan from the heat. Mix the vegetables with the pork and add a little salt.

Make the Won Ton Dough as given on page 48, then cut it in half. Mark each half into eight portions. Cut off one portion of dough, then cover the rest. Roll out the portion of dough on a surface dusted with cornflour to form a thin circle about 10 cm (4 in) in diameter. Place a little of the meat mixture in the middle, pressing it together neatly. Brush the dough with a little lightly whisked egg white, then fold the side nearest you over the filling. Fold the sides of the dough in over the filling. Brush with egg white and roll up neatly to make a miniature spring roll. Repeat with the remaining dough and filling.

Heat sufficient oil to deep-fry the parcels to 190°C/ 375°F/Gas Mark 5 or until a cube of day-old bread browns in about 30 seconds. Fry the parcels until they are crisp and golden, turning them several times during cooking. Drain well on kitchen paper and serve piping hot.

Braised Chicken with Rice Sticks

SERVES 4

2 dried Chinese mushrooms

150 ml (¼ pt) hot water

2 boneless chicken breasts, skinned

1 carrot

1 tbsp oil

1 tsp sesame oil

1 red pepper, de-seeded and cut into 2½ cm (1 in) squares

4 spring onions, finely grated diagonally

1 garlic clove, chopped

1 piece of lemon grass

2½ cm (1 in) piece fresh root ginger, sliced

225 g (8 oz) tin bamboo shoots, sliced into thin strips

3 tbsp light soy sauce

¼ quantity Chinese-style Stock (see page 53)

225 g (8 oz) ribbon rice sticks

1 tbsp cornflour

3 tbsp dry sherry

Place the mushrooms in a bowl or mug. Add the water and cover, then leave to soak for 30 minutes. Drain the mushrooms, reserving the soaking liquid, and discard the stalks if they are tough, then slice the mushroom cap. Cut the chicken breasts across into fairly thick slices. Cut the carrot into 5 cm (2 in) lengths, then slice them very thinly lengthways into wide strips.

Heat the oil and sesame oil in a flameproof casserole. Add the pepper, carrot, spring onions, garlic, lemon grass and ginger. Stirfry for 2 minutes, then add the bamboo shoots, soy sauce and stock. Strain the soaking water from the mushrooms and add it to the saucepan with the mushroom slices. Heat until simmering, then add the chicken. Cover and cook gently for 30 minutes.

Towards the end of this time, cook the rice sticks according to the instructions on the packet, then drain and rinse them under cold water.

Blend the cornflour with the sherry. Stir the cornflour mixture into the sauce in the casserole and bring to the boil, stirring. Add the rice-sticks and simmer for 2 minutes. Serve at once.

Spicy Duck with Mango and Rice Sticks

SERVES 4

4 boneless duck breasts, skinned

2 tbsp soy sauce

2 garlic cloves, crushed

1 tbsp sesame oil

25 g (1 oz) fresh root ginger, peeled and cut into fine strips

2 tbsp hoisin sauce

2 tbsp dry sherry

350 g (12 oz) ribbon rice sticks

2 tbsp oil

1 bunch of spring onions, finely grated diagonally

350 g (10 oz) tin jelly mushrooms, drained

1 mango, peeled, stone removed and flesh cut into small pieces

50 g (2 oz) roast cashew nuts

Cut the duck breasts across into thin slices. Mix them with the soy sauce, garlic, sesame oil, ginger, hoisin sauce and sherry. Leave to marinate for 3–4 hours.

Cook the rice sticks according to the instructions on the packet.

Heat the oil in a large frying pan or wok. Use a slotted spoon to add the duck pieces, removing as much of the marinade from them as possible. Stirfry them briskly for 4–5 minutes, then add the remaining marinade with the jelly mushrooms. Heat through until the sauce is sizzling hot.

Drain the rice sticks and turn them into a dish. Mix the mango with the duck and sauce and immediately turn the mixture out on to the rice sticks. Serve at once.

Pork and Baby Corn Chow Mein

SERVES 4

225 g (8 oz) baby sweetcorn

225 g (8 oz) fresh or dried Chinese
egg noodles

1 tbsp oil

1 tsp sesame oil

175 g (6 oz) lean boneless pork,
cut into fine strips

25 g (1 oz) fresh root ginger, peeled and
cut into very fine strips

1 red pepper, de-seeded and
cut into fine strips

6 spring onions, grated diagonally

1 tsp cornflour

3 tbsp dry sherry

2 tbsp soy sauce

150 ml (¼ pt) chicken stock

Blanch the sweetcorn in boiling water for 2 minutes, then drain well. Cook the noodles according to the instructions on the packet or add fresh noodles to boiling water and bring back to the boil, then reduce the heat and cook for 3 minutes. Drain well and set aside.

Heat the oil and sesame oil in a large frying pan or wok. Add the pork and ginger, and stirfry until the meat is lightly browned in parts and just cooked.

Add the sweetcorn and red pepper and continue to stirfry for 2–3 minutes more. Then, add the spring onions and cook for a further 1 minute.

Blend the cornflour with the sherry, soy sauce and chicken stock, then stir the mixture into the pan and bring to the boil, stirring all the time. Add the noodles and toss them with the mixture for 2–3 minutes, until hot and well coated. Serve at once.

Spicy Beef Chow Mein

SERVES 4

450 g (1 lb) rump steak or frying steak

1 tbsp cornflour

1 tbsp fermented black beans

3 tbsp dry sherry

2 tbsp soy sauce

½ tsp five spice powder

1 garlic clove, crushed

1 tsp sesame oil

1 green chilli, de-seeded and chopped (Cook's Tip, page 80)

350 g (12 oz) fresh or dried Chinese egg noodles

2 tbsp oil

1 red pepper, de-seeded and cut into small squares

1 green pepper, de-seeded and cut into small squares

1 onion, quartered and cut across into small squares

300 ml (½ pt) chicken stock

Cut the beef across the grain into very thin slices (partially freezing the steak makes this easier). Place the meat in a non-metallic dish, add the cornflour and mix well. Then mix in the black beans, sherry, soy sauce, five spice powder, garlic, sesame oil and chilli. Cover and leave to marinate for 3–4 hours.

Cook the noodles according to the instructions on the packet or add fresh noodles to boiling water and bring back to the boil, then reduce the heat and cook for 3 minutes. Drain well.

Heat the oil in a wok or frying pan. Add the red and green peppers and onion. Stirfry for 2 minutes, then use a slotted spoon to drain the marinating juices from the beef and add the beef to the wok or pan. Stirfry until it is sealed and browned. Add the stock to the marinade, pour it into the wok or pan and bring to the boil, stirring.

Add the noodles and toss them with the meat and peppers until they are thoroughly reheated. Then, transfer the Chow Mein to a serving dish and serve at once.

Stirfried Squid with Rice Vermicelli

Most fishmongers and supermarkets sell prepared squid sacs, but if you buy whole, fresh squid, read the Cook's Tip below for advice on how to prepare them.

SERVES 4

350 g (12 oz) rice vermicelli

8 squid sacs (see Cook's Tip), thinly sliced

salt and freshly ground black pepper

2 tbsp cornflour

4 tbsp groundnut oil

2 red chillies, de-seeded and finely chopped
  (see Cook's Tip, page 80)

4 garlic cloves, finely chopped

6 spring onions, finely grated diagonally

2 tbsp light soy sauce

2 tbsp fish sauce

Soak the rice vermicelli in boiling water for about 3 minutes to soften the noodles, then drain well.

Toss the squid rings with salt, pepper and cornflour.

Heat the oil in a large frying pan or wok. Add the chillies and garlic and cook for 1 minute. Then add the squid rings and fry them briskly for a couple of minutes, until lightly browned. Use a slotted spoon to remove the squid rings from the pan and set aside.

Add the spring onions to the pan or wok, then add the vermicelli. Continue to fry for 2–3 minutes, turning rather than stirring the vermicelli. Add the soy sauce and fish sauce. Return the squid to the pan or wok, mix lightly and serve at once.

COOK'S TIP

To clean whole squid, first pull the head and tentacle parts out of the sac (the tentacles may be cut off the head and these can be fried if wished). Remove the fine, opaque quill that runs down the length of the inside of the sac. Then wash the sac, rubbing off the mottled skin from the outside to leave the sac clean and white.

Crispy Prawn Chow Mein

SERVES 4

225 g (8 oz) dried fine Chinese
  egg noodles

6 dried Chinese mushrooms

4 tbsp oil

1 tbsp sesame oil

1 large carrot, cut into fine
  matchstick strips

8 spring onions, grated diagonally

1 tbsp cornflour

6 tbsp soy sauce

6 tbsp dry sherry

350 g (12 oz) peeled, cooked prawns

Cook the egg noodles according to the instructions on the packet, then drain well.

Soak the mushrooms in a small basin in hot water to cover for 20 minutes, then drain, reserving and straining the liquid to remove any grit. Discard any tough stalks and slice the mushrooms.

Heat 1 tbsp of the oil and 1 tsp of the sesame oil in a large frying pan. Tip in the noodles and spread them out evenly, pressing them flat with the back of a spatula. Fry the noodles until they are crisp and golden underneath. Slide the noodles out on to a plate. Add another tbsp of the oil and tsp of the sesame oil to the pan. When the oil is hot, turn the noodles back into the pan, uncooked side down. Brown the underneath of the noodles, then slide them out on to the plate. Turn the noodles into a large serving dish, cover loosely with foil and keep hot.

Add the remaining oil and sesame oil to the pan. Stirfry the carrot, spring onions and mushrooms.

Blend the cornflour with the soy sauce, sherry and liquid drained from the mushrooms in a measuring jug. Make up the mixture to 450 ml (¾ pt) with water, then pour it into the pan and bring to the boil, stirring.all the time. Boil the sauce for 2 minutes.

Reduce the heat and stir in the prawns. Heat, without boiling, for 2 minutes. Pour the prawns in sauce over the noodles and serve at once.

Pan Stickers

These are cooked by frying and braising – the results are very tasty! A good non-stick frying pan with a lid is ideal for cooking these.

MAKES 24
FOR THE PAN STICKERS
1 dried Chinese mushroom
100 g (4 oz) minced pork
100 g (4 oz) minced steak
2 spring onions, finely chopped
1 garlic clove, crushed
1 tbsp finely chopped tinned bamboo shoots
1 tbsp soy sauce
1 tsp sesame oil
2 tsp cornflour
1 quantity Dim Sum Dough (see page 49)
cornflour, for dusting
1 egg, beaten
oil, for frying

FOR THE DIPPING SAUCE
tbsp soy sauce
4 tbsp dry sherry
1 spring onion, finely chopped

First, make the Pan Stickers. Place the mushroom in a small bowl or mug, pour in hot water to cover it, then leave to soak for 30 minutes. Drain well, reserving the soaking liquor, and remove the stalk if it is tough. Chop the mushroom finely, then mix it with the pork, steak, spring onions, garlic, bamboo shoots, soy sauce, sesame oil and cornflour. Pound the ingredients together well until thoroughly and evenly combined.

Make the Dim Sum Dough as given on page 49, then divide it in half. Mark each half into twelve equal portions. Cut off one portion and keep the rest of the dough covered. Press out the dough into a circle, then roll it or press it out further into a circle measuring about 57½ cm (2–3 in) in diameter on a work surface lightly dusted with cornflour.

Place a little of the meat mixture in the middle of the circle of dough and brush the edge of the dough with a little egg. Fold the dough over the filling to form a shape like that of a miniature pasty. Pinch the edges of the dough together to seal in the filling. Continue shaping and filling the pan stickers, using all the dough and filling.

Pour a thin layer of oil into a large frying pan (preferable one with a lid, or find a saucepan lid or plate that can be used to cover the pan later). Heat the oil and fry the Pan Stickers until they are golden underneath, then turn them over. Strain the reserved soaking liquor from the mushroom and add enough water to make it up to about 200 ml (7 fl oz). Pour this into the frying pan (you may have to add a little more water if the pan is large as the bottom of the pan needs to be completely covered).

Bring the water to the boil. Then reduce the heat and cover the pan. Braise the Pan Stickers for 15 minutes. Remove the lid and continue cooking until all the liquid has evaporated and the Pan Stickers are again frying. Continue to cook until they are browned on this second side, then carefully lift them out of the pan. Serve at once.

Wind-dried Sausage with Spinach

If you have not yet discovered Chinese sausages, then you have a real treat in store. They are sold in vacuum packs in oriental supermarkets, but, if you are not keen on offal or liver, check the ingredients and pay a little more for a pack that does not have liver listed significantly high on the list.

SERVES 4
4 wind-dried Chinese sausages
350 g (12 oz) fresh or dried Chinese egg noodles
3 tbsp oil
1 tbsp grated fresh root ginger
225 g (8 oz) baby sweetcorn
1 garlic clove
1 bunch o f spring onions, finely grated diagonally

4 celery sticks, cut into fine matchstick strips

100 g (4 oz) spinach, grated

100 g (4 oz) mange-tout

100 g (4 oz) button or closed cap mushrooms, thinly sliced

2 tsp cornflour

200 ml (⅓ pt) chicken stock

3 tbsp dry sherry

2 tbsp light soy sauce

Steam the sausages over boiling water for 20 minutes, or until tender. Cut the sausages diagonally into thin slices.

Meanwhile, cook the noodles according to the instructions on the packet or add fresh noodles to boiling water and bring back to the boil, then reduce the heat and cook for 3 minutes. Drain well.

Heat 1 tbsp of the oil in a large frying pan. Add the noodles and press them down into the pan. Cook until crisp and golden underneath, then slide the noodle cake out on to a large plate or platter. Add another tbsp of the oil to the pan. Invert the noodles into the pan, press down and cook as before. Transfer to a large plate and keep hot.

Heat the remaining oil in a large frying pan or wok. Add the ginger, sweetcorn, sausage slices and garlic. Stirfry for 2 minutes, then add the spring onions, spinach, celery, mange-tout and mushrooms. Blend the cornflour with the stock, sherry and soy sauce, then pour the liquid into the pan and bring to the boil, stirring.

Pour the sausage and vegetable mixture over the crispy noodles and serve at once. Cut the noodles into sections as you serve the mixture (if the noodles are sufficiently crisp when fried, then they still retain some crunch after the sauce has been poured over them).

Above: Wind-dried Sausage with Spinach

Vegetable Chow Mein with Deep-fried Bean Curd

SERVES 4

225 g (8 oz) firm bean curd

1 tsp sesame oil

2 tbsp cornflour

salt and freshly ground black pepper

pinch o f chilli powder

oil, for frying

350 g (12 oz) fresh or dried
  Chinese egg noodles

2 tbsp oil

2 leeks, thinly sliced

1 red or yellow pepper, halved, de-seeded
and cut into thin strips

225 g (8 oz) tin bamboo shoots, drained
  and cut into thin strips

225 g (8 oz) tin of water chestnuts,
drained and sliced

1 carrot, cut into fine matchstick strips

150 ml (¼ pt) vegetable stock

4 tbsp light soy sauce

4 tbsp dry sherry

1 tsp cornflour

¼ head of Chinese leaves, grated

Cut the bean curd into small cubes of about 1 cm (½ in) each side, then gently mix the sesame oil with them. Mix the cornflour with plenty of salt and pepper, and a pinch of chilli powder. Once the sesame oil is well mixed with the bean curd, tip the cornflour mixture over and mix lightly to coat all the pieces. Heat sufficient oil to deep-fry the bean curd to 190°C/375°F/Gas Mark 5 or until a cube of day-old bread browns in about 30 seconds. Deep-fry the bean curd until it is a pale golden colour, then drain well on kitchen paper.

Cook the noodles according to the instructions on the packet or add fresh noodles to boiling water and bring back to the boil, then reduce the heat and cook for 3 minutes. Drain well and set aside.

Heat the oil in a wok or large frying pan. Add the leeks, pepper, bamboo shoots, water chestnuts and carrot. Stirfry until the leeks and carrots have lost their raw texture without becoming soft (about 3–5 minutes).

Mix the stock, soy sauce and sherry into the cornflour, then add to the pan and bring to the boil stirring.

Add the Chinese leaves and noodles to the vegetable mixture. Mix well, then add the bean curd. Continue to mix the Chow Mein until it has thoroughly heated through (about 2 minutes). Serve at once.

Noodles with Japanese Fish Cake and Vegetables

SERVES 4
FOR THE NOODLES

2 slices Japanese fish cake

1 carrot

1 leek

100 g (4 oz) mange-tout

¼ head of Chinese leaves

350 g (12 oz) udon noodles

salt

300 ml (½ pt) chicken stock

12 large, cooked prawns

FOR THE DIPPING SAUCE

6 tbsp Japanese soy sauce

2 tbsp sake

1 tsp sugar

150 ml (¼ pt) Japanese-style Stock
  (see page 53)

pinch of wasabi

1 spring onion, finely chopped

Japanese fish cake bears no resemblance to the European product of the same name. Kamaboko, the Japanese name for it, is a smooth-textured loaf, sometimes with a red exterior, bought cooked and in slices. It is served as part of the celebratory New Year menu. I have taken the ingredients out of their authentic context in this recipe to make a light noodle dish.

First, prepare the dipping sauce. Heat the soy sauce, sake, sugar and stock, stirring until the sugar dissolves. Bring to the boil, then remove from the heat and leave to cool. Add a small pinch of wasabi and stir in the spring onion, then pour the sauce into small dishes.

Now, prepare the noodles, fish cake and vegetables. Cut the fish cake into matchstick-size strips. Cut the carrot and leek into matchstick-size pieces also. Top and tail the mange-tout and shred the Chinese leaves.

Cook the noodles in boiling salted water for about 15 minutes, or following the instructions on the packet, until tender. Meanwhile, bring the chicken stock to the boil. Add the carrot and leek and simmer for 1 minute. Then add the mange-tout and cook for a further minute. Finally, add the Chinese leaves and bring back to the boil. Add the prawns and remove the saucepan from the heat. Leave to stand for 2 minutes.

Drain the noodles and divide them between four bowls. Carefully spoon the vegetables and prawns over the noodles, then pour the stock over them. Top with the pieces of fish cake and serve at once.

Fried Noodle Snack

SERVES 4

225 g (8 oz) fresh or dried
  Chinese egg noodles
100 g (4 oz) French beans, cut
  into 5 cm (2 in) lengths
3 tbsp oil
2 eggs, beaten
1 bunch o f spring onions,
  finely grated diagonally
1 garlic clove, crushed
1 large carrot, cut into fine
  matchstick strips
175 g (6 oz) cooked, peeled prawns
4 tbsp Japanese soy sauce

Japanese fast food stalls stir up quick dishes of Chinese-style egg noodles with vegetables and prawns or meat like this. This recipe is ideal for making a quick, tasty lunch or supper.

Cook the noodles according to the instructions on the packet or add fresh noodles to boiling water and bring back to the boil, then reduce the heat and cook for 3 minutes. Drain well and set aside.

Add the French beans to a pan of boiling water, bring back to the boil, then drain the beans.

Heat a little of the oil in a large frying pan. Add the eggs and cook until they are beginning to set underneath. Then, lift the edges of the omelette off the pan and allow the unset egg on the top to run on to the hot surface of the pan. When the omelette has set completely, slide it out on to a plate and cut it into small squares.

Heat the remaining oil in a large frying pan or wok. Add the spring onions, garlic, carrot and French beans. Stirfry for 2 minutes, then stir in the prawns and noodles. Stirfry for a few minutes, until heated through, then sprinkle in the soy sauce and add the omelette squares. Mix well and serve at once.

Hiyamugi

SERVES 4

FOR THE NOODLES
2 eggs, beaten
1 tsp Japanese soy sauce
a little oil
350 g (12 oz) hiyamugi
salt
4 spring onions
8 button mushrooms
7.5 cm (3 in) piece of cucumber
16 cooked, peeled prawns

FOR THE DIPPING SAUCE
300 ml (½ pt) Japanese-style Stock
15 g (½ oz) dried bonito fish
4 tbsp Japanese soy sauce
4 tbsp sake, 1 tsp sugar
1 tsp finely grated fresh root ginger

This is a Japanese dish of cold noodles, hiyamugi being thin, white noodles of vermicelli thickness. To be authentic, ice cubes ought to be added to the noodles and cold water is sometimes poured over them. Then the noodles and other ingredients are lifted from the water and dipped into sauce before being eaten. I have not added water or ice directly to the noodles in this recipe, but you can do so if you wish.

First, making the dipping sauce. Heat the stock with the bonito fish until boiling, then strain it into a clean saucepan and stir in the soy sauce, sake and sugar. Bring to the boil, stirring, then remove from the heat. Add the ginger and leave to cool.

Meanwhile, prepare the noodles. Beat the eggs with the soy sauce. Heat a coating of oil in a frying pan. Pour in the egg mixture and cook until they are beginning to set, then lift the edge of the omelette and allow the raw egg on top to run on to the hot surface of the pan. When the omelette has set, slide it on to a plate.

Cook the hiyumagi in boiling salted water for 8–10 minutes, or according to the instructions on the packet, until just tender. Drain and rinse under

cold water, then leave to drain.

Cut the spring onions finely on the diagonal. Slice the mushrooms thinly and cut the cucumber into fine matchstick strips. Cut the omelette into small squares.

To serve the hiyumagi, divide the noodles between four dishes. Top with the prepared ingredients and serve with the dipping sauce. If liked, the dishes of noodles can be served on a bed of crushed ice.

Above: Hiyamugi

PASTA SALADS

Pasta is good cold. It takes a salad dressing well and complements full-flavoured ingredients by providing the bulk they need if they are not to become overwhelming.

Unfortunately, the reputation pasta salads have for being gaudy is a result of concoctions that are so often served at buffet parties – where any old pasta shape will do. Take a look at the better alternatives in this chapter.

Salad of Smoked Haddock with Lemon-dressed Tagliatelle

A strong, lemony dressing matches the robust flavour of the smoked fish.

SERVES 4

675 g (1½ lb) smoked haddock

grated rind and juice of 2 lemons

350 g (12 oz) fresh tagliatelle verde

salt and freshly ground black pepper

300 ml (½ pt) soured cream

1 tsp Dijon mustard or other mild mustard

4 tbsp chopped fresh parsley

2 tbsp chopped fresh dill

225 g (8 oz) fresh, thin French beans,
    cut in half or shorter lengths

1 red pepper, de-seeded, quartered and cut
    across into thin slices

Place the fish on a heatproof plate that fits over a large saucepan. Bring some water to the boil in the saucepan, sprinkle the fish with the lemon juice, cover tightly with foil and cook over the boiling water for 15 minutes, or until just cooked, then remove from the saucepan and leave, covered, until cool. You may have to do this in two batches if you do not have a sufficiently large plate.

Cook the tagliatelle in boiling salted water for about 3 minutes, or until tender. Drain well and rinse under cold water, then drain again.

Mix the lemon rind with the soured cream, mustard, parsley and dill. Add salt and pepper to taste, then toss this lemon dressing with the pasta. Transfer to a serving bowl or single plates or dishes.

Add the French beans to a saucepan of boiling salted water. Bring back to the boil and cook for 1 minute. Add the red pepper and boil for a further 30–60 seconds, then drain well.

Flake the smoked haddock flesh off the skin in fairly large pieces, discarding any stray bones as you do so. Lightly mix the fish with the beans and pepper, taking care not to break up the flakes. Serve the fish mixture on the pasta base so that it may be tossed with the pasta before being eaten.

Pasta Salad with Bacon and Pesto

SERVES 4

225 g (8 oz) short pasta spirals

salt and freshly ground black pepper

2 large oranges

225 g (8 oz) baby spinach leaves,
 washed and grated

4 spring onions, finely chopped

1 bunch of watercress, leaves only

6 rocket leaves, grated

4 large sprigs of parsley, roughly chopped

450 g (1 lb) rindless bacon, diced

½ quantity Pesto (see page 67)

Cook the pasta in boiling salted water for about 15 minutes or according to the instructions on the packet, until just tender. Drain and rinse briefly under cold water, then leave to drain completely.

Cut the top and bottom off each orange. Then stand the orange on a board and cut off all the peel and pith, working down the side in overlapping strips. Holding the orange over a bowl to catch the juices, use a serrated knife to cut between the membranes dividing the segments, removing each section of orange.

Mix the spinach, spring onions, watercress, rocket and parsley. Place this salad base in a bowl or on plates.

Dry-fry the bacon, stirring occasionally, until the pieces have browned and are crisp. Drain on kitchen paper.

Toss the orange and bacon with the pasta and add pepper to taste, then pile it on top of the salad leaf base. Top with Pesto and serve (the Pesto is mixed with the pasta and leaves as the salad is eaten to act as a dressing).

Pasta with Crab Dressing

SERVES 4

175 g (6 oz) soup pasta shells

salt and freshly ground black pepper

2 x 50 g (2 oz) tins dressed crab

100 g (4 oz) cream cheese

4 tbsp plain yoghurt

1 tbsp snipped chives

1 tbsp chopped fresh parsley

6 tomatoes, peeled (see Cook's Tip,
  page 72) and sliced

½ cucumber, peeled and thinly sliced

sprigs o f parsley, to garnish

A couple of tins of inexpensive dressed crab make a good dressing for these simple first-course cocktails. Serve thinly sliced rye bread as an accompaniment, arranging black and light bread by overlapping slices of each colour alternately on a platter.

Cook the pasta in boiling salted water for 5–10 minutes or according to the instructions on the packet, until tender. Drain and leave to cool.
Mix the dressed crab with the cream cheese, yoghurt, chives, parsley and salt and pepper to taste. Toss this dressing into the cooled pasta.

To serve, arrange the tomato and cucumber slices on four plates or shallow dishes to form a border for the cocktail, then pile the pasta mixture into the middle. Garnish with sprigs of parsley and serve.

Salad of Pasta with Roast Peppers

I used fusilli col buco (long spirals, which were available in a local supermarket) for this, but short spirals or twists can be substituted. I would not use spaghetti, tagliatelle, linguine or any of the longer pasta shapes – somehow they are not quite right.

SERVES 4

225 g (8 oz) fusilli col buco

salt and freshly ground black pepper

2 red peppers

2 green peppers

2 yellow peppers

1 red or white salad onion, thinly sliced

4–6 large sprigs of basil, grated

3 tbsp balsamic vinegar

1 tsp caster sugar

1 tsp mild, wholegrain mustard

1 tbsp chopped fresh marjoram

2 tbsp walnut oil

100 ml (4 fl oz) good virgin olive oil

Cook the pasta in boiling salted water for about 15 minutes or according to the instructions on the packet, until tender. Drain and rinse under cold water, then leave to drain.

Peel the peppers by charring them singly over a gas flame or place them all under a very hot grill. When the outside is blistered and blackened, rinse under cold water and rub off the skin.

Cut out the stalk and core of the peppers from the top, then carefully remove any remaining seeds from inside. Rinse out and dry the peppers on kitchen paper. Slice the peppers, then layer them in a wide, shallow dish, with the pasta, onion and basil (it is a good idea to start with a thin layer of peppers, then add half the pasta, then most of the remaining peppers, reserving a few rings to go on top of the last layer of pasta, but it is not important to follow this pattern).

Whisk the balsamic vinegar with plenty of salt and pepper, the sugar, mustard and marjoram until the sugar has dissolved. Then, whisk in the walnut and olive oils. Trickle the dressing over the salad, cover and leave to stand for 1–2 hours before serving.

Pasta Salad Niçoise

This makes an excellent lunch or light meal.

SERVES 4

225 g (8 oz) penne

salt and freshly ground black pepper

100 g (4 oz) fine French beans, halved

1 green pepper, de-seeded and diced

450 g (1 lb) tomatoes, peeled, de-seeded and quartered

225 g (8 oz) tin tuna in oil

50 g (2 oz) tin anchovy fillets

16 black olives, stoned

4 eggs, hard-boiled and quartered

1 garlic clove, finely chopped

3 tbsp cider vinegar (or wine vinegar if preferred)

3 tbsp olive oil

croutons (see Cook's Tip page 219)

Cook the penne in boiling salted water for about 15 minutes or according to the instructions on the packet, until tender. Drain, rinse in cold water and leave to drain.

Add the French beans to boiling salted water, bring back to the boil, cook for 1 minute, then drain and rinse under cold water. Leave the beans to drain.

Mix the pepper and tomatoes in a large bowl. Drain and reserve the oil from the tuna and anchovies. Flake the tuna and add it to the pepper and tomatoes. Cut the anchovy fillets into short pieces and add them to the salad. Mix in the olives, penne, French beans and eggs.

Whisk the garlic and vinegar together with a little pepper (the oil from the anchovies and the fillets themselves will be sufficiently salty to season the salad). Then gradually whisk in the reserved oil from the tins and the olive oil. Pour this dressing over the salad and mix well. Finally, toss in some croutons and serve.

Left: Salami and Pasta Salad

Salami and Pasta Salads

These make a satisfying lunch or they can be served in smaller portions and divided between shell dishes or glasses for a light first course. Serve with warmed crusty bread.

SERVES 4

225 g (8 oz) small pasta shapes, such as elbows or ditali

salt and freshly ground black pepper

225 g (8 oz) good-quality Italian salami
  (see Cook's Tip page 219)

1 small courgette, very lightly peeled, halved and thinly sliced

1 bunch watercress, leaves only

1 red onion or other mild salad onion, chopped

10 stuffed green olives, thickly sliced

4 tbsp pine nuts

8 quails' eggs

good olive oil

1 lemon, cut into large wedges

Cook the pasta in boiling salted water for about 10 minutes or following the instructions on the packet, until tender. Drain well.

Meanwhile, cut the salami into strips and mix them with the courgette, watercress, onion and olives.

Dry roast the pine nuts in a small, heavy-based saucepan over a low to medium heat and shake it often so that they cook evenly until lightly browned.

Place the quails' eggs in a saucepan and pour in cold water to cover them. Bring to the boil, then cook for 3 minutes. Drain, rinse under cold water and remove the shells.

Toss the hot pine nuts with the freshly drained pasta and trickle over a little olive oil. Mix well and place in a bowl. Cover and leave until warm. Lightly toss the salami mixture with the pasta and divide it in between four plates. Halve the quails' eggs and arrange them on the salad. Garnish with lemon and serve at once, offering extra olive oil to trickle over the salad to taste.

COOK'S TIP

To make croutons, trim the crusts off medium-thick slices of bread and cut them into 1 cm (1½ in) squares. Heat a mixture of butter and olive oil in a large frying pan. Add the bread cubes and turn them in the hot oil with a slotted spoon. Fry the bread cubes, turning them regularly with the slotted spoon, until they are crisp and golden. Drain on kitchen paper.

COOK'S TIP

To make this salad special, it is essential to buy good quality salami from a good delicatessen or Italian grocers. If you do buy from a specialist shop you will find a terrific range, including coarse-textured and extremely spicy types. I you are limited for choice to a poor selection at a small supermarket, then have a look at the packed meats – you may find that a choice of bresaola (cured beef) or Parma ham are preferrable alternatives.

Pasta Salad with Fresh Dates

SERVES 4

225 g (8 oz) pasta shapes (such as
   porcini-flavoured, mushroom shapes,
   penne or rigatoni)

salt and freshly ground black pepper

4 celery sticks, sliced

4 tbsp pine nuts

50 g (2 oz) walnuts or pecan nuts,
   roughly chopped

225 g (8 oz) fresh dates, stoned and sliced

1 bunch of watercress, leaves only

4 tbsp chopped parsley

1 tbsp chopped mint

handful of fresh basil leaves, grated

3 tbsp balsamic vinegar

1 garlic clove, crushed and chopped

1 tbsp walnut oil

100 ml (4 fl oz) olive oil

Cook the pasta in boiling salted water for about 15 minutes or according to the instructions on the packet, until tender.

Blanch the celery in boiling salted water for 1 minute, then drain well.

Dry roast the pine nuts in a small, heavy-based saucepan over a low to medium heat and shake it often or stir so that they have browned lightly and evenly. Mix the walnuts or pecans, pine nuts, dates, watercress, parsley, mint and basil in a large bowl.

Whisk the balsamic vinegar, garlic and salt and pepper to taste in a bowl, then slowly whisk in the walnut and olive oils. Pour the dressing over the nut and date mixture.

Drain the cooked pasta and add it to the bowl, toss well and cover until cooled before serving.

INDEX

A

Ariso 13
agnellotti (agnollotti; agnolotti) 10
agnolini 10
all'uovo 9
almonds 60, 140, 177
Amatriciana Sauce 126
amori (amorini)10
anchovy
   and Green Olive Paste 66, 170
   Lemon Anchovy Butter 63, 170
anellini 10, 98
Apricot and Almond Gems 177
Arrabiatta Sauce 138
artichoke(s)
   and Bacon Lasagne 190
   Bottoms with Parma Ham
   and Peas 144
   Soup with Walnut-dressed Pasta 90
asciutta 9
asparagus
   pasta 16
aubergine(s)
   Pasta-filled 185
avocado
   Fresh Tuna Sauce 109
   Patty Pan and Avocado Topping 147

B

Bacon
   and Artichoke Lasagne 190
   Broad Beans with 145
   Pasta Carbonara 72
   with Pasta Salad and Pesto 215
baked pasta 178-193
bamboo steamers 196
barley pasta 14
basil
   pasta 16
   Pasta with Garlic and 68
   Pesto 61
bavette 10
Bay and Garlic Oil 75
bean curd
   and Rice Stick Soup 93
beans and pulses
   broad beans 145
   chickpeas 126
   flageolet 116
   French beans 132, 218
Béchamel sauce 56, 218
beef
   and Lager Soup 83
   Cannelloni 166
   and Chestnut Stew 104
   Hot Sauce 122
   Meatballs 120
   Pan Stickers 206

   and Rich Pork Stuffing 158
   Spicy, Chow Mein 204
   Spicy Beef Soup 84
   Stuffing 153
beetroot
   dough 41
   and gammon Sauce 125
   Quick Bortsch with Uzska 88
   with Uzska 173
   vacuum-packed 125
   bigni 10
bigoli 10
Blackcurrant Circles 177
Blue Cheese and Cucumber Sauce 135
boil-in the bag pasta 17
Bolognese Sauce 57
Borsch, Quick, with Uzska 88
Boscaiola Sauce 127
bows, pasta 127, 128, 135
Braised Chicken with Rice Sticks 202
Braised Turkey with Fennel 98
bresaola 219
Broad Beans with Bacon 145
broccoli 102
brunch 164
Brussels sprouts 104
bucatini 116, 126, 143
buckwheat pasta 15
butters 62-64

C

Cabbage Soup with Spätzle 89
campanelle 10
candele 10
cannelle 10
cannelloni 10
   Baked Spinach and Ricotta 169
   Beef 166
   Turkey, with Lemon Sauce 166
canneroncini 10
canneroni 10
capellini 10,143
capellini spezziati 10
cappelletti 10, 83, 100, 114
   making 150
   Pheasant, with Dried Morels and
   Oyster Mushrooms 162
Carbonara, Pasta 72
Carbonara-style Leeks with Horseradish 140
cardamom-spiced dough 41
carrot(s) 104
   dough 45 garnishes 197
   and Parsnip Soup with Crispy
   Pasta 91
   casareccia 10
casonsei 10
cauliflower 104
Celeriac, Creamed, with Baby Spinach
and Dill 144
Celery Leaf Spätzle 47
champignon pasta 16

cheese
   Baked Spinach and Ricotta
   Cannelloni 169
   Blue, and Cucumber Sauce 135
   Dolcelatte Dressing with Fennel and
   Olives 136
   Eggs with Stilton and Beans 132
   Feta Circles with Walnut Oil and
   Olives 170
   Garlic, with Sun-dried Tomatoes 136
   Goats', with Grapes and Bows 135
   and gammon Ravioli with Broccoli
   and Leeks 164
   and gammon Stuffing 155
   Herbed, and Walnut Topping 68
   Macaroni 72
   Parmesan Cheese Gnocchi 45
   Parmesan Gnocchi 45
   Parmesan and Oregano Gnocchi 43
   Ricotta Gnocchi 43
   sauce 54
   Spicy Brazil Nut and White Cheese
   Topping 66
   Spinach and Ricotta Stuffing 157
   Walnut Tortellini Tossed with
   Cucumber and Stilton 168
chestnuts 104
chianti speciality pasta 17
chicken
   Braised, with Rice Sticks 202
   Contemporary Cock-a-leekie 104
   Creamed, Stuffing 152
   Gnocchi-topped 101
   and Leek Broth with Mushroom
   Cappelletti 83
   Mediterranean Medley 98
   Noodle Soup 82
   and Spinach Roulade 161
   Supreme 115
   and Vegetable Lasagne 193
Chickpeas with Chickpeas 126
chilli(es) 80
   Arrabiatta Sauce 138
   Curls 197
   garlic and, pasta 16, 66
   Oil 75
Chinese dim sum 196-208
Chinese-style Stock 52
Chopped Herb Omelette with
Mushrooms 132
Chow Mein
   Crispy Prawn 205
   Pork and Baby Sweetcorn 203
   Spicy Beef 204
   Vegetable 208
cicatelli di San Severo 10, 123, 141
circles, pasta 150, 170
Clam Sauce 109
cocktail(s)
   Little Pasta 64
Coconut Cream 84
conchiglie 10
conchiglie rigate 10

Contemporary Cock-a-leekie 104
corallini 10
corn see sweetcorn
cottura 9
courgette(s)
   and Basil Salad 132, 114
   preparation 146
   sautéed 101,114
   Soup 88
crab
   and Sweetcorn Soup with Crunchy
   Pasta 78
Crispy Prawn Chow Mein 205
croûtons 218
csipetke 22
cucumber
   and Blue Cheese Sauce 135
   garnishes 197
   and Prawn Sauce 114
   and Stilton Tossed with Walnut
   Tortellini 168
cumin-spiced dough 41, 65, 66
curry-spiced dough 41, 65, 66, 91

D

Dashi see Japanese stock
dates
   Fresh, with Pasta Salad 220
dim sum 296-208
   dough see dough
dinner parties 100
ditali 11, 91, 218
ditalini 11
Dokelatte Dressing with Fennel
and Olives 136
dough
   cutting 33
   dim sum 49, 198, 206
   Eggless Pasta 40
   flavoured 41
   kneading 32
   mixing 31
   Pasta 40
   Rich Egg Pasta 40, 161, 162, 164, 166, 168, 170, 173, 177, 188
   rolling 32
   Won ton 48, 198, 200, 201
   dressing
   Ham and Olive 125
duck
   Spicy, with Mango and Rice Sticks
   202
   with Sweet Ginger Sauce 116

E

Eggless Pasta Dough 40
egg(s)
   Carbonara-style Leeks with
   Horseradish 176
   Chopped Herb Omelette with
   Mushrooms 164

Creamed, with Smoked Salmon 129
noodles see noodles
pasta all'uovo 9
Pasta Carbonara 72
Poached, with Creamed Watercress 160
Puffed, on Pasta 131
Rich Egg Pasta 40
Sauce 54
and Smoked Haddock Sauce 112
with Stilton and Beans 132
elbows, pasta 218

F

Farfalle 11
farfallini 11
fennel
    and Almond Sauce 140
    with Braised Turkey 98
    Dolcelatte Dressing with Olives and 136
fettuccine 11 , 119, 143
    squid-ink 108
fideos 22
fischietti 11
fish
    Seafare's s Hotpot 96
    Simple Fish Sauce 108
    Smoked Fish Hotpot 97
    see also individual fish
Fishball Soup with Rice Vermicelli 78
fresine 11
Fried Noodle Snack 210
fruit compotes for pasta 18
fruit-filled pasta 18
fusilli 11
fusilli col buco 217
fusillier col buco 11

G

Galuska 22
Gammon Parcels 164
garlic
    Butter 62, 170
    Cheese with Sun-dried bmatoes 136
    and chilli pasta 16, 66
    flavoured pasta 16,17, 65
    Oil 75
    and Oregano Spatzle 47
    Pasta with Garlic and Basil 68
    and tomato pasta 17
garnishing, oriental 197
genovesini 11
Gingered Lamb with Broccoli 102
glistrozzapreti 11, 141
gnocchetti sardi 11
gnocchetto 11
gnocchi 11
    Baked Semolina 45
    Gnocchi-topped Chicken 101
    Kopytka see Kopytka

Parmesan Cheese 45
Potato 42, 43, 44, 119, 120, 141
semolina 101
Spinach 42
Goats' Cheese with Grapes and Bows 135
gomiti 11
Goulash 120
gramigna 11
grapes
    Goats' Cheese with Bows 135
Grecian lamb Casserole 96
Greek Salad 216
Greek Yoghurt Topping 65, 170

H

Haddock
    Salad of Smoked, with Lemon-dressed Tagliatelle 214
    Smoked, and Egg Sauce 112
    Smoked, Lasagne 182
ham
    Artichoke Bottoms with Parma Ham and Peas 144
    and Beetroot Sauce 125
    and Cheese Ravioli with Broccoli and Leeks 164
    and Cheese Stuffing 155
    and Olive Dressing 125
    Pasta Carbonara 72
herb(s)
    Almond and Parsley Paste 60
    Butter 62
    Chopped Herb Omlette with Mushrooms 132
    dough 41
    Garlic and Oregano Spatzle 47
    Herbed Cheese and Walnut Topping 68
    Lemon and Herb Rolls 67
    Olive, Oregano and Garlic Dough 41
    Oregano and Parmesan Gnocchi 43
    Pasta with Garlic and Basil 68
    Pesto 61
    and Red Pepper Paste 68
    Spatzle 47
    Tarragon Oil 75
    Tarragon Sauce 54, 190
    Uszka with Chives and Tarragon 173
    vinegars 75
Hiyamugi 210
horseradish 140, 173
Hot Beef Sauce 122
hotpot(s) 95-104
    Smoked Fish 97
    of Venison Meatballs 102

I

garganelli romagnoli 11
is malloreddus lunghi 11

J

Japanese
    fishcake (Kanaboko) 209
    specialities 209-211
    stock (dashi) 53, 93

K

kamaboko 209
Kamut 15
kasnudln 22
knedle 22
knedliky 22
kneidlech 22
Kopytka 22, 44
Kreplach 22

L

Lamb
    Gingered, with Broccoli 102
    Grecian Casserole 96
lasagne 57, 112, 114, 166
    al Forno 181
    Bacon and Artichoke 190
    Chicken and Vegetable 193
    making 180
    Mushroom Ring 188
    Prawn Pots 182
    Seafood 186
    Smoked Haddock 182
    Spinach 190
    Turkey and Chestnut 186
lasagnette 11
lasanki 22, 33
le emiliane 12
leek(s) 104
    and Broccoli with gammon and Cheese Ravioli 164
    Carbonara-style, with Horseradish 140
    and Chicken Broth with Mushroom Cappelletti 83
    Contemporary Cock-a-leekie 104
    and Pumpkin Stuffing 152
    with Spinach 101
lemon
    Anchovy Butter 63, 170
    dough 41
    and Herb Rolls 67
leniwe pierogi 22
linguine 12, 116, 144
Liver with Peppers and Pine Nuts 128
Lobster and Spinach tipping 112
lumache 104, 122, 123, 141, 157
    Stuffed 158

M

Macaroni 12, 68, 79, 192
    Cheese 72
    milk pudding 18

maccheroni 12
mackerel
    Smoked, and Lemon Stuffing 152
mafaldine 64, 119, 120, 123, 125, 131
malfattini 12
mango
    Spicy Duck with Rice Sticks and 202
    Spicy Okra and 141
Meatballs 120
Mediterranean Medley 98
minestra 23
Minestrone 86
i mista pasta 12
misto corto 12
Mixed Olive and Pepper tipping 67, 170
mohn nudeln 18
mushroom(s)
    champignon pasta 16
    Chopped Herb Omelette with 132
    crimini 127
    Dark Mushroom Sauce 143
    dried 119, 173
    Fresh Shiitake and Mange-tout with Mushroom Ring 188
    Pheasant Cappelletti with Dried Morels and Oyster Mushrooms 162
    porcini pasta 16
    Sauce 54
    Soup with Watercress 41
    Stuffing 154

N

Niçoise, Salad 218
nidi 12
noodles
    arrowroot vermicelli 21
    bee hoon 20
    chow mein 20, 203, 204, 205, 208
    Crispy Won ton 48, 198, 201
    cutting 33
    egg 20, 58, 82, 203, 204, 205, 206, 208, 210
    Fried Snack 210
    Hiyamugi 21, 210
    ho fun (hor fun) 20
    instant Chinese 17
    ishiguro yahaimo soba 20
    with Japanese Fish Cake and Vegetables 209
    kua teaw (kway teow) 20
    laksa 21
    lokshen 18, 23
    lokshyna 23
    marufuji samen 20
    matzo meal 23
    mee hoon 20
    rung bean thread or transparent 20
    maeng myun 20
    nai you mein 20
    noky 23
    ramen 21
    rice sticks 20, 93

rice vermicelli 20, 78, 84, 204
saifun 20
sanuki somen 20
sen lek 21
sen mee 20
sen yai (wide rice) 21
sev 20
shirataki 20
spatzle 23
tarhonya 23
tomoshiraga somen 20
trahana 23
udon 20, 209
wheat, fresh 82
wheat flour, dried 20
woon sen 21

O

Offelle 12
Oils, Flavoured 75
Okra, Spiry, and Mango 141
olive(s)
    Bread 70, 86
    Dolcelatte Dressing with Fennel 136
    doughs 45
    Feta Circles with Walnut Oil and 170
    Green, and Anchovy Paste 66, 170
    Mixed Olive and Pepper tipping 67, 170
    Pasta in a Greek Salad 216
orecchiette 12, 90, 184
organic pasta 14
oriental
    pastas 19-21
    specialities 194-211
orzo 23, 96
oysters
    Hidden 83

P

Paglia e fieno 12, 102, 119
Pan Stickers 206
pansotti 12
pappardelle 12, 123
Parma Ham 72, 127, 144, 219
pasta
    coloured 28, 104, 115
    cooking 34-36, 150
    dough see dough draining 36, 161
    dried 34, 37
    equipment for making 30-31
    flavoured 16-17, 41, 60, 62, 66, 127
    freezing 37
    fresca (fresh) 9, 36, 37
    from other countries 22-23
    home-made 30-33
    ingredients 9
    instant 17
    Italian 10-13
    kneading 32
    low-protein 14

machines 31, 32, 33
portions 35
quick-cook 17
serving 28-9, 36
specialist 14-15
storing 37
pasta verde 60, 62
pastes 60, 66, 147
pastine 13
Patty Pan and Avocado Topping 147
peaches, dried 119
pea(s)
    Artichoke Bottoms with Parma Ham and 144
pelmeni 23
penne 13, 98, 127, 138, 216, 218
    mezzani 13
    mezzanine 13
Pepperonata Round 188
pepper(s)
    Liver with Peppers and Pine Nuts 128
    and Mixed Olive Topping 67, 170
    Pepperonata Pasta Round 188
    Pork and Pasta 184
    Red, Paste with Sun-dried tomatoes 71
    Salad of Pasta with Roast 217
    and Turnip Sauce 143
perciatelli 13, 120, 143
perline 13
pesto 61
    Pasta salad with Bacon and 215
    Turkey with Flageolet Beans and 116
pheasant
    boning 100
    Cappelletti with Dried Morels and Oyster Mushrooms 162
    Galantine with Walnut Cappelletti 100
    Pierogi 23, 174
Pierozki, Fruit 229
pine nuts
    Liver with Peppers and 128
Piquant Diced Lamb 123
Piquant Pork and Prawn Soup with Coconut Cream 84
Pistou Soup 86
Polish poppy seed pudding 18
porcini pasta 16
pork
    and Baby Sweetcorn Chow Mein 203
    Pan Stickers 206
    and Pasta Peppers 184
    Pierogi 174
    Rich, and Beef Stuffing 158
    Satay-style, with Egg Noodles 282
Sweet-and-sour Won Jans 200
Potato Gnocchi see gnocchi prawn(s)
    Butter 64
    Cucumber and Prawn Sauce 114
    Har Kaw 198
    Lasagne Pots 182
    and Pasta Bisque with Rouille 80

Seafarer's Hotpot 96
prosciutto see Parma Ham
    Puffed Eggs on Pasta 131
Puffy Deep-fried Won Jans 48
pulses see beans and pulses Pumpkin and Leek Stuffing 152
Puttanesca Sauce 139, 170

Q

Quadretti 13

R

Radiatori 13
radish roses 197
Ratatouille 138
ravioli 13
    Ham and Cheese, with Broccoli and Leeks 164
    making 150
    trays 31
rice and millet pasta 15
rice pasta 14
rice sticks 20, 202
Rich Egg Pasta see dough
Rich Pork and Beef Stuffing 158
Rich Ragoût 122
rigatoni 13, 98, 123, 127, 141
rings, pasta 98
Rosemary Oil 75
ruoti 13

S

Sage Oil 75
salad(s) 212-220
    Courgette and Basil 132, 192
    Greek 216
    Niçoise 218
    Pasta, with Bacon and Pesto 215
    Pasta with Fresh Dates 220
    of Pasta with Roasted Peppers 217
    Salami and Pasta 218
    of Smoked Haddock with Lemon-dressed Tagliatelle 214
salami
    Italian 219
    and Pasta Salads 218
salmon
    Creamed Eggs with Smoked 129
    Salmon-stuffed Shells 157
    smoked salmon pasta 16
    sauced dried pasta 17
sauce(s) 54
    Amatriciana 126
    Arrablatta 138
    Béchamel 56, 114
    Blue Cheese and Cucumber 135
    Bolognese 57
    Boscaiola 127
    Butter 54
    Cheese 54

Chicken Supreme 115
Clam 109
Cucumber and Prawn 114
Dark Mushroom 180
dipping 206
Egg 54
Fennel and Almond 140
Fresh Tina 109
Garlic Cream 58
Ham and Beetroot 125
Hot Beef 122
Hot-and-Sour 58
Lemon 166
Light, Fresh Jamato 55, 120, 170
Mushroom 54
Parsley 54
Puttanesca 139, 170
Rich Tomato 45, 54, 120, 170
Seafood 110
Simple Fish 108
Smoked Haddock and Egg 112
Swordfish and Tomato Sauce 114
Tarragon 54, 190
Turnip and Pepper 143
White 54
White Wine 56
sauerkraut 174
sausage(s)
    Chickpeas with Chickpeas 126
    Chinese 206
schlick krapfen 23
Scotch Lamb Sauce 148
Seafarer's Hotpot 96
seafood 186
    Chowder 79
    Clam Sauce 109
    cleaning 110
    cleaning shellfish 110
    Crispy, Chow Mein 205
    Cucumber and Prawn Sauce 114
    Hidden Oysters 183
    Lasagne 186
    Little Pasta Cocktails 64
    Lobster and Spinach Topping 112
    Prawn Butter 64
    Prawn Har Kow 198
    Prawn Lasagne Pots 182
    Sauce 110
    Seafarer's Hotpot 96
sedani 13
semolina
    Baked Semolina Gnocchi 45
    gnocchi 101
sevyian 18
shells, pasta 64, 80, 96, 97, 109, 112, 114, 122, 146, 157
Simple Fish Sauce 108
soba 20
Soufflé-topped Pasta 184
soup 76-93
    Artichoke, with Walnut-dressed Pasta 90
    Bean Curd and Rice Stick 93

Beef and Lager 83
Cabbage, with Spätzle 89
Carrot and Parsnip, with Crispy Pasty 91
Chicken and Leek Broth with
Mushroom Cappelletti 83
Chicken Noodle 82
Courgette 88
Crab and Sweetcorn, with Crunchy
Pasta 78
Fishball, with Rice Vermicelli 78
Hot-and-sour 58
Minestrone 86
Mushroom, with Watercress 91
Piquant Pork and Prawn, with
Coconut Cream 84
Pistou 86
Prawn and Pasta Bisque with Rouille
80
Quick Bortsch with Uzska 88
Seafood Chowder 79
Spicy Beef 84
Thin Tomato, with Spinach Tortellini
90
Won Ton 93
soup pasta 80, 83, 86, 183, 184, 185
spagellini 13
spaghetti 13, 57, 64, 72, 109, 114, 116,
120, 122, 125, 126, 131, 139, 143, 144
black olive 17
Spätzle 23, 46, 89, 119, 120
batter 47
flavoured 47
spelt pasta 14
Spiced Anchovy Butter 62
spiganarda 13
spinach
Baby, with Creamed Celeriac
and Dill 194
Baked Spinach and Ricotta
Cannelloni 169
and Chicken Roulade 161
dough 41
Fresh, and Spring Onion Cream 140
Gnocchi 42
Lasagne 190
Leeks with 101
and Lobster Topping 112
pasta 16
and Ricotta Stuffing 90,157
with Wind-dried Sausage 206
spirals, pasta 88, 97, 114, 127, 128, 144, 146,
215
spring onion(s) 173, 198
squash, patty pan 147
squid
black squid pasta 16, 63, 108
preparation 204
Stirfried Squid with Rice
Vermicelli 204
steamers 196
stelline 13
stews 94-105
stir-fries

Squid with Rice Vermicelli 204
stock 52, 53
stuffed and filled pasta 148-177
stuffing
Beef 153
Creamed Chicken 152
Ham and Cheese 155
for Lumache 158
Mushroom 154
Pumpkin and Leek 152
quantities 150
Rich Pork and Beef 158
Salmon 157
Smoked Mackerel and Lemon 152
Spinach and Ricotta 157
Walnut 100,155
suessen nudelauf 18
swede(s)
Terrine 192
sweet pasta 18, 174-177
Sweet-and-Sour Pork Won Tons 200
sweetcorn
Baby, and Pork Chow Mein 203
corn, tomato and chilli pasta 16
corn and parsley pasta 15
corn pasta 15
corn and spinach pasta 16
corn and vegetable pasta 14
and Crab Soup with Crunchy
Pasta 78
Swordfish and Tomato Sauce 114

T

Tagliatelle 13, 64, 72, 78, 114, 116, 119, 120,
128, 131, 143, 144, 214
Salad of Smoked Haddock with
Lemon dressed 214
verdi 108, 112, 115, 125
tarragon 173
Oil 75
Sauce 54, 190
tomato(es)
Arrabiatta Sauce 138
dough 41
Fresh, with Pasta 70
garlic and pasta 17
Light Fresh Sauce 55, 120, 170
Rich Tomato Sauce 45, 54, 120, 170
Sun-dried with Garlic Cheese 136
Sun-dried with Red Pepper Paste 71
Thin Tomato Soup with Spinach
Tortellini 90
tomato pasta 17
topping(s)
calorie-counted 27
Greek Yoghurt 65, 170
Herbed Cheese and Walnut 68
Lobster and Spinach 112
Mixed Olive and Pepper 67, 170
Patty Pan and Avocado 147
Spicy Brazil Nut and White Cheese 66
torchietti 13

tortellini 13, 90
filling and shaping 150
Walnut, Tossed with Cucumber and
Stilton 168
tortiglioni 13
trenette 13
truffle(s)
Butter 62
tubetti 13
tuna
Sauce, Fresh 109
turkey
Braised, with Fennel 98
Cannelloni with Lemon Sauce 166
and Chestnut Lasagne 186
with Flageolet Beans and Pesto 116
turmeric dough 41
Turnip and Pepper Sauce 143
twists, pasta 102, 144

U

Uszka 23, 88,173

V

Varenyky (varieniki) 23
vegetable(s)
Medley 146
Ratatouille 138
stock 52
see also under individual vegetables
venison
with Dried Peaches 119
Hotpot of Venison Meatballs 102
Stroganoff 119
vermicelli 13, 84, 86,131
arrowroot see noodles
rice see noodles
Vinegars, Flavoured 75

W

Walnut(s)
dough 41
and Herbed Cheese Topping 68
oil 170
Stuffing 100, 155
Tortelhhi Tossed with Cucumber
and Stilton 168
Mushroom Soup with 91
Poached Eggs with Creamed 131
wholemeal pasta 15, 25
Wind-dried Sausage with Spinach 268
Winter Salad 297
Won Ton(s) 21, 58, 93, 198-201
Crispy Parcels 201
dough see dough
noodles see noodles
Puffy Deep-fried 48
Soup 93
Sweet-and-sour 200

Z

Zacierki 23
Ziti 13,119
Zitoni 13